DRAWING OUT LAW:
A SPIRIT'S GUIDE

The Anishinabek Nation's legal traditions are deeply embedded in many aspects of customary life. In *Drawing Out Law*, John Borrows (Kegedonce) skilfully juxtaposes Canadian legal policy and practice with the more broadly defined Anishinabek perception of law as it applies to community life, nature, and individuals.

This innovative work combines fictional and non-fictional elements in a series of connected short stories that symbolize different ways of Anishinabek engagement with the world. Drawing on oral traditions, pictographic scrolls, dreams, common law case analysis, and philosophical reflection, Borrows's narrative explores issues of pressing importance to the future of Indigenous law and offers readers new ways to think about the direction of Canadian law.

Shedding light on Canadian law and policy as they relate to Indigenous peoples, *Drawing Out Law* illustrates the past and present moral agency of Indigenous peoples and their approaches to the law and calls for the renewal of ancient Ojibway teaching in contemporary circumstances.

This is a major work by one of Canada's leading legal scholars and an essential companion to *Canada's Indigenous Constitution*.

JOHN BORROWS is a professor and Law Foundation Chair in Aboriginal Justice in the Faculty of Law at the University of Victoria and Robina Professor in Law and Public Policy at the University of Minnesota Law School.

JOHN BORROWS (KEGEDONCE)

Drawing Out Law

A Spirit's Guide

UNIVERSITY OF TORONTO PRESS
Toronto Buffalo London

© University of Toronto Press Incorporated 2010
Toronto Buffalo London
www.utppublishing.com
Printed in Canada

ISBN 978-1-4426-4068-9 (cloth)
ISBN 978-1-4426-1009-5 (paper)

Printed on acid-free, 100% post-consumer recycled paper with
vegetable-based inks.

Library and Archives Canada Cataloguing in Publication

Borrows, John, 1963–
    Drawing out law : a spirit's guide / John Borrows.

    Includes bibliographical references and index.
    ISBN 978-1-4426-4068-9 (bound). – ISBN 978-1-4426-1009-5 (pbk.)

    1. Ojibwa law.   2. Native peoples – Legal status, laws, etc. – Canada.
    I. Title.

    KE7749.C6B67 2010   342.7108'72   C2010-900711-5

This book has been published with the help of a grant from the Canadian
Federation for the Humanities and Social Sciences, through the Aid to
Scholarly Publications Program, using funds provided by the Social
Sciences and Humanities Research Council of Canada.

University of Toronto Press acknowledges the financial assistance of the
Canada Council for the Arts and the Ontario Arts Council.

 Canada Council   Conseil des Arts   ONTARIO ARTS COUNCIL
for the Arts   du Canada   CONSEIL DES ARTS DE L'ONTARIO

University of Toronto Press acknowledges the financial support of its
publishing activities by the Government of Canada through the Book
Publishing Industry Development Program (BPIDP).

*To Jeeneequae, my mother, and Chik'chik'chikaudesae and Keegitah,
my daughters.*

Contents

PART FOUR: BEEBON   Ideas: The Fourth Hill

Preface: N'gii-pawaudjige[1]

I really don't want to write this preface. I would rather readers went directly to chapter 1 and read the book on its own terms, without the aid of this introduction. This would introduce you more quickly to an Anishinabek legal method. It would allow you to struggle in a direct manner with the book's central questions. Turning immediately to chapter 1 would also allow you to more sharply encounter with greater intimacy the particular Anishinabek methodology I am trying to follow in this work (though, of course, there is more than one Anishinabek intellectual method).[2] To dive into the deep end of this text, I encourage you to skip the next few pages and come back to the preface when you have finished the last chapter. If you find yourself wondering 'what's the point?' once you begin reading, you can always come back to the preface for more explanation. Even if the work becomes too alien or confusing, I hope you do not turn back here immediately. Ironically, reading the preface could also cause you to miss important elements of the text. Nevertheless, I want to make sure that readers have a degree of choice about how to proceed through this book. For those who desire greater context before proceeding further into the work, or desire more explanation after you have finished reading it, I offer the following reflections, on the advice of wise counsellors.

This book was conceived of and written in layers. Its cyclical development began its formal life as a Foreword to the first edition of the *Indigenous Law Journal*.[3] While the present book originates from a relatively recent essay, the work is much older in many ways. It stretches back into some of my earliest memories with my grandparents, parents, aunts, uncles, and cousins. In other important respects, the book significantly predates me. At the same time, this work is very current. It covers the period of time during which I have worked as a law professor in various Canadian and American law schools. While the reflections that follow are not strictly autobiographical at times, they mirror the experiences I gained over the last twenty years of my life. At the same time, it is crucial to note that many of the events and characters found herein are of a composite nature. They are drawn together from a kaleidoscope of people, places, and ideas, and do not necessarily represent one place or person. They are also very much a product of what I have read in this period; the work of Dr Basil Johnston, an Elder from my reserve, deserves special acknowledgment in this regard. The influence of his work can be felt in almost every chapter.

Thus, care should be taken not to read everything found in this work in a literal way. Readers are encouraged to search for the deeper symbolism embedded in the broader structure and finite particulars of this work. As this book intermixes constituent fictive and non-fictive elements, it is important to re-emphasize that all references to people, events, institutions, organizations, or locales are not be taken literally, as this is a creative work of a philosophical nature that amalgamates, fuses, merges, combines, and synthesizes historical eras, personalities, places, and ideas.

As such, it is my hope that readers do not linger on the supposed literal, real-world physicality of any individual in this book; rather, I encourage readers to feel the spirit of the characters and look through them into the larger issues they encounter. This should allow readers to generalize and synthesize ideas in a way that goes beyond any single set of experiences and opinions. This approach is consistent with a form of Anishinabek literacy that tells stories through the words of supernatural beings, past leaders and ancestors, animals, plants, insects, or rocks. I learned this method of storytelling from my Anishinabequae mother, who would communicate about the world around her through her indirect teaching style and third-person perspective. This was in contrast to the more direct style of teaching of my Yorkshire-born father. My mother spoke in her way to explore ideas and events in a manner that freed us to question the larger forces at play in what we were experiencing and hearing. She was the major carrier of culture in our home, encouraged by my father's love and support. Thus, in line with an Anishinabek method, the characters in the following pages function as conduits for further reflection, rather than as specific personalities that should attract real-world approbation or blame.

I use this methodology because of the opportunity it presents to step

back and reflect upon what I have learned from an Anishinabek perspective. As such, the book is very much the product of how I reason
about and understand Anishinabek law. I feel as if I am being more can-
did in communicating my insights in this book than is the case with my
other work, notwithstanding this work's somewhat unconventional
style. What follows may be too ambiguous, vague, or obscure for some
readers because of its deep and sometimes hidden roots in Anishinabek
and common law language and culture. Notwithstanding these challenges, I hope that some people may see within these pages an ancient,
rich, contemporary but nevertheless still developing Anishinabek legal
perspective.

Despite its challenging methodology I have tried to write the book
in a way that my Anishinabek grandparents, parents, and adult children would understand. They are my first audience. I hope that in writing in this manner, my future great-great-great grandchildren will also
find it somewhat accessible. In this regard, the book does not always
follow the conventions of published Canadian legal scholarship. In
fact, the central images and ideas that follow were broadly composed
while I was asleep. They are largely the product of dreams I shared
with my daughter a few years ago as we went running each morning through our neighbourhood. As we enjoyed the new light of each
day, I would tell her what I had learned the night before and I would
discuss with her what I thought these dreams might mean. After some
time of thoughtful silence, she would often add her own ideas about
their possible meanings, and help me speculate about how they all fit
together. As this went on for a few weeks, I came to feel like each chapter was simultaneously dreaming itself into existence *and* giving me an
opportunity to develop a deeper relationship with my (then) teenage
daughter. These dreams and discussions enabled me to share with her
how I experienced the world as an Anishinabek man involved in legal
education. After some weeks, I began to write down what I was learning from these dreams and conversations. The chapters in this manuscript quickly began to take shape and I saw a potential book in their
midst. At some point in the process, at the end of a day's writing, I
developed the practice of calling my mother, father, and sister at home
on the reserve to get their feedback on what I was thinking. For three
months I experienced a wonderful pattern: dream, discuss, write, discuss, dream, discuss, write, discuss, et cetera.

At the end of the summer when this work was almost complete, I
found myself back home on the Cape Croker Indian Reserve, *Neyaashi-*

inigmiing. With a draft manuscript in hand, my family set aside a portion of each day to listen to me read from this book. Their wonderful generosity and kind attention allowed me to further develop my ideas. These experiences embedded the work more deeply in the world of Anishinabek clan and kin. Our family is linked to the otter (*nigig*) dodem, and I have felt the strength that comes from this connection in my work. Furthermore, I was energized as I realized the story was literally living as oral tradition in the lives of people who are closest to me. Though interspersed with periods of writing, the book you are holding in your hands first lived an oral life – through my initial talks with my daughter, to my weeks-long recitation of this work in the comfortable surroundings of my parents' and sister's home. I rewrote portions of the book as a response to my family's feedback and, when I was finished, I once again sought their insights in accordance with our traditions.

Thus, four years after our initial dream-world discussions, my daughter read and responded to a draft of this work while on mid-term break from Dartmouth College. We spoke once again about its images and meanings. My mother, sister, and father also read the book at this point and we engaged in another round of intense discussions, intermingled with laughter, tears, teasing, and encouragement. The book subsequently went through a similar process as I taught Anishinabek law from these pages to students in a Tribal Courts class at the University of Minnesota Law School. I also benefited from Vancouver Island author Jack Hodgin's thoughts on an earlier draft. He helped me identify a better way of organizing the book. My colleagues Ben Berger, Hester Lessard, and Jeremy Webber also made helpful suggestions in relation to some of the theoretical issues discussed herein. I am also grateful to the anonymous readers who reviewed this book for the University of Toronto Press. Their comments were very helpful. While all errors are my own, I am grateful to everyone for their feedback on the stories and ideas I shared with them. In addition, I want to express my gratitude to the Trudeau Foundation for its financial support while I travelled through Anishinabek territory in the United States and Canada to complete this book. Furthermore, the book has been published with the help of a grant from the Canadian Federation for the Humanities and Social Sciences, through the Aid to Scholarly Publications Program, using funds provided by the Social Sciences and Humanities Research Council of Canada.

From the moment it dawned on me that what I was experiencing could be turned into a book, I recognized I had to sustain the oral dimension of this work. Since I initially encountered many of the ideas found in these chapters as images in dreams, I decided to represent them in pictographic form to the best of my remembrance and ability. The Anishinabek have a long history of recording dreams, songs, and stories in this manner.[4] Thus, at the beginning of each chapter I have provided illustrations related to the ideas within each chapter that take inspiration from other forms of Anishinabek literacy. The images are meant to function as mnemonic devices or memory aids for those who want to subsequently 'read' the book in oral form. While understanding these images requires a different set of skills than those taught in law schools, their presence provides readers with an opportunity to access ideas in subsequent readings without having to use the English text. In this light, I hope readers feel empowered to remember and develop their own interpretations of what they see and read in images. Since these representations are not meant to be formalized in their meaning, like those found on Midewewin scrolls or other sacred texts, they can take on a life of their own. They represent my dreams. They replicate images of scrolls discovered by me with my family's help. As offered in this book, they are not meant to be read within a single interpretive tradition. Thus, the ideograms can be adapted and reformulated to suit the recipient's purposes. In my view, legal traditions are often at their most relevant when they continually change and address ideas their creators did not necessarily envision. As such, I hope readers partially see this work as an invitation to creatively develop Indigenous legal traditions in accordance with their own familial and community standards. Perhaps this work will even inspire the development of further books and writings that convey thoughts in accordance with distinctively Anishinabek and other Indigenous forms of literacy. We may yet see the development of books that more richly rely upon our own pictography.

In studying the accompanying images and text, I also hope readers will see that Anishinabek legal traditions are drawn from places other than courts, legislatures, lawyers' briefs, or law professors' lectures. Indigenous laws can be revealed in broader ways. They are nourished by a grandparent's teachings, a law professor's reflections, an animal's behaviour, an engraved image, and a landscape's contours. Anishinabek law can grow from an ancient story recast in a contemporary light, or through a community's restorative justice efforts. These laws are sourced in the thunder and lightning, in animal creation narratives, individuals' efforts, educational creativity, community resistance,

Canadian legal doctrines, comparative law's insights, family members' relationships, community deliberations, Windigo stories, and our experiences with and reflections on the Great Mystery. Readers who desire a more explicit discussion of Anishinabek laws in 'Western' legal and philosophical terms (and how they can be understood and applied in an intersocietal context) should consult my work *Canada's Indigenous Constitution*, a book written simultaneously with this one. The thesis of that book is that Indigenous laws can be recognized and affirmed in a Canadian context, and can also be justified through 'Western' legal argumentation. In contrast, the book you are holding in your hands draws more heavily on Anishinabek forms to justify multi-juridical engagement. As a result, the arguments in this book are made in implicit terms and in a manner that is more consistent with varying Anishinabek philosophical traditions. In this book, there is a greater scope given for readers to use their agency by drawing their own conclusions about the meanings hidden in the text. An examination of both works will reveal that I believe Anishinabek and other North American legal traditions and philosophies can be brought into conversation with one another. However, a close study of both works will also illustrate my view that the tone and method of engagement across cultures should change with the context in which the debate is set. The differing voice and style of these two books exemplifies the point that legal pluralism is alive and strong, but should not be reduced to one kind of argument that creates a fused or shared horizon. Readers who are interested in the implications of my approach should compare and contrast the methods and ideas in this book with those found in *Canada's Indigenous Constitution*.

In the end, this is a book about cycles, circles, seasons, and rounds, and how our choices interact with the seemingly stable repetitive recurrences seen in most of our lives. I have been conscious of my connections with the past, present, and future in this work. Despite the linear nature of much of common law scholarship, I hope this book is received in a context that finds a life in the complex interactions of different people's life patterns. This hope lies close to the heart of the standards encouraged in this work. We all have a degree of power to make choices about what we encounter in this world, despite the differing limitations, opportunities, and constraints we each experience within the context of our cultures. This is the law as I see it.

PART ONE: MINOKMI

Issues: The First Hill

DAEBAUJIMOOT[1]

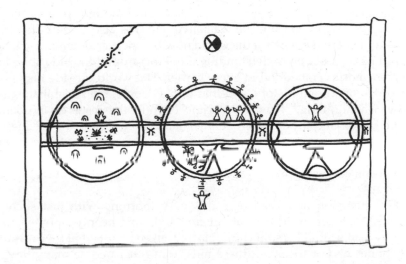

Mishomis sat for some time, contemplating the morning's conversation with his grandson. It was often like that at this time in his life. Long days reflecting on an even longer life, peppered with fleeting moments of real-time human association. Yet when he was a younger man it seemed as though he never had a moment's peace. He had worked hard as a labourer in many different fields: logger, painter, plasterer, farmer, and road builder. This kept him busy from sunup to sundown; except for that time he spent working in films. California had been a welcome change for a while, but it was also a very demeaning place, especially during the Depression. So he eventually moved back to the reserve, Grapes-of-Wrath-style, and resumed his life on the land. He would work twelve-hour days, and then when he came home it always seemed that something else was pressing, calling his attention. A door to hang, a net to repair, an old car needing attention, or a family problem to resolve; the demands seemed endless. No time to rest. He also drank a little too hard through some of these periods. Life drowned in cold, deep waters. Whole years were washed from his mind. Gone: *gausee-ibeegaewin*. Too much living had been lost to those dark spirits, and he knew they always lurked nearby, threatening to submerge him.

But now as he sat silently in his old chair, he could also remember the quiet times. Hunting, fishing, talking with his wife and friends – there were periods of peaceful reflection. Thinking back, all in all, he was grateful life had unfolded the way it did. He was happy to live out his last years close to those experiences, painful though some of them were. They reminded him he was alive. He was also grateful for the time to try to make sense of the world now that he was older, to see if he could pass on a little understanding. Looking around his old cabin, he saw memories embedded in every corner. The world outside his door recorded his recent history, and that of his people, the Anishinabek of Neyaashiinigmiing.[2] It was the same beyond the reserve's borders. Lake Huron and the Saugeen Peninsula archived a rich knowledge of how to properly live with the land. When he thought about all this, he longed to tell others about what he had learned. He was always glad when someone stopped by and asked him to share these things with them.

His grandson had been here this very morning with just such a request. A recurring dream about four hills had been occupying the young man's mind for some time. He had asked about what they meant. Mishomis had heard about these hills from other people many times. Basil had first told him about them when he was a younger man.[3] The four hills of life, as they were called, taught the Anishinabek about life's seasons. They represented many teachings about how to live in balance with the world. As Mishomis' thoughts returned to his grandson and his dream, he reflected on life's repetitions and the struggle it took to climb through them. The four hills symbolized that journey. They represented the fact that many of the most important issues a person confronts in life often manifest themselves at a very young age. Then, as you grow older, you continue to cycle through them and encounter them over and over again. It was like climbing boundless hills. While these issues may be experienced differently each time, this does not make each journey any less difficult. And this knowledge certainly does not prepare you for your first encounter. Certain issues remain with us all our days; only our perspective on them changes. Our interpretation grows.

Mishomis could see why his grandson wondered about his dream. He was struggling to understand and overcome the challenges that confronted him on his journey. A law professor's life was easy in some ways; his grandson's life certainly seemed to be more stable than his own had been. At the same time, Mishomis could appreciate some of the challenges his grandson encountered. While they would often dive into deeper subjects, most conversations about his work turned on the disruptiveness of Canadian law. He could relate to that; Mishomis had seen how the law had so deeply dispossessed too many around him. To counter this problem, his grandson's main preoccupation seemed to centre on the reinvigoration of Anishinabek law in contemporary settings. He was searching for ways to more fully draw out law from the world around them. They had returned to the topic this morning when he once again asked about his dream. His grandson seemed especially interested in the first hill.

It reminded Mishomis of his own dream, many years back. He had been given a similar lesson. For as long as he could remember, Anishinabek people had been taught to give the highest regard to their dreams. He was told that they possessed great power. In fact, some dreams could not be shared because they were too sacred. Others could be openly spoken of only if they were not connected to some ceremonial rite of passage. And still other dreams could be widely circulated, because they contained more generalized lessons. In his own dream, from that long-ago day, Mishomis had also been taught about the first hill, though in a different way from his grandson. Mishomis' dream had occurred shortly after he first left home. He had started a new job which he really enjoyed. He was glad to free himself from the constraints around the reserve, and was happy to be earning some money for a change. But he was also a little homesick for family and friends, and he found himself often wondering about them. One night he fell asleep thinking about these things, and had a powerful experience that had stuck with him all the years of his life. It taught him a great deal about the issues his grandson was now reflecting on, concerning the first hill.

In his dream, Mishomis had returned to the reserve to visit with his family. He always enjoyed their company, and was looking forward to relaxing and enjoying a peaceful weekend with them. One of the first things he did upon his arrival was to visit with his Aunt Mary and have supper with her. Aunt Mary's Ojibway name was Wausiiyaunce. He drove over to her brand new house, and admired the order which she brought to the place. No matter where she lived, she always had a few flowers around her yard. It was one of the tidiest places at Neyaashiinig-miing. Mishomis climbed on the porch and knocked on her gleaming white door. This set off Waubegeeshig and Nag'anal'mot, who barked and howled their welcome. After a few moments, Aunt Mary looked through her front window and saw that it was her nephew. She opened the door, gave him a big hug, and welcomed him in. His mother soon joined them, walking the few steps from her house across the way.

As he thought of that experience, Mishomis couldn't stop himself from filling in the details of the dream. He knew from many visits to Wasiiyaunce's *wakau-igun* that it usually smelled of roasted duck or pheasant. Sweetgrass hung in every window, adding to the rich fragrance of her home, especially after a hot, sunny day. He was sure they took their time visiting over their food. From what he could remember from his dream, though, he clearly recalled that when they were finished eating they decided to drive down to the lake and take in its beauty. The mixture of rock, water, and stone had a prehistoric quality. So, they got into his aunt's ancient blue jalopy and set out for the bay. In those days, the old dirt road would have been lined with tall timothy grass, rusty alfalfa, Queen Anne's lace and blue creeping bellflowers. As they were getting close to the water, they noticed a small island just off the shore. It had a towering pine tree, *zhingwuak*, growing on it. None of them remembered ever seeing it before. They were curious about how the tree got there. One of the limbs of the giant extended over the water towards the shore, and on the limb was a man. Mishomis and his aunts were perplexed as to what the man was doing there. As they got closer, they eventually noticed that the man on the branch had his hands in a bundle of sticks. They were heaped in a twisted pile, their bulk shadowing the water below.

When they stopped the car and focused their gaze, Mishomis realized that the man's hands were in an eagle's nest. It was a shocking violation of a sacred space. Mishomis called out to him to stop. As these words reached the upper heights of the tree the man lifted a baby eaglet, *migizi*, from inside its home and perched it on the side of the nest. The young bird shrieked in distress, its small, white body quivering with fear. Mishomis called out a few more times and heard his voice ricochet around the lake. His shouting attracted attention of other people in the community, though the man in the tree did nothing to restore the bird to its home. As Mishomis persisted in his pleas, people from the reserve started gathering on the shore to see what was happening. Despite the growing crowd, no one came to the eaglet's aid. It was unnerving. He felt someone needed to do something, so he took matters into his own hands. He waited until he could delay no longer. He rushed into the knee-deep water and ran as fast as he could to reach the island and tree. He wanted to prevent the man from harming the small bird.

Mishomis was too late.

As he reached the trunk the frail life was cast over the side of the nest. The eaglet was too young. It fell into the water below. It briefly thrashed on the surface before drowning in the waters along the shallow shore.

Mishomis was enraged. He started to climb the tree to restrain the man. Yet, just before he could reach him, the man set another baby eaglet on the side of the nest. He rested it there for a second, and then cast it over the edge too. It was only at this point that Mishomis was able to stop the man from further harming the nest, and they came down from the branches. They awkwardly climbed down from the trunk together.

When they got to the bottom of the tree, there were a considerable number of people encircling the shore, watching the proceedings. No one had moved or said anything. Mishomis marched the man through the water and back towards the silent group. It was deathly quiet. The only sound was the water splashing about their feet. Then, from within the midst of the crowd, a First Nations police officer stepped forward. He was an imposing figure, bringing his full authority to bear. He looked Mishomis in the eye and proclaimed: 'I'm arresting you for disturbing the peace.' Mishomis was stunned. He struggled to regain his voice and feebly protested: 'I'm trying to help. This person, here,' he said pointing, 'he's the one that was causing the problem.' The officer's stern silence brushed his words aside. Mishomis persevered; gaining his strength and composure he went on: 'He should be arrested, not me! Look what he was doing! I was just trying to help. Don't you remember me? I just came home to visit my Auntie Mary, I was –.' Just then, the officer interrupted him mid-speech; his severe demeanour broke. Hearing Mary's name caused him to look at Mishomis in a different light. The officer's eyes took on a warmer glow as a smile crept across his face. He reached out in greeting as he began to laugh. He shook Mishomis' hand and said: 'Welcome home! Sorry about that. We don't always know who to trust around here … but now I know who you are. You're Jonah. I heard you were having supper at Mary's place tonight. Now I remember. I hope you'll forgive me. As you know, justice works differently around here. It's all relative,' he said, laughing at his own joke. The officer continued, 'I really didn't realize who you were, but not to worry. I know your family; you're OK. You're free to go.' At that point, Mishomis' dream ended and he woke up. The dream was still vivid over sixty years later.

As Mishomis sat in his old cabin remembering the experience and thinking about his grandson's question concerning the four hills, he pondered over what it all meant. There were many issues wrapped up in his dream's symbols that had guided his own life. He had learned much from its images. He felt his grandson was getting a similar message in his dream, too. His vision of the four hills had much to teach him about life.

Mishomis began to chronicle in his mind what his own dream meant to him. When he was younger, he wanted to make a difference in the wider world. He particularly wanted to help his people. This dream gave him some important cautions in that respect. In those early days, his first thought regarding the dream was that he could not do anything of significance to help others if he did not remain known to his community. The reaction of the police officer to his efforts taught him that much. He knew he had to keep his association and attention focused on the everyday experience of others if he was going to be able to do anything helpful. As time went by, he also realized he not only had to remain close to the people of his home reserve, but he also had to get closer to people from the other communities in which he participated, Indian and non-Indian. Anishinabek law was all about relationships. He believed his dream contained this general lesson that his grandson was now being taught with the four hills. While we are growing, we must be careful not to become detached from those around us in our attempts to assert our interests before the wider world. If we do, we run the risk that others will not accept our actions, even when our deeds are well-intentioned and right.

As he grew older, a second lesson from the dream settled in his mind. There are always *some* people in our own communities who are casting the power of our future away, 'over the side of the nest.' Then, remembering his grandson's dream, he thought, there are *some* people on each hill who have no regard for the real power in their midst. They push away that which would most help them reach their destination. This is done in different ways. Children are too often abused and/or taken away from those who love them. He first encountered this when he was a young man. He had been playing on the beach with his sister when the Indian Agent and the minister said hello to them on their way to his parents' house. It had been one of those hot, sticky summer days. He remembered because of the waxy shine on the preacher's face.

After the pair visited with his mother across the road, the two came down to the beach, wearing their black woollen suits, smelling of sweat. They spoke and smiled in greeting. The Agent said that his sister would be going away to school that fall. He told her how she would enjoy it. There would be lots of other young girls there. She would learn to read and write, cook and sew. He said she would have an adventure. His sister just looked at both men, not saying a word. When they left, her dark eyes filled with tears. She had spoken about this day to him before, told him of her fears. They had both seen other children from the reserve leave in this way. They had heard about the horrible things that happened to those who attended residential school. When the visitors were gone, his sister didn't say anything to anyone, for the remainder of the summer. When she came back from school six years later, she spoke a lot more, in a way she never had before. The problem was that no one could understand her or her new language and ways. Now, most people said nothing to her. Just as in his dream, people encircled the shores of her life and stood in silent watchfulness, not knowing what to do, sometimes not even wanting to respond

Mishomis witnessed the reverberation of this issue down the years, as his sister struggled to fit back in on the reserve. She had to climb through many rough spots. She looked for approval in all the wrong places when it wasn't forthcoming from those formerly close to her. She eventually fell in with someone who gave her too much attention and she could never quite escape his abusive grip. For her, it was like being in residential school all over again. After trying to alleviate her pain with too many bottles, with their sharp spirits, her children were taken from her by child welfare workers. It started another cycle that replicated the past. While this was all done in the name of her children's 'best interests,' which was true in some ways, Mishomis couldn't help but wonder if his sister's grandchildren would suffer the same fate with their kids. He would hate to see them taken by the authorities, but he knew it was a distinct possibility. Too few people around the reserve were learning the skills they needed to be good parents, to raise healthy kids. Love and trust were being shattered through a cycle of removal, abuse, and removal again. He thought it strange: what was considered to be in a person's 'best interests' at one moment in their life could become the exact opposite when viewed down the corridor of years. His sister was now a born-again Indian, attempting to find her place at home. She was now alcohol free. He hoped that she could stop annoying people long enough to find a measure of peace in her life.

Mishomis stood up from the couch; it was hard to get up at his age. He slowly made his way to the bookcase. Some of his best friends rested on those shelves. Kant, Mill, Plato, Charlie Brown, Isaac Asimov, and Farley Mowat. They were good people, all of them, at least in his opinion. His life was richer from the time spent with them. He traced his finger along the top edge of their spines. He stopped at one well-used book and picked it up. It was the Bible. It remained one of his favourites. He liked the thought that the old stories of tribal peoples continued to have resonance for many today. Browsing through it for a moment, a small piece of cardboard fell from its leaves and skimmed through the air onto the floor. Mishomis slowly bent down to retrieve it. It was two-and-a-half by three-and-a-half inches. Looking at it for a moment, and slowly turning it over in his hands, he thought his grandson must have put it there when he was a young boy. It was an old Orland Kurtenbach hockey card from the Vancouver Canucks' second year in the NHL. The teal, green, and white on the sweater still looked bright to him. He wondered how many people had seen the parallels to the Montreal Canadiens' crest and name in those early years. Turning the card over Mishomis read the words: 'Kurt is one of the best fighters in hockey.' Then, looking to the place marked by the card in the book, he saw that someone had underlined with red pencil the words: 'And in the second year of the reign of Nebuchadnezzar, Nebuchadnezzar dreamed dreams, wherewith his spirit was troubled, and his sleep brake from him.'[4]

Mishomis knew that dreams could teach people about power. They could be directed to kings, countries, and ordinary citizens. Dreams could tell them about violations of trust and conflict in those relationships. They could cause restlessness and trouble people's spirits. Like Nebuchadnezzar's experience, dreams could even shape the times and seasons of the world. He saw this in his grandson's dream, and he remembered it from his own earlier experience. All through his life he saw that children were not the only ones who were suffering from the abuse of others. Many people were being knocked down on their climb through the hills of life. They were thrown from the nest, cast out of their homes without kindness or compassion. While Mishomis was mostly aware of individuals who had caused or experienced these problems, he also knew that whole nations could suffer this fate. Like the young Jewish nation in the book he held; like his people today. Their sacred spaces had been violated. They were cast out and scattered by others in their own lands. Their climb up the first hill was cut short, shattered by a stone cut from a mountain without hands.

Individual parallels were also legion. When Mishomis looked around him, he knew that too many women were beaten or abused, raped and assaulted. Their views were often minimized and they were excluded from community participation.[5] Men also encountered abuse, though its contours could, at times, be quite different.[6] He also saw how community factions were encouraged, and how 'rivals' were destructively isolated from political, economic, and social influence. Language was employed throughout the community, and indeed, across the country, that was disrespectful of the convictions and feelings of others. He thought of how all this offended the laws of his grandmothers and grandfathers. Some people even mischaracterized others' words and intentions in order to make their own arguments appear stronger and more persuasive. Reflecting on these pathologies in his own community, Mishomis had to honestly ask himself, in thinking about his own dream: 'Am I also the man in the nest?' It was a necessary question. If the trickster taught him anything, it was that people could be simultaneously charming and cunning, selfless and selfish. One moment they could be kind, and the next they could play mean tricks.[7] He was no exception.

Mishomis put the book back on the shelf and ambled over to the window. A few small, porcelain elves sat amongst other *pau-eehnssiwuk* crowded next to the dusty pane at the base of the casement. Pulling back the curtains and looking out through the glass, he saw that Georgian Bay lay blue before him, framed by snow-covered escarpments and a vast, grey sky. The scene was rich with beauty. The Cape Croker Indian Reserve is surrounded by water and rocks, and shrouded with cedar, hemlock, and birch. The early spring melt had barely begun, with small rivulets only just beginning to drain from the sleeping land. As Mishomis looked over the lake, he thought of his own two brothers; they were drowned in its waves last winter. Sometimes he wondered if the Creator was the man in the nest. Life cast away so easily, watching but seemingly doing nothing.

It was disturbing to think of all the wasted and broken lives around the reserve. And it saddened him to see how hesitant some people could be around here, when others needed their help. Of course, he knew that people in many cultures generally stood at the edge of most issues and watched. While there were a few illustrations of how people would take action if they were pushed beyond measure, for the most part he saw silent watchfulness as rhetoric, politics, law, and philosophy became increasingly disconnected from the actions and understanding of people 'at home.' Participation too often occurred at a distance, through the legislatures, band council, media, or courts, with little active involvement from those whom their actions would most personally affect.

Yes, he thought to himself, his grandson could gain important insights about how he should live if the young man worked at understanding his own dream. Most of the issues he could see in the first hill were traced back to what was learned from childhood. There was much to gather from the traditions taught in those first years. Their best traditions needed to be encouraged, taught, and reinvented in every generation. Whole nations could take counsel from their formative teachings and experiences. This was the heart of knowledge, though it grew with you over the years. He remembered visiting with his friend Ernie a few years back and having an experience that reinforced this idea.

Mishomis had been working in Vancouver at the time, and was invited to visit with his friend. Ernie joked that he wanted to show him how 'real' Indians lived. 'Come home with me to Kingcome,' he said. 'You'll eat like royalty. When the tide goes out, our table is set. All you have to do is go down to the beach and collect your supper. All is provided for us. We have the best place in the world.' He went on, 'You Eastern Indians don't understand what it's like to be surrounded by the kind of abundance we enjoy. Eating bannock and scones, with a bit of corn soup for variety? Who would want that? And your dances! Let me tell you. You guys look like a bunch of dressed-up chickens, prancing around at your pow-wows. Wait till you see the Big House: our masks, poles, blankets, coppers, and drums. You'll see bears, killer whales, and eagles in our feasts. Now that's dignified. That's dancing.'

After piling on the teasing for a few more minutes, Ernie persuaded Mishomis that he should visit the north-west coast. A few weeks later, they boarded a small prop-engine plane and flew from Vancouver to Campbell River. Then they caught a floatplane travelling further north, flying back to the waters just off the mainland, to a place called Kingcome Inlet. It was just about the most beautiful area he had ever seen. Green-forested mountains rose steeply out of liquid-blue oceans to scrape against cloud-mottled skies: *kitug-auniquot*. Plants of a hundred varieties sprang to life on the shores at the head of the fjord. Nourished by the incoming tide's exchange with the out-flowing river, a nutrient-rich environment welled up from the depths of the sound. When they landed, they took an old, flat-bottomed tin boat with an oil-belching motor to the river's mouth. They then travelled up a ways, against the strong current, before heading to shore. From there they transferred their stuff from the boat to the bed of a pickup truck, because the river was too unpredictable to go any further. The vehicle bounced along beside the river up the valley for a time, before stopping again. The last leg of the journey was accomplished by taking another boat across the river, where the truck stopped adjacent to the village: Muusgamaaw Tsawataineuk, Kwagiulth village, home to approximately eighty people.

Mishomis spent three days visiting with Ernie, his family, and members of the community. They had a feast from the sea. Halibut, clam fritters, chowder, salmon, crab, and eulachon were in abundance. Ernie was right; he had never eaten so well. At the end of his time in the valley, Mishomis was taken to their Ceremonial Big House. It was an eighty or ninety-year-old structure with beautiful house posts and carvings. It was a place to be respected. There were benches all around the sides with a screen at the front where preparations were made; it was a place of activity. A sand/dirt floor grounded the one-hundred-by-thirty-foot structure in the strength of the valley in which it stood. With Mishomis in tow, Ernie walked around the House, going clockwise from post to post in the corners. He explained in great detail the representations the wood engravings depicted. He told the stories of their origins with visible pride. They spoke of events as old as the mountains around them. At the same time, they spoke of teachings as relevant as today. The figures on the poles were bright, lively, and beautiful. However, as he was going around the room he stopped at the last pole, to the right of the door. He pointed out gashes, where someone had taken an axe to the figure and partially defaced it. With a note of shame, Ernie said, as Mishomis remembered it: 'This is what our people have done in the day of their sadness. Some of us forgot who we were, where we came from, and the laws we were given. We turned against that which would most help us remember. Our people are beginning to recall their power, their origins, but this pole stands as a reminder that we must never again forget.' When they finished their tour, they stepped out into the veiled sunlight of the deep mountain basin. Mishomis thought of Ernie's words and remembered the lessons of casting baby eaglets over the side of a nest.

Now, six decades later, standing at the window of his cabin he looked across the bay. The years sometimes felt like days. His daughter's new house stood half way up the cape. Its black shingles poked through the trees. He was proud of her; she loved others. She was strong. The small figure of his great-granddaughter could be seen playing in the snow. 'What of her origins?' he wondered. 'Would they be sustained? Would they guide her future well? Would she be thrown from the nest, or would she climb the hill?' He thought about how children were the soul of a people, their foundation. He knew that what happens to them is eventually experienced by all. It is the lesson of Kingcome, the lesson of the first hill.

Making these connections, he remembered a story his grandfather once told him about the woodland trickster Nanabush. In its own way, it also spoke of hills and nests. It taught important lessons about children and their future. Mishomis remembered how, as Nanabush was walking from village to village, he noticed that the air was devoid of laughter. Everywhere he went, silence followed. Yet the sun shone brightly. The breeze was alive with the smell of cedar and fresh water. Even the moon stood out against the azure blue sky. 'Why no laughter?' he thought. It was a beautiful day. Nanabush was curious.

As he approached one small encampment, it appeared to him that the place seemed empty. The dogs that should be playing around the edges were missing. There were no mothers by the fire. No men were repairing the nets nearby. Emerging from the woods, Nanabush cautiously stepped into the village. The people who had fashioned the clearing had made it almost perfectly round. The community lay on the shore of a gleaming lake, with towering pine and broad maple trees bordering the site. Looking across the village, he saw seven large wigwams spread around the circle. He noted that they needed attention; the bark coverings were damaged and worn. The meadow in which they sat was overgrown. Nanabush circled the village four times before stepping into its central precincts. Only when he had gained this vantage point did he detect some movement inside a lodge. The people inside moved so slowly; they seemed weary. He wondered who they were. He approached cautiously before calling out: '*Ahnee*! How are you?' Inside, there was a slight shifting and a feeble voice. Thinking he heard an invitation, he pulled back the weathered deerskin flap covering the entrance. Nanabush came face to face with a small woman with bright dark eyes who was sitting with her grandchildren. He noticed others were slouched against the surrounding walls. After some time the grandmother leaned forward, with great effort. Looking down at her gnarled fingers she said: '*Ah-kokoosk-kahgoon*. Nanabush, what brings you here? We are so tired.'

Nanabush answered, 'I wanted to see where everyone was. The land was so quiet without their activity. Where is everyone? Why are you tired?'

The old woman spoke, 'It's our children. They are so sad. They say they have nothing to do, and they mope around the lodge all day. They have affected everyone. No one feels much like doing anything because they are so sad. Please leave us alone, Nanabush: *booni-atoon*. Outsiders are not welcome here. We are too weary. We don't want any of your tricks.' She then leaned back against the wall and closed her eyes in silence. Nanabush stared at her for a moment, before pulling the door flap down over the opening.

Rebuffed, he stood up. Nanabush thought about what the old woman had said as he walked away from the home. He returned to the middle of the village and stood before its central fire, thinking about what he had heard. He didn't like to be ignored, insulted, and dismissed; he was both sad and angry. He looked, listened, and felt the world around him in the deepest way he could – *mau-mino-aubiwin*. After some time, he picked up the sound of soft laughter. Straining to hear the source, he followed its echoes to the edge of the village, into the woods, and towards a small stream some distance away. He eventually came to stand beside a brook whose waters gushed with the sound of laughter as they tumbled over the rocks: *gausk-waewae-idjiwun*. He looked at the rocks, pebbles, and sand lying in the bed of the stream. He pondered their effect on the water. He walked along the banks gathering a few of the small, coloured stones as he went. He filled his pouch. Then Nanabush walked back to the centre of the village.

'*Ahnee!*' he called. 'Come. See. *Ondauss*.' No one came, the first time. His second call produced the same disappointing results. On the third invitation, a few Elders slowly made their way to stand beside him. When Nanabush called the fourth time, seeing the Elders, the rest of the village eventually joined the circle. They stood around the fire in the centre of the community, its embers almost extinguished. Nanabush looked at their faces and felt an oppressive sadness. The air seemed dead with the weight of their sorrow. He finally spoke, and reproved the people for their foolishness. He chastised them for forgetting their power of re-creation and regeneration. He then reached into his pouch and took a pile of stones from the brook in his hands. He held them out in front of the people, turning in every direction to show what he had gathered.

Then, with a burst of energy, Nanabush flung the rocks into the air.

The people stepped back in surprise. They recoiled and covered their heads, bracing themselves against the coming onslaught. They felt they had been tricked again. Stones were about to rain down upon them. In that moment, many berated themselves for following their Elders to the circle. Nanabush wasn't to be trusted.

As they looked up, still shielding themselves, a new thing happened.

Unexpectedly, as each coloured stone reached its zenith, it suddenly transformed. As each one fell, it became nearly weightless, and changed in mid-flight. Each one's colours became even more vibrant. Some were yellow, others turquoise, orange, or green. Some were mixed, iridescent in the sun. Soon the stones started to flicker and waver, catching the currents of air above the circle.

They started to dance in the breeze: *maemaengawauh-winugauwin*. Then they became butterflies, flying about the clearing. Eyes went wide below.

The flurry of activity above caused a stir of excitement to pass through the group. The children reached their hands into the air to try to catch them. The butterflies swirled through their grasp, though each one stayed just out of their reach. The children smiled. They gathered energy from their play. After a while, laughter could be heard from the tiny voices of the children gathered around Nanabush. The adults stood a little taller too, and they soon began to join in the chase.

Grins broke out; mothers and fathers playfully tussled with the kids, sometimes lifting them high into the air.

The dogs eventually entered the fray, barking and weaving between the legs of the people of the village.

And the butterflies sailed on, over and around the people wherever they could be found. A reminder of the gift of laughter, and the beauty and joy life could bring.[8]

Mishomis smiled at the thought. Nanabush had taken something that was seemingly ordinary and transformed it to create new life. He wondered how many other people remembered these deeper laws about hope and healing. The land and their old stories had much to teach them about how to live well in the world. He could hardly wait to tell his grandson – his dream could do much to deepen his insight into these issues. The powers of regeneration and re-creation were literally at hand.

W'AUD-ISSOOKAE[1]

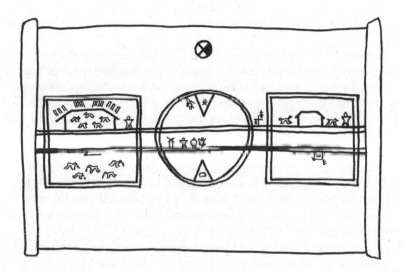

'Indian Dogs and the Law.' The young man thought someone should write a law review article about this subject one day. It would be a great topic because it would reveal many things about Indian reserves. People throughout Indian Country would understand the subject's significant, representative nature. Dogs were probably the first point of contact on most of the reserves he had visited, though the Canada Mortgage and Housing Corporation (CMHC) clapboard bungalows were a close second. Dogs were mercurial, bearing the shifting personalities of those they lived with. Their behaviours sometimes reminded him of Nanabush. A focus on their legal status and behaviour could reveal much about life around them. Such an article could be doctrinal and discuss band by-laws regulating dogs in Indian Country. It could develop the interpretation of these laws by various legal institutions. Or the piece could be socio-legal, exploring the interaction between customary norms associated with dogs in traditional Indian cultures and the adoption of more formal rules since Indigenous contact with colonial societies. Even better, he mused, a whole theoretical structure could be developed from such a study: 'Critical Indian Doggie Studies.' It could use hermeneutical methodologies to great effect. Or maybe someone could devise a few formulas and strive for predictive analysis with their theory: 'Law and Dogenomics.' He laughed to himself. Good title, he thought – but maybe it was a little too hidebound. He considered all this as he walked past the old Indian Agent's house at the crook in the road on the shore of McGregor's Harbour, *wikwedons*. It was besieged by dogs.

The dogs had certainly taken their toll on the place. In fact, they made a good case for adverse possession, having dug holes in the yard, through the fence, and under the foundation. He wondered what the old Agent would think if he saw the house today. The barbells and broken-down exercise bench out front would probably be weighed and found wanting. He might also object to the black Iron Maiden sticker on the centre of the living room window. Weeds were everywhere, and junk was strewn through the yard. The building must have been something grand in its time, though. It was one of the few stone houses standing on the reserve. No doubt it was built to impress when it was thought Indians needed such lessons. Made of tan, multilayered limestone bricks, it overlooked the bay and surrounding precincts. From its generous two-sided porch, the Agent would have been able to survey the activities of all who passed. He would even have been able to keep his eye on the Chief living on the other side of the harbour. Such was the positioning of the house on the reserve. It paralleled the Agent's position in the legal hierarchy known as the *Indian Act*.[2]

The young man continued past the house as he wound his way around the bay. He passed his uncle's old brick farmhouse, destroyed by arson twenty years ago. Only a blackened stone chimney remained in the clearing to mark the death of the family's dream. Then the young man was at the field in front of the Catholic church. He always admired the tarpaper home across the corner there. A sign in its window read Built Without Taxpayer Dollars. He then turned left and walked to the end of Jones Point. He stopped before the foundation of his great-grandfather's house, where it had stood a generation ago. Snow piled in the shadows of broken-down walls and took defence in scattered hollows where the sun could not reach. Lilac bushes and gnarled apple trees surrounded the stones. Buds on the otherwise empty branches promised the return of new life with spring. He turned and faced the water, admiring the spot his ancestors had chosen to live. The ice was almost completely out of the harbour. He walked down to the beach, across the road in front of the site. Generations of children must have played there. His great-grandfather had been born on that very shore. He was wrapped in moss and bearskins in those first few years of life; Aunt Irene used to love to tell such details about him. The young man then looked back the way he came and saw the Agent's house across the bay, diminished by both time and distance.

He knew most reserves in the United States and Canada had Indian Agents appointed by the federal government to oversee Indian 'development' and facilitate the assimilation process.[3] Some tribes even had whole bureaucracies assigned by the government to look after their affairs, called Indian Agencies.[4] Agents and Agencies were supposed to be the last word in the community on such diverse issues as band expenditures, land surrenders, the passage of laws, the running of schools, the building of infrastructure, and the general economic and social climate of the reserve. He remembered the quote from George Manuel he had to memorize in grade twelve: 'It was the job of these new white chiefs to displace our traditional leaders in their care over our day to day lives in order to bring our way of life into line with the policies that had been decreed in Ottawa.'[5] He thought this statement about summed up their purpose. He had been told, however, that the Indian Agents of his reserve had been a rather incompetent lot, though their official, legal capacity certainly made them a force in the community.[6] The shifting sands of Indian agency caught his thoughts and caused him to reflect on its influence on issues with which he was familiar.

In his own life he had seen many different views of Indian agency. He could still remember his first real encounter with the subject. It was in his grandparents' pitched wood log cabin many years before. In fact, he could see the escarpment that shielded the small house at its base; it was beyond the Johnston cottages across the bay. The old cabin was in the middle of nowhere, the centre of an amazing world. He remembered an earlier day, sitting beside his grandmother's wood stove in her old chair, having not spoken for ages. He had probably been about ten at the time. After a couple of hours of non-stop conversation, Mishomis, Nokomis, and his mother went silent. They turned their attention to him. They suddenly seemed to realize he was there. After a moment's reflection, Nokomis said something like, 'He's so quiet. He must be listening to everything we say: *Bzindamowin*.' The young man recalled feeling good about her words. He had tried to sit still so as not to disturb them. He didn't want them to stop or change a thing they were saying because of his presence. At that moment, he had struggled to blend into the room. He remembered that they seemed to consider him for a moment, and then go on talking.

And they did talk. He learned of *Kwoabnise*, *Windigo*, *Mishi-bizheu*, and Wolverine: creatures that stalked the darkness and brought terror to those who were careless. They spoke of how the world was alive, or animate,[7] fires walked along the escarpment, and water lit up the night. Trees spoke to you when you passed by them. Even the dead were living and would visit if you needed them, or if they needed something from you. This was agency. It was all part of Neyaashiinigmiing, the Cape Croker Indian Reserve in what is now called Ontario, Canada. His mother's ancestors made this land home from time of memory. She had grown up in that place where they sat, on this territory, and in those three little rooms. And listening to his family's stories at ten years of age, understanding dawned on the young man that he, too, was growing up. He was becoming a part of the place and sharing in its memories. Similar moments throughout his childhood entwined themselves with his own experiences. They shaped his understanding of the world around him. They helped him glimpse another kind of agency that had great influence on the reserve.

Standing there on his great-grandparents' beach, he thought of many experiences connecting and separating him from that time: his life on the farm, high school in Barrie, an early marriage and then university. He thought of time spent in law school. How in those years, like in that old cabin, he once again had sat very quietly. He couldn't recall speaking in class more than ten times. In contrast with his time at the cabin, his silence wasn't because he didn't want to disturb, but because what he heard was disturbing. The stories seemed so different. Everything felt cold and lifeless. The people spoken of were detached from any context. Law school seemed to embody a distorted type of agency, and it reminded him of the Indian Agent. It felt repressive. It was not like the Anishinabek concept his grandparents taught him. In the law school, case after case piled one on top of another, where background barely mattered and facts were only the shadows of reasons for the decision. And the places he studied had no spirits, only uses, divisions, and remainders. And the dead were, well ... *dead*. Apparently they could only be relevant vicariously, through criminal law and civil remedies. The stories did not connect him to any place; in fact, they seemed to sever him from the world he knew. They created a realm of interchangeable and abstract concepts that obscured the vast range of choice available to both those observing and those involved in its administration.

At university, he learned that one effect of this concealment was that very little protection was accorded to Aboriginal rights and freedoms.[8] Lives were unduly 'susceptible to government interference' as a result.[9] Interference came through the suppression of Aboriginal choice in numerous fields, such as governance,[10] land use and ownership,[11] parent-child relationships,[12] economic development,[13] religious practices,[14] association,[15] due process,[16] and equality.[17] Those who created and administered the law had not ensured that Indian peoples were 'endowed with institutions and rights necessary to maintain and promote their identities against the assimilative pressures of the majority.'[18] As time passed, this led to even greater governmental interference, as Indians were not extended the institutional means to resist the violation of their rights.[19] The absence of remedies to contest the injustices they faced contributed to their unacceptable socio-economic status within a generally prosperous society.[20] Law, he saw, had largely hidden Indian agency from public view, obscured by a heavy stratum of Canadian federalism.[21]

Yet he knew that people's immersion under the structures of others was not always from a failure of effort to make it otherwise.[22] He knew this from stories like those heard at his grandparents' house. His Mishomis helped him understand that Indians were not passive objects in the sweep of colonial history. His Nokomis taught him that Indians exercised their will to contest and sometimes subvert institutions and ideologies imposed on them. Despite their best efforts, he also knew his people encountered great difficulties in turning these intrusions around. They were buried under levels of law and bureaucracy that had little to do with their understanding and aspirations for their place in the world.

The young man looked up at the oak trees standing beside him. He glanced back over his shoulder at the apple trees and lilac bushes surrounding the old place. His great-grandfather had planted many good things here. He also nourished and grew that which was passed on to him. After millennia of self-rule, he became an elected chief on the reserve under the provisions of another government's rules. Prior to that, through the seven previous generations, his family had served as chiefs through heredity and community consensus.[23] Yet he had to submit to the federally enacted *Indian Act* to be recognized by the Dominion government as the representative of his people.[24] It was the only way the government would allow the community to receive the benefits of treaty promises secured by his father a short time before. He worked for close to fifty years as a chief and councillor and struggled to make it relevant to the values and activities of the people he served. The Act contained a detailed code that imposed a structure on Indian communities largely inconsistent with their ancient teachings and traditions. Passed in 1876, it sought to change them into middle-class Victorian citizens by transforming their identity,[25] land holding systems,[26] traditional governance structures,[27] spiritual observances,[28] economies,[29] and community citizenship rules and entitlements.[30]

As if these changes were not enough, an Indian Agent – like the man who once lived across the way – was inserted into this dysfunctional scheme.[31] His great-grandfather found it difficult to integrate the Act's authoritarian proscriptions with the consensual approach to governance common to Anishinabek political and legal thought. His success in responding to community needs was most often achieved in spite of the *Indian Act*. He had to take great steps to preserve the Indian's agency at Cape Croker. He had to make many hard choices to prevent it from being undermined by the legislation's substitution of an Indian Agent.[32]

As these thoughts trailed through his mind, a small breeze picked up the water and splashed it against the sand at the young man's feet. His eyes followed the line of the waves around the harbour to the far shore. Sizing up the bay, he estimated that it was about a mile around. It was good moorage for the few commercial fishing boats his cousins would launch here in a few weeks. In the summer it would shelter a different kind of vessel, as tourists' sailboats from around the Great Lakes would gather every weekend. Taking it all in, the young man thought that the view here was probably not that much different from when his great-grandfather stood on the same spot over one hundred years ago. Except for the large, white water tower below the second bluff, he imagined it looked much the same. He was glad he came home for the weekend.

It was good to be home, to have the land teach him again and trigger many memories. It was his legal archive. He had not thought of those early times in the cabin for quite a while. He had also forgotten how jarring his law school experience had been. He had become somewhat used to its strange ways through graduate school and teaching in law schools these past few years. Now, thinking about these experiences in a fresh light, he turned his mind back to his dream from the night before. His conversation with his grandparents this morning had been helpful, too. He again wondered how the four hills related to his life and the things he was doing at the university. He knew the issue of Indian agency was somehow important in figuring out the answer to these questions. Many legal issues played a powerful role inhibiting and unburdening the power of choice and accountability on the reserve. He wanted to trace their connections.

In his mind, he reviewed the legal history he had been teaching in his classes. In doing so, it was a little like seeing the first hill again; a lot of broken hopes piled at the bottom, and a great deal of immaturity. Only a few issues were successful in rising to the top. He considered the Supreme Court of Canada's virtual silence on the issue of Aboriginal peoples' place in society for nearly one hundred years. By ignoring issues of Indian agency in such a stark way, this institution tacitly reinforced the claims of others to power over Indians. It enabled others to pull them down. It wasn't until 1973 when the Court released *Calder v. A.G.B.C.* that the situation started to change.[33]

The Court's recognition that Aboriginal title was a justiciable right, and not solely a moral or political concern,[34] finally raised the issue of Indian agency to the level of public consciousness.[35] It elevated the notion that Aboriginal peoples had un-extinguished legal interests that could potentially protect them from the types of abuses experienced during the first one hundred years of Confederation. Furthermore, the *Calder* case also suggested that Aboriginal rights had as their source an authority that originally lay outside of the common law and constitutional legal structures. This unique source was 'the fact ... that when the settlers came, the Indians were there, organized in societies and occupying the land as their forefathers had done for centuries.'[36] As such, the Court said that Aboriginal rights did 'not depend on treaty, executive order or legislative enactment,' as most freedoms did. They were 'pre-existing rights' that had their own logic 'indigenous to their culture [though] capable of articulation under the common law.'[37] The effect of the *Calder* decision for Aboriginal peoples was profound. Indigenous legal and political issues arose to occupy a permanent place in Canada's political and legal landscape.[38] Much like those of his dream, they had taken a few feeble steps forward up the first hill.

He then reflected how, not quite ten years later,[39] this trajectory continued. Indigenous issues rose even higher within Canada's legal terrain when they were recognized and affirmed in section 35(1) of the

Constitution Act, 1982.[40] He thought of all the fuss this had caused when such protections should have been there from the start. The open-ended nature of the provision's wording, 'the existing Aboriginal and treaty rights of the Aboriginal peoples of Canada are hereby recognized and affirmed,' left much room for subsequent negotiation, interpretation, and manipulation. The politicians tried to define these rights through a series of constitutionally mandated First Ministers' conferences.[41] When they were in session, the young man would come home from school each day and turn on the TV. He loved to watch them dance around the table with their fancy, frustrating debates. The prime minister, provincial premiers, and the leaders from the major national Aboriginal organizations struggled with one another to give Aboriginal rights meaning. After their failure, he was at law school in time to study the Supreme Court's watershed decision of *R. v. Sparrow*[42] in 1990. The Court then went on to render no less than twenty-five decisions dealing with the rights of Aboriginal peoples in Canadian society in little over a ten-year period.[43]

The decisions swirled through his mind. He had read them so many times. He tried to catalogue their effects. On the one hand, he saw how Indigenous rights had climbed to national consciousness. In *R. v. Sparrow* the Court recognized that existing Aboriginal rights could include fishing for food, social, and ceremonial purposes. The *R. v. Gladstone* decision affirmed that in certain instances, where evidence warranted, Aboriginal peoples could claim rights to fish for commercial purposes. *Blueberry Indian Band v. Canada* recognized a fiduciary duty on the part of the government to treat Aboriginal lands with trust-like precision and to act towards them in good faith. *Delgamuukw v. British Columbia* affirmed that Aboriginal title included the exclusive right to use traditional territories for a wide variety of purposes for the benefit of the community, if the government had not eliminated the right by extinguishing it. *R. v. Badger*, *R. v. Sundown*, and *R. v. Marshall* (I and II) lifted treaty rights above non-treaty uses of lands and resources to protect agreements negotiated by Indigenous peoples that are often over two hundred years old. Duties of consultation, accommodation, and good faith were imposed on the Crown through the *Haida*, *Taku*, and *Mikisew Cree* cases. These and other decisions re-inscribed Aboriginal issues on a Canadian legal structure that had built over the country's Indigenous systems. He saw promise in these developments. They contained a view of Indian agency that was respectful of the principles he was taught as a young boy.

On the other hand, he saw much that was troubling in these cases. He was painfully aware of how the same decisions that protected Aboriginal rights simultaneously hid strong currents that threatened their erosion. For example, he knew that *Sparrow* outlined a test which allowed for so-called justifiable infringements of Aboriginal rights. *Gladstone* extended this test to allow for the infringement of Aboriginal rights in cases where the interests (*not* the Constitutional rights) of other Canadians might be affected. *R. v. Badger* and *R. v. Marshall* (I and II) applied this infringement test to treaties. He thought it was wrong that non-Aboriginal governments were given power to unilaterally reduce treaty rights. Treaties, as negotiated instruments, set out the limits of each party's power over the other in the agreement. They were based on mutual consent. This principle was undermined if the government could act alone. He remembered how his friend Mary-Ellen had tried to persuade the Court to adopt the better position when she appeared before them in *Badger*. He was sad she had not been able to convince them. Then he reflected on how *Delgamuukw* had further corroded Aboriginal rights, despite its high promises. Some had even written about this in law review articles.[44] The *Delgamuukw* Court suggested that a broad range of governmental objectives could justifiably infringe Aboriginal rights. As he taught numerous times, the Court wrote that 'the development of agriculture, forestry, mining, and hydroelectric power, the general economic development of the interior of British Columbia, protection of the environment or endangered species, the building of infrastructure and the settlement of foreign populations to support those aims, are the kinds of objectives that ... can justify the infringement of [A]boriginal title.'[45] The list of objectives that could wash away constitutionally recognized Indigenous rights was sweeping. It threatened the very core of Aboriginal rights as constitutional rights, if they could be overridden by the non-constitutional interests of other Canadians. He wished he could draw these harmful laws out of Canadian jurisprudence, and replace them with something more settling for Indigenous peoples. Yet rights became even less secure in the *Bernard and Marshall* case, where the Court did not even get to the threshold issue of recognizing Aboriginal title. It concluded the Mik'maq people of Nova Scotia were historically too nomadic to possess such rights. As he reviewed each case in his mind he could feel how they were a little like the sand at his feet; like the people on the first hill. The erosion and cruelty was incessant.

Despite the strengthening spring sun, he was beginning to get chilled thinking about all this. Standing on the shore, he felt winter's reluctant retreat. Beebon's snow and stiff winds hung tenaciously to the new season's edges. The young man pulled his coat more tightly about his neck and quickly made his way back around the bay. When he arrived at the Indian Agent's house he stopped for a moment. All he could hear was the barking and growling of dogs inside the old place. *Niikimo Animook.* The story of their creation always fascinated him: cut down from a giant and then grown from the earth for the protection and companionship of humans. The noise inside the old house grew as he stood there. It was unlike anything he had heard before; in fact, it sounded destructive to him. He decided to knock on the door of the old Agent's house to see if something was wrong. He was also curious to see what it was like. He had never been inside before.

As the young man unlatched the metal gate, a few inquisitive faces lifted up to look at him. A grey, wire-haired husky and a mixed lab/beagle ambled over to where he stood. The beagle nuzzled him as the young man walked up the path and the husky sniffed him from behind. Approaching the porch he noticed a malamute/shepherd cross lay sleeping on the top stair. He stepped over it and knocked on the door. After some commotion inside a large black Irish Setter nudged the door open. It was the dog who often stayed at his uncle's house; his name was Nag'anal'mot. He looked up at the young man, who heard, 'Can I help you?' He could almost swear the voice came from the dog, but when he looked closer it just stared back in silence. He peered around the partially opened door to see what kind of trick this was, when he heard the invitation once again. He couldn't be sure who was speaking. The voice seemed to come from the direction of another dog he could see. He wondered if someone was fooling around with a speaker inside the house. He didn't like the ambiguity. The uncertainty of knowing who was speaking reminded him of some of the storytellers and writers he knew around the reserve. Since he couldn't tell who was talking to him, the young man yelled into the air: 'Who's there? I can't see you. I heard all the noise from the road and wondered if you were OK.' When he finished calling out, a few more dogs walked into his line of vision and stared back at him. He tried pushing himself even further into the room, but Nag'anal'mot lightly growled and blocked his way. Then, from somewhere near the back of the house, a gravel-spiked voice barked back: 'I'm OK. Sorry about the noise, I was just fooling around with some friends. Come back tonight; we're having a party. I'll show you around the place.' With those words, the Setter at the young man's feet backed into the house and the door closed behind him on its hinges.

The young man gazed at the grimy door inches from his nose, wishing he hadn't stopped at the house. Now he would have to come back tonight. It was rude to turn down invitations from others on the reserve. He didn't want people thinking he had forgotten his manners because he had been away. He was also suspicious about the way someone had made it appear as though the dogs were talking. He didn't want people teasing him, and was anxious to get to the bottom of this mystery. The young man also wanted to know more details about who was speaking to him, and why they wouldn't fully reveal themselves. He knew that indirection was sometimes an Anishinabek practice. It was employed to encourage listeners to use their own agency when interpreting messages. But was that the case here? It could be frustrating trying to figure out life on the reserve. Anyway, the young man thought to himself, he wanted to learn more, so he would return tonight. As he walked away from the house he also reminded himself that he was curious to see more of the place. He wondered what a decaying agency would look like.

As night fell, the young man found himself back on the old house's front porch. He knocked as before. As he did so, the door swung open from the force of his knuckles gentling rapping against the wood. This time, no one welcomed him. Just like his earlier visit, he once again peered around the door. It was too dark to see much. 'Can I come in?' he called out. There was virtually no sound, at first. Then, from the back of the house, he heard a noise. Barely audible chords of some tinny heavy metal music grew in intensity. After a minute or so, the young man caught a line of the lyrics, 'Eyes that shine burning red ... Dreams of you all through my head.' It was *Black Dog* by Led Zeppelin, one of his favourites. Rising in crescendo, the song eventually washed over the house. When Jimmy Page's guitar screamed out at the song's end, the music was at its loudest. At that moment, a door at the back of the house burst open. A pack of dogs swirled into view, bumping and rustling through the corridors. They seemed frenzied by the pulsating beat.

The young man pushed the door fully open and rushed into the house when he realized what was happening. Passing through the narrow entrance, his arms became entangled in the fur-lined walls. It was eerily disconcerting. Looking around, he could barely make out what seemed like long pelts and skins dangling on the rungs of the tight corridor. He burrowed his way through the mess to reach the large living/dining room just beyond. Fifteen or twenty dogs circled the space, running and crashing into each other from all directions. The room was in complete disarray. The dogs seemed out of control. Their frenzied actions were destroying the place. The man took a closer look at them. He wanted to see if he could recognize any from his early morning walks around the reserve. He saw they were of all types and breeds, but he wasn't familiar with any one of them. He did notice one thing similar amongst them, though – they had no tails. It seemed they had all had cropped tails, and the young man wondered why anyone would do that to them.

Looking around the room, he tried to call out again over the noise, but no one answered. A few animals jumped up and barked at him, but other than that there was no reply. He showed himself around the house: the kitchen, bedrooms, and bathroom. The place was in chaos. While the house must have been impressive at one time, it was now in bad shape. Everywhere he wandered, he saw nothing but dogs and the trail of destruction they were leaving behind. Dogs were even in the closets. While the young man had a bad feeling about what he was seeing, he couldn't shake the impression that the place had the distinct feel of a party, or a feast. The atmosphere was somehow charged with energy and the dogs seemed to be getting more rambunctious and excited as time passed. After half an hour waiting and wandering, the man was growing tired of the surrounding anarchy. He wondered why someone would let their home fall to this level of disorder. It offended him, and seemed to be a deep transgression of higher Anishinabek legal ideals. It was just plain, poor stewardship. The law professor within him couldn't help but see the parallels to what was happening to the earth around him both on the reserve and beyond. He didn't feel like joining the dogs in their destructive reverie.

When enough of the evening had passed, it became clear to him that he would never know who invited him to the house, so the young man made his decision to leave. As he turned to exit, a large rottweiler at his side lifted its back right leg and soaked the chair by the living room door. The dog looked at the young man and panted as a pool of warm urine puddled around them. It almost seemed pleased with itself. It was obvious to the man that these dogs needed some discipline. They needed order. They had no respect for their environment. Wherever the owner was, he thought to himself, he could not sit here and let the dogs destroy the house. Wondering what to do to clear them from the home, an idea from an old Nanabush story came to him.[46]

The young man jumped to the cushion of a nearby couch. He cupped his hands around his mouth and yelled in his loudest voice: '*Ishkode*! *Ishkode*! *Ishkode*! Fire! Fire! Fire!' Then he went running through the house clapping, waving his arms, and stomping on the floors in an attempt to frighten and chase the dogs away. After a few minutes, his actions seemed to be working. The dogs were thinning out. They poured out of the various rooms and funnelled through the front hall with its narrow corridor. There, they became entangled in a bottleneck for a time. The dogs writhed in confusion, tearing at one another and at the furs lining the foyer walls. They used their teeth to rip free from the mat of twisted bodies. Taking random chunks from their pile, they rushed out into the night with flesh and hair clutched in their mouths.

When the hall was nearly cleared of the dogs, the young man managed to chase the last of them out into the yard. They all stood around eyeing one another with pelts clenched in their jaws. In the dim light, the young man thought the dogs looked like they had tails in their mouths. They were each of a different size and shape. Whatever had been lining the hall now hung from what looked like the wrong end of their crop-tailed bodies. As the dogs mingled on the lawn, they cautiously began to approach one another from behind, apparently searching for something. The sight caused a random thought to pass through his mind; it was like the Nanabush story, too. He always saw dogs sniff each other's backsides whenever they greeted. They seemed to have an obsession with the practice, as if they had lost something that was rightfully theirs, seeing if the other had mistakenly taken their tail. The scene reminded him of the people of the reserve and those of the world beyond them. Quietly laughing at the idea, he also saw himself reflected in their actions. He realized that agency could be a funny thing, when you looked into it. The thought made for a good end to the day – Indian Dogs and the Law might be a good field of inquiry after all.

PAUWAUWAEIN[1]

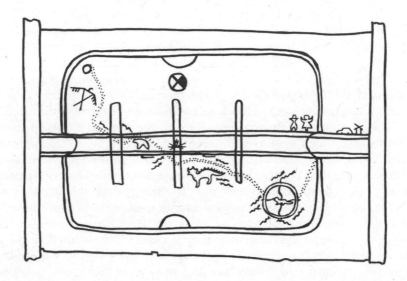

Nokomis drove out the old road behind her house. The trail began as little more than two ruts through a field. She had to be careful with all the mud; she didn't want to get stuck. While she loved being outside in the spring, if something should happen she didn't want to have to walk back to get help. It was a day to spend alone enjoying the silence of the woods. She was looking forward to seeing how the old place had weathered the seasons. She ached for its peace and serenity. There was a lot to think about today. It had been ages since she had visited the ancient site. Her grandson's dream had awakened old memories for her. She hadn't felt like this in a long time: *amajise*. It was invigorating. She wondered what the earth would teach her today.

On her way out, she passed an old Studebaker and a fishing boat. They had rested in her field at the back of her house for ages, rusting into the bedrock and rejoining the land. Her son never did get around to fixing much that lay around the place. It was a shame she thought, it would have been nice to drive the old car again. She eventually left the field behind and tunnelled through the forest. Branches scratched along her car doors. Last fall's weeds and jagged, loose rocks scraped against the car's undercarriage. She didn't mind. It was a welcome sound, reminding her of earlier times. She had often come this way as a young woman. The first time was by horse and wagon, gathering wood and doing some trapping with her family. As they moved through the forest, she would leave the trail from time to time and go exploring. It was always easy to catch up with the old cart later on in the day. She loved the tangle of the woods, the hidden treasures in every corner. It was during one of those forays almost sixty years ago that she made her discovery.

Events from that long-ago day flooded her mind as she drove deeper into the bush. She must have been about twelve years old at the time. An old, sun-lit meadow had first caught her attention. Then the abandoned apple orchard in the clearing intrigued her. The circular symmetry of the trees' placement made her wonder who had once lived so far back in the woods. Even at that time, there had been nothing around for miles and she couldn't recall anyone ever mentioning that people had lived back here. No one but the Anishinabek had ever used the surrounding country. Since her grandfather had signed their treaty, the area had always been Indian reserve land. Now, driving through the bush, she recalled that earlier day in the meadow. She had looked around for a while, searching the ground for clues as to its past occupancy. Nokomis had been sure she would find something; in her younger days she had a good eye for detail. Yet when she finished looking through the grass and scrub, it was only then that she looked up to notice the escarpment towering over her in the clearing. She had been so sheltered walking through the bush, and then so focused on the ground once she arrived, that she had failed to look up when she entered the old grove that first time. She recalled her shock when she finally took her bearings.

An immense rock wall had loomed above her, giving her vertigo. When she regained her balance she remembered looking at the meadow in a different light. She guessed that whoever once lived there probably wanted to be close to the bluff. She wondered what the attraction was, and made her way to its base to examine it more closely. It had not been an easy climb for Nokomis, even in her childhood. Looking back on the experience, it reminded her somewhat of the climb her grandson described from his dream this morning. The hill was thick with shrubs, jagged rocks, and stones. Moss covered the floor. Boulders the size of houses piled one upon another. They had been sheered by ice from the towering cliffs before her. As a young girl Nokomis climbed between, around, and over them as she advanced. Her hands and knees had been bloodied and torn. Crouching to wipe her reddened palms, she had smeared them over some moss. As she did so she lost her balance, and her hand plunged through the foliage covering the ground and into a large hole. She nearly fell in. After steadying herself, she had studied the hole more closely. She remembered that a cool breeze had risen from the opening she had made in the moss. She immediately knew that it must have been connected to a larger cavern below. She climbed down off the limestone shelf and explored the crevices that cut into its sides.

Now, as she drew closer to the old site, she turned off the car and sat in silence. A lot had happened to her since that earlier day. Nokomis hoped she still had enough strength to make it back there. Age could make you so foolish. But she had to go. Age also brought wisdom, and she wondered if her grandson's dream contained another key to understanding what it all meant. She offered a short prayer and got out of the car. Orienting herself, she looked around. A blue jay's call echoed through the trees. Barren branches stirred in a slight wind. *Deendehnsuek* flew into view and passed into the tangle before her. Taking their presence as a sign, she lined herself up with a rise in the escarpment's first hill and ambled into the woods, towards the place she first came to know as a young girl.

Twelve hours later, back in the old cabin by the bay, Nokomis was still gone and Mishomis was worried. She left that morning and the day was now past. He called his grandson, but there was no answer. His cabin next door was dark. When they spoke earlier he had mentioned his invitation to the Agent's old house. Mishomis thought the young man must still be there. While he hoped his grandson was having fun, he also wished he would hurry home. Mishomis was anxious and wanted to talk to someone. He couldn't help but wonder if his wife was OK. She had been gone for too long. The lone police officer on the reserve couldn't be reached and no one answered the phone at his daughter's home. Mishomis didn't know what to do. He was too old to navigate through the woods in the dark to see if she was all right. Nokomis had been so insistent about visiting the old site again. 'Told her she shouldn't go without someone else,' he said aloud. She was too old to help herself if she had an accident.

Mishomis tried to calm himself by watching TV. It was no use. *The Teletubbies* were not much solace. The strange *pau-eehnssiwuk*, from some distant land puzzled him. He sometimes found them captivating, but not tonight. Even the baby's head in the sun seemed agitated. It was the first time he wondered why the show aired at nine o'clock at night. Were four-year-olds up this late these days? He wished they could pull in another station, but reception was limited on the reserve. He turned off the set and sat in the dark. Across the road, the waves lapped against the shore. Their gentle rhythm brought the comfort he couldn't find from the TV.

Half an hour later the low rumble of an engine startled him out of a light sleep. Lights flashed and slid across his wall as he looked up. Mishomis creaked out of his chair and peered out the window, hoping to see his wife's car. He was a little disappointed to realize it was only his grandson's Cherokee pulling into the driveway next door. At that moment Nag'anal'mot, the neighbourhood dog, began to bark at the car. For some reason Nag'anal'mot was always hanging around the place when his grandson was home. When Mishomis heard the young man's front door slam, he picked up the phone and called him again. 'Can you come over, grandson? I need your help.' In a few minutes the young man was at the door.

'What's wrong Mishomis? Why did you call? Are you all right?'

'It's your Nokomis. She left this morning, and she's not back yet. I don't know what to do. I was hoping you could go look for her and bring her home.'

'Where'd she go? I'll go get her right away.'

The old man explained that she had driven out to the bluff behind the house. 'Do you remember the meadow near the escarpment where we used to do those ceremonies with you?' Mishomis asked.

The young man nodded and said, 'I think so. Isn't that where those seven old apple trees were planted in a circle?'

Mishomis confirmed his grandson's memory, and told him he would likely find Nokomis nearby. He said, 'There's actually more to that place than we ever showed you. We were waiting until the time was right. Your Nokomis went out there today because of what you said about your dream this morning. It prompted her to check something we have been safeguarding for you. We were going to show you one day, but that's beside the point just now. Nokomis has been gone too long. I'm afraid she might have fallen or hurt herself. Do you remember how to get to the meadow?'

The young man nodded affirmatively.

'Good. All you need to do is drive along the trail out back until you find her car. It'll probably be parked in the middle of the road near the wooden cross we tacked onto that large *zhawae-meesh* tree near the meadow. I'm sure our markings will still be there; no one but us ever goes back that far. If you don't find her on the road, just remember to follow that rise to the right of the road beside our old tree. You stay on that ridge for about a quarter mile until you come to the clearing.'

'I think I remember how to get there Mishomis, though I've never been in the dark. I'll need your flashlight.'

Mishomis rifled through a nearby drawer and handed his grandson a flashlight. 'You'll need this for sure. If you don't find her on the way, she probably won't be in the meadow when you get there. You'll have to shine your light on the escarpment across the field. It will probably take some searching, but you'll see the big stone under the bluff that we painted red, white, black, and yellow. Remember it from the ceremonies? It's lined up with the ridge you'll be following when you enter the meadow. Nokomis is probably in an old lodge nearby. That's why she went back there today. We discovered the place years ago but we never told you about it because the time wasn't right. It's under the Chicago Black Hawk-like Indian profiled on the escarpment face. The stars look bright enough tonight that you should be able to see the rock's nose standing out against the sky. She'll probably be in the cavern near the escarpment, just under the stone Indian.'

'Do you think she'll be able to hear me from the meadow if I call out to her?' the young man asked.

'I'm not sure. You might have to walk towards the coloured rock if she doesn't respond. She'll probably hear you once you get close enough. Once she calls back, just follow her voice.'

The young man prepared to leave as Mishomis walked him to the door.

As they parted, the old man said, 'Don't forget to turn your cell phone on this time. I couldn't reach you when you weren't home earlier. I want to know how she is as soon as you find her.'

Forty-five minutes later, the young man found his grandmother's car where Mishomis said it would be. It was next to the old beech tree. The car was empty. He shone his flashlight through the window to see if she had left a note. He saw nothing. The young man then walked around the car and found the ridge his grandfather had told him about. He vaguely remembered it from ceremonies last summer. He entered the forest, and was careful to keep to the ridge as he walked into the gloom. Along the way he stumbled over rocks and old roots and kept running into sharp branches. It was tough going, but the young man arrived at the meadow twenty minutes later. Since Nokomis had not hurt herself along the ridge, he assumed she must be where Mishomis said.

When he entered the meadow he was taken aback. It was a stunning sight. Standing in the opening under April stars, the Milky Way lay frozen in the sky. Winter-maker and the Three Canoes could be clearly seen paddling along the Path of Souls leading to the land of the dead. *Kiwedin'anang*, *Mishi-bizheu*, and *Waasnode* were also vibrant in the sky. Many beings with their laws and stories were visible in the heavens tonight. The stars lit up the trees circling the clearing and threw into sharp relief the white limestone escarpment wall rising above the field. He could see the Black Hawk warrior profiled on the rock face; it was silhouetted perfectly against the rising night sun. Seeing the sky, the young man remembered it was the breaking of the snow shoes moon: *popogamii-giizis*. Its clarity and sharpness brought him back to how cold it was out here; he understood why Mishomis was worried.

The young man called out to his grandmother, but there was no answer.

He then raised his flashlight and shone it above the trees on the opposite side of the meadow, searching for the coloured rock. After a few minutes he found what he was looking for, and began his walk towards it. He entered the dark forest again, hoping he was staying true to the direction he was headed. As he walked, the young man soon discovered he was on a sharp incline, and had to climb over and around many rocks and boulders. It was slow going, and he fell more than once. Scrambling in the dark, he scraped his hands and knees on more than one occasion. However, with determination he climbed the hill and eventually came to the base of the bluff. The trees did not grow right against the cliff, so he scanned his flashlight along the wall, searching for the overhanging Indian-faced rock. It was a few hundred yards to his right so he had to clamber around a final boulder to reach the destination. When he rounded the last big rock, he saw a sliver of light spill from a fissure in a crevice just ahead. At once he called to his grandmother, and he heard her respond from within the cavern walls.

Nokomis invited the young man to come in.

It was a low entrance facing towards the east. The young man bent down and had to creep through on all fours. Crawling out of the darkness, Nokomis helped him up through the narrow passage. She spoke his name in Anishinabemowin, and took him in her arms. It reminded him of entering a sweat lodge. Light from the fire illuminated the large cavern within; shadows danced across fractured walls. He could smell cedar, sweetgrass, sage, and tobacco mingling in the air. The man looked to his grandmother for explanation. Nokomis was quiet for a few minutes before she finally spoke.

'I was only twelve when I found this place. I almost fell through a hole in the sky that day,' she said, motioning with her chin towards the cavern roof. 'When I felt a breeze through the opening, I wanted to know what was on the other side. So I explored around the base of this cave after I climbed down from the top. It took some time, but I eventually found a rock leaning against the crevice you just came through. The rock looked a little like a door and was etched with a small red figure. It was just like one my grandfather used to make. I think it was an otter, which excited me because that's our dodem. As I said, it was laid across the entrance here. *Nigig* is a powerful sign of medicine and preparation, and I wondered what was concealed behind it. So I moved the rock and wriggled my small body through the passage within.

'When I first came through, it was like being born into another world. I could hardly see anything at first, but the warmth of the place was welcoming. Sizing the place up, I felt my way around its edges. Because it was bigger than our cabin, I thought the place would have been a good home. When my eyes adjusted to the dim, I was astonished. I saw there were platforms on the walls just above my reach. At first I was frightened; we used to send our dead to the next life by placing them high above the ground in this way. I was afraid I was disturbing a grave site. I almost left, but curiosity got the better of me. On closer inspection, I saw that these ledges had containers, pots, and wooden bundles on them. There were no bones or skins like you would find in a burial. I was so excited. I took my bearing and then ran from here to find my family.

'When I told my father what I had found, he was very surprised at first. However, it didn't take him long to say how happy he was I had been led there. He approved of my finding. He said it was our family's old ceremonial lodge. It used to belong to his grandfather, and he was its caretaker before he died. Our ancestors have been coming here for generations. They had cleared the meadow and planted the seven trees. It was our spiritual home for generations before we ever settled at Cape Croker. This lodge has been used by your family for at least one hundred and fifty years.'

Looking above him, the young man saw that platforms still lined the walls. Objects loaded them down. Nokomis invited her grandson to sit by the fire with her. 'I want to show you something. I was so intent on studying these things,' she said, pointing at some vessels by the blaze, 'that I lost track of time. Then, by the time I was finished doing my work, it was too dark to return. I didn't want to risk hurting myself walking back to the car. So I sat here and continued looking. I thought I'd wait until morning light, and then make my way home. But now that you're here, it's perfect. I came here this morning because of your dream. I thought it might soon be time to share this all with you. I now feel that it is the right time. Do you want to learn about what I was studying?'

The young man looked at his grandmother with awe. He could hardly wait to begin, but at that same moment he thought of his grandfather waiting at home. 'I would be honoured to have you teach me, Nokomis. Just let me call Mishomis. He was worried, and sent me to find you. He'll be relieved to know you're all right. I told him I'd call when I found you. I'll see if I can reach him on my cell. I'll let him know we'll be a while.'

The young man reached into his pocket and flipped his phone open. The signal was weak inside the cave. 'I can't seem to get a signal in here,' he said. 'Let me just step outside to see if it's any better out there.' His grandmother waved him out, and he crawled into the night and found a high spot on a rock. It was handy having cell phones on the reserve; they came that year the new tower was installed at Tobermory. Sometimes getting a signal could be tricky, but he found you just had to be creative and stand in the right place.

It didn't take many rings before Mishomis picked up the phone. The old man was relieved. He was glad to hear things were fine. The young man explained the situation and told him of Nokomis' invitation to stay the night in the cave. Mishomis was very happy to hear he would be learning more about their ways. He also told the young man to tell Nokomis he was glad she was all right, and that he hoped they had a good night together. He was going to bed. With the conversation at an end, the young man switched off the phone and made his way back towards the cave.

Once again he crawled through the entrance to find Nokomis waiting for him. She motioned for him to sit on the opposite side of the fire. He was full of anticipation. His heart was racing in his chest, and he heard the rush of his blood pounding through his throat and ears. He could hardly contain himself. He felt as if his ancestors were gathering on the other side to witness this moment. His spirit soared. When the young man and his grandmother were comfortably seated, he reached into his coat and took out a small, round pouch of cloth, tied together at one end. He passed it across the fire, and she received the small portion of tobacco while she smiled and bowed her head to him.

When she looked up at him once again, Nokomis began, 'I was deeply impressed with that dream you told us about this morning. It reminded me so much of what I have learned in my own life over the years. But more than that, it triggered memories of things I'd seen in this place. There are some interesting images around here that look a lot like the things you were describing in your dream. As I said, I wanted to come here and see if I could connect them and decide what to do. I'm sorry I took so long and put you to all this trouble tonight, but I had to see them again before I made a final decision. The pots on the boards above have etchings that are similar to those you saw in your sleep. There are also petroglyphs under the platforms that should be familiar to you. But what really motivated me were the scrolls that our family has passed down through the years. They contain our history and important teachings. The pictures and representations are very close to what you described, only there is so much more. Once I got here, I knew I wanted you to see them. I knew it was time to show you.'

The man could hardly believe the richness that lay all around him. He also knew they would enable Nokomis to tell him things that went well beyond the images. He was excited to hear about their connection to his recurring dream of the four hills. He had heard of places like this before, but never realized one was so close. Now that he was in the presence of such powerful beings in a sacred place like this, he was over-awed. He was also humbled.

In a quiet voice he asked his grandmother: 'Why didn't you ever tell me about this place?'

'As I said, I didn't know if you were prepared,' she replied. 'But don't feel bad. I have only told a very few people about this place. It was a big part of my mother's and father's life when we were younger, and our grandparents came out here with us when they were alive. They all said I should only share it with those who could make the proper connections. So I've kept it quiet, though I am glad your Mishomis sent you tonight. He used to come here a lot, too. You are ready to see what's here. It'll help you to piece together that dream of yours, connect it in ways beyond what you told us this morning. I have no doubt that your interpretation today was a good one, though I think you'll see that there's so much more to it than what you said.'

Reaching into a long, brown container beside her, Nokomis pulled out a bundle of sticks. The sticks had cloth and bark wrapped around them, which she carefully separated. The scrolls were frail in her hands. When she had finished unrolling four or five on the ground before her, she looked up at her grandson. Firelight bounced off her darks eyes. She smiled. 'Thanks for putting the salt in my coffee this morning, grandson. Nanabush is getting bold.' He couldn't suppress his smile; they were always playing tricks on each other.

Then, calmly looking him in the eyes, Nokomis said, 'I hope you don't mind those ants befriending you below. You're sitting on their home.' Laughing, he looked down; sure enough, the heat from the fire had brought an anthill to life where he sat. He jumped up and danced around the lodge, shaking his arms and brushing the ants to the floor. She had done it again. He couldn't let his guard down with her. Even at a time like this, there was a place for humour. She was continually teaching him about the importance of balance in his life.

Gently chuckling at his small mishap, Nokomis said to her grandson, 'Come sit on this side of the fire with me. The ants won't be as anxious to visit you here.' She smiled again, and then signalled a truce, the palms of her hands upraised over her knees. Carefully, the young man moved clockwise around to her side of the fire and sat next to the scrolls. Each was about a foot long, with dark engravings sunk into the underside of the birch bark. He was careful not to brush against them. They looked like they would easily disintegrate.

Nokomis began again, 'When I found these, they were tightly sealed in hollowed logs. There was some kind of pitch covering both ends of the wood. I guess that was meant to keep out the bugs and air. I think this treatment, along with the dryness in here, helped my grandfather preserve them. It probably protected them beyond their natural years. Anyway, whenever we came in here, we had to break their seals each time to read them. With repeated use, it doesn't take long to realize the scrolls quickly decay. So each generation is tasked with reading and becoming familiar with their contents, and then we have to recopy them. Over our lifetime, Mishomis and I have made a few texts of our own, too. We have recorded some of what we have been taught and learned for future generations. Our traditions are always being renewed. What you see sitting along the platforms is the result of generations of work. We keep them sealed in here so that they are always ready for a future day. It's our way of drawing out law. I hope you'll make some scrolls yourself one day when you feel like you have something important to pass along. Perhaps you can make them a part of your next book.'

The young man looked around at the cavern again, and noticed the different sizes and shapes the ledge-like structures supported. In the clutter of ceramic, wood, and rocks, he could see some of things to which she was referring. Nokomis followed his eyes with interest as the young man looked around.

'Notice how there are four platforms, grandson? They each face a different direction: east, south, west, and north. The shelf over the passage you came through is at the east. Later, if you take your flashlight, you'll see rock markings under each platform that mark their cardinal direction. You'll also see different symbols for various teachings related to those directions replicated on these scrolls. But that's for another time. Let me show you the scrolls. I think you'll see why I stayed late.'

Nokomis took a stick and pointed to the first scroll on the rock beside him. It looked tanned in the firelight. 'You read the scrolls from east to west, or left to right, in this fashion. This scroll shows the four orders of creation: earth below, the water world, earth above, and the sky realm.' She pointed out the scroll's division into four equal sections. 'A lot like your hills, aren't they? Only their orientation is more completely vertical, less horizontal. Each level is guarded by different beings, serving as guides to those who pass through.' He looked more closely for a few minutes.

Then, pointing to lowest section of the scroll, Nokomis continued. 'See this figure here? It looks like an otter. *Nigig*. It represents the beginning of wisdom and knowledge. *Nigig* is beneath and behind the first line, on the earth below. He is the guide and guardian of this realm, the first order. Surrounding him is a circle, with points in the four cardinal directions. That's his lodge.' The young man also noticed snakes surrounding the circle, but didn't want to interrupt Nokomis' train of thought by asking about them.

'Then,' she said as she traced the stick up the scroll, 'you see these dots, originating inside the otter's circle? They go up and cross the line just over him and enter a rectangular lodge above the first level. The dots represent *Nigig*'s journey from the world below to the water world above. He's going to the second level. Much like when a baby's conceived, as it passes from the spirit to water in its mother's womb. *Mishi-bizheu*, the water lion, holds power within this realm. You know from our time on the lake that we must always be wary of him, leave offerings, and make sure he is not provoked.' The man also observed people standing outside the water lodge, joined with fish, birds, and other animals. Nokomis ignored them and waved her stick further up the diagram.

'Here, and here,' she said, pointing at two separate spots on the scroll, above the water level. 'These are the last two orders, guided respectively and guarded by bear and thunderbird. *Mukwa* and *Animikee*. You'll notice the dots that began in the otter's circle continue meandering all the way up through the other orders. They cross lines separating the second from the third level, and the third from the fourth level. On their way, they pass through the lodges housing *Mishi-bizheu* in the water, and *Mukwa* on the earth above. Then they terminate in this circle at the top. It's the sun, the place of thunderbird. That's his lodge in the sky.'

The young man marvelled at the intricacy of the drawings and the symmetry of their placement. Small, dark lines in the birch laterally bisected the pictures, creating a precise geometry of vision.

'We don't have the time it would take to explain all this tonight,' Nokomis said. 'For now, it's enough to know that the scrolls depict travels through four orders. To begin, let's just focus on the first level. These other four scrolls on the floor here detail what the first level represents. That's what I thought I'd look at while I waited for morning to come. Then you showed up. I hope we'll have time to study the other orders another day. There are dozens of scrolls that develop what the other pictures mean. In fact, this cave itself is something of a scroll. If you could unfold the walls from its entrance and lay them flat on the ground, you would see images similar to these pictographs on its walls. The cave is divided into four orders, and petroglyphs near the floor portray the same journey. I hope we have time to explain them all before I'm too frail to come here anyone.'

Looking at his grandmother, the young man felt an overwhelming sense of awe. Ever since he was young he knew she had wisdom, but he never guessed what secrets she had locked in her mind. Now, seeing this place, he realized how little he knew about her or his own family. He saw how little he really knew about their teachings. He wondered how he could know anything if he didn't even know his own heritage, especially when he thought he had listened and studied so much all his life? It made him think. He had always told his students you need to be ignorant to learn. He now felt a tinge of shame about how carelessly he sometimes tossed around the phrase. Staring into the void of your own real ignorance was unnerving.

'Tell me again what you said about that first hill in your dream this morning, grandson. I want to be sure I understood.' After relating it to her once more, Nokomis picked up one of the scrolls beside her and quickly passed it to her grandson. Excited once more by his dream, she rushed to speak. 'Look at this; you'll see you were right. The first hill did introduce issues. Your vision told you about these issues in the context of babies and very young children. It is hard to come into the world. As you saw, a lot don't make it. Others are severely scarred even before they take their first steps. In the scrolls, it's somewhat the same. Passing from the realm of spirit to water is fraught with challenges for children. That's what the dark black line separating the levels represents. Strong medicine is needed to bring you through. That's where *Nigig* comes in. You need a guide and a guardian. That's his role. Otter's wisdom is found here. When a child was born in the past, the woman who assisted with the delivery became the child's second mother. She was the *N'd'odissiim*, the woman who set me and my mother free.[2] There is even a ceremony to celebrate and acknowledge her role. The teachings on these scrolls impart knowledge that parents need to guide children through conception and birth, through the first level. They show *Nigig*'s way. Medicines are also revealed on the scroll for this purpose. They give ideas that will help them be good guardians, too.

'But then it gets really interesting. The scrolls expand in scope. They teach about knowledge that's necessary to face many issues in life which have dependence at their root. They go far beyond childhood and parenting. When I hear you talk about the law, I often think communities and nations could also take counsel from what's found in here. The scrolls talk about the development of choice. They prompt its proper use when self-reliance has not fully taken hold. Guidance is also given on how you must make decisions. This is key when the people around you have not yet properly developed or used the choices available to them. I think I heard you call it agency. We talked a lot about that word when I lived in the city with you, that year I went to college. The scrolls develop what you call agency. No matter what your stage of development, if dependence is an issue, they teach you about your responsibilities.'

Nokomis stopped and stared into the fire, stirring the embers with her stick. 'Do you think these scrolls have some important messages you could use in teaching about the law?' She looked up at her grandson again, searching his eyes: 'In a very real sense, you know, these teachings are our law, Anishinabek law.'

They sat in silence for a long time. The young man examined the medicines related to conception and birth and noticed which plants were especially helpful. He studied the steps that were needed to ensure the continuation of life. *Nigig*'s lodge was full of pictograms related to these issues. He thought about what these teachings meant for the law and reflected on what he taught at school. Once again, he marvelled at how the approach of the two systems seemed so different. The case of *Racine v. Woods* passed through his mind. It was a child welfare case that discounted a child's identity as she grew older. So many Native children were taken from their parents without making proper connections when they came into this world. It was certainly happening on the reserve. He knew many children around here who experienced this· struggle in scaling the first hill.

As he thought about the different cases he taught that harmed new life, his attention riveted on an even darker decision: *Stenberg v. Carhart*.[3] He hated to think about it. He had been troubled since rereading it yesterday afternoon. In *Stenberg*, the U.S. Supreme Court described how some doctors terminated early life in unwanted pregnancies through a procedure called a D&X. The Court said that the 'fetus' arms and legs are delivered outside the uterus while the fetus is alive. Witnesses to the procedure report seeing the body move outside the woman's body. The abortion procedure has the appearance of a live birth.' Then, he remembered the detail, 'With only the head of the fetus remaining in utero, the abortionist tears open the skull,' and 'witnesses report observing the portion of the fetus outside the woman react to the skull penetration. The abortionist then inserts a suction tube and vacuums out the developing brain and other matter found within the skull ... the heart of the fetus may continue to beat for minutes after the contents of the skull are vacuumed out.' In reading the case, the young man recalled that the Anishinabemowin word for fetus is *wizhigin*, meaning: it is formed. In the light of these teachings, the treatment described by the court sounded so cold, hostile, and demeaning. He was sure the people who were involved in the procedure meant well, but he wasn't sure about the effects of what he read. Equality jurisprudence in Canada paid attention to both intention and effects, but had recently de-emphasized effects. Studying the case gave him a flashback to his first-year law school experience. When he read *Stenberg* he sat quietly, not because he didn't want to disturb, but because what he was learning was so disturbing. Thinking about this case, the conversation with his grandfather this afternoon came to mind. He reflected on throwing baby eaglets from their nests. He paused on that for a moment before returning to the imagery of his own dream: small people gathered in blood at the base of the first hill.

He looked at the third scroll lying on the ground. The snakes gathered outside otter's lodge were shown in detail. Some enclosed it and were trying to crush its contents. Others were following Nigig's path and had spread out along the way; sometimes they were solitary and sometimes in pairs. Nokomis had said dependency was a hard thing to live through when she explained this scroll. Examining the pictures more closely, he thought of the multiple dependencies found in the creation of life. Not only were the fetus and infant dependent as they grew, but mothers faced their own challenges in this regard. If abandoned by partners, or forced to forgo other opportunities to deliver and raise a child, they too could face crushing dependence, though not always. Economic, biological, and sociological context mattered to the consequences that flowed from such decisions. In teaching the law he had often struggled with these issues. The idea that 'woman should not be a passive recipient of a decision made by others as to whether her body is used to nurture a new life' made sense to him.[4] He liked much of what the *Morgentaler* case had to say in that regard.[5] As the Supreme Court of Canada noted, a woman's life, liberty, and security were centrally implicated in such matters.[6]

Yet despite the truth of these facts, he also wondered if there were better ways to examine the question. He wondered about the alternatives. As a law professor, he knew that framing what was at issue in a case made a huge difference to its reasoning. A decision-maker always had a choice in this regard. The young man wondered about the role of choice when a woman participated in the creation of new life through reproductive acts. What were men's responsibilities at that moment? Were alternatives available that didn't always pit mothers against their developing children if the pregnancy was unwanted? What could the courts do about men who were abusive, or who sought to control women in these circumstances? Could the conflicting dependencies, agencies, and lives be addressed and respected? He couldn't help shake the feeling that Canadian law had not yet even come close to reconciling these interconnections. It had not really framed the issue in a way that would promote a broader resolution.

As he looked at the scrolls, he thought he saw things differently. He felt there was much more to the issue. It seemed as though others could be involved in raising children if there were dependencies in those early months and years. In the scrolls he saw there were those who weren't otters journeying on with the young. It wasn't always biological families who raised their children. This was confirmed in his own experience. Many of his cousins and friends grew up with two or three families. They experienced love, direction, support, and belonging in each of these settings. They generally grew to be well-adjusted adults. He saw this pattern on many reserves, despite the challenges that continued to exist.

When community resources were more attentive to the dependencies encountered in unwanted pregnancies, both the dependencies and pregnancies were reduced. Others took up the task of raising children. Fathers were compelled to bear a greater burden of responsibility, financial and otherwise, for the pregnancies. Mothers facing the consequences of their pregnancies received greater support to reduce social, economic, and psychological stress. Such actions acknowledged and respected the agency and dependency of women, the fetus, and young children. It confirmed the responsibilities of mothers, fathers, communities, and nations to the seventh generation of those yet unborn. Of course, there were many more issues involved that also needed attention, but he saw something in the scrolls that taught the need for reconciling agency and accountability in reducing dependency.

Reflecting on his own experience of adoption, the young man knew more could be done. He and his partner had desperately wanted to adopt. They had spent years preparing and had the desire and resources to help. However, every time it seemed a child was coming to their own maturing family, the arrangements they made would always fall through. He and his wife had wanted so badly to have a new life join their home, but, try as they might, there were just too few babies up for adoption for the number of couples wanting them. They could have raised many more children, and would have gladly done so. The law seemed to create additional problems when it treated life's creation as *only* an individual decision that did not recognize its community context. In this respect he felt the courts had narrowed choice for women, the fetus, communities, and other parents. In the same vein, he thought legislatures had missed connections that would expand agency, while acknowledging and resolving dependencies.

This line of thought started the young man thinking about the scrolls' wider implications involving nations and peoples, as his grandmother briefly mentioned. In thinking about this, he saw the necessity of addressing issues of dependency and agency within a country to facilitate development. Yet he knew this would not be an easy task. Many unwanted nations rested in the bodies of other, more powerful nations. Those nations did not want to contemplate the smaller group's agency or growth. A desire to terminate their development was often manifest by the larger power.[7] They felt a need to exercise full control; it was said their sovereignty and autonomy would be threatened if they didn't. This sometimes led to steps being taken to end the weaker power's existence. They could be cut up, divided, isolated, and removed.[8] Dismemberment even took place in the name of democracy. Principles of popular will justified the diminishment of choice for many nascent nations. Couched in the language of agency, the liberty and security of the majority was held out as a reason to override minority rights. Dominance through such force was often a means and excuse to end or stifle a weaker nation's development, under the cloak of principle and legitimacy. This was why the International Declaration on the Rights of Indigenous Peoples was important to so many Native nations. They wanted to end practices aimed at their termination.

The young man looked at his grandmother bent over scrolls beside him, studying in the dancing light. He was grateful for all she taught him and the connections she had helped him make. There was so much he did not understand. He knew he had more to learn at school from studying the many perspectives people held on these issues. He also knew he could learn more about this from his grandmother, too. Nokomis helped bridge the gap between the legal worlds in which he walked. Tonight was perhaps the most profound experience he had ever had in that regard. However, the young man knew he still had much to learn.

He couldn't help but wonder if, in staying out here tonight, Nokomis had not manipulated things so that they could spend this night together. She was a complex woman, in her effortless way. The realization made him think he'd never know that question's answer. Yet she would tell him many things, as confirmed by the scrolls in their hands this evening. Pondering his shortcomings, he watched as she stirred ash and embers beneath dying flames. Sparks broke loose and floated above the wood. She reached behind her to put another log in the hearth.

Watching the light grow, the young man asked, 'Nokomis? Do you think we'll ever fully understand the implications of our decisions? There just seems to be too much to learn. There are so many complica-

tions, half-truths and blind-spots in what we think we know. I sometimes feel so weak and foolish.'

Nokomis let the words hang in the air for a time as she formulated
her answer. Finally she said, 'We'll only know ourselves when we're
ready to honestly ask the right questions. To take this step, we need to
find greater clarity surrounding our most pressing issues. I've found
that clarity is enhanced when I see things in the light of creation's
sacred nature. The great mystery of life sometimes gives us unexpectedly generous answers when we view the world in this way. I can never
be sure of what I am hearing, though. It often seems as though the universe is silent.' They sat by the fire many more hours, talking about and
applying the principles from the scrolls. Their conversation touched on
their lives, the reserve, and country. They spoke of the grandson's concerns at law school. They discussed the cases he was teaching and writing about. They both gained a lot by studying the first order that night.

Then, as sunlight began to illuminate the cave's eastern door,
Nokomis gathered the scrolls and began to bundle them together. She
took great care to ensure they were carefully rolled up. Placing them
back in their containers, she looked at her grandson. She thought of
herself discovering this place so many years ago as a twelve-year-old
girl. She felt the weight of her age as she said, with a note of sadness
in her voice, 'Be sure you live by what you learned tonight grandson,
and by so living, pass it on. Our traditions must be lived to be relevant,
but it requires great effort to acquire and apply them. You have a choice
about what laws you should follow as you climb through life. Those
choices are strengthened when they remain connected to the earth and
all that we can learn from her, including being careful where you sit.'
She continued, smiling, 'I hope you remember these truths and have
the wisdom and stamina to make the journey.'

When Nokomis was finished speaking, she slowly rose from her
place and stood before the fire. Her grandson stood, too, following her
lead. Placing some tobacco in the fire, Nokomis offered a prayer for the
new day: *waubun*. When she was finished, she handed him the scrolls
and asked him to place them above the entrance, where the new morning light grew.

DAEB-AWAEWIN[1]

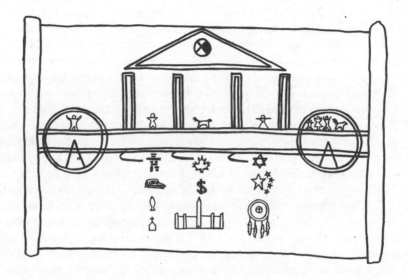

Nag'anal'mot lazed in the front yard, waving the flies away with his tail. As soon as spring arrived, *bugoksens* swarmed in droves, never giving a moment's peace. He sat up and scratched behind his ears, working hard to satisfy the itch. Certain spots were getting difficult to reach the older he got. When he was finished, he settled his chin back onto the lawn. Tufted grass and bare dirt rolled out to the road a few yards away. Beyond was a new crop of weeds, and the bay. A few fishing boats lay in the water, resting from their early morning run. Escarpments filled in the background, stretching the horizon, holding the sky in its place. But the scene did little for him; being mostly colour-blind, everything was washed in grey. He could still pick out movement though; he was more sensitive to it because of his condition. A couple of dogs trotting down the road in the distance caught his eye. He watched the smaller claim each mailbox they passed. Their territory stretched all around the harbour. As they got closer, he made out their shapes. A corgi and otterhound was his guess. Curious, he jumped up and ran over to them, eager to check out their tails.

On the other side of the bay below the escarpment, the young man was preparing to leave. An hour later, Nokomis and Mishomis bid their grandson goodbye. He was leaving for the city to teach his class tomorrow afternoon. He crawled into his car and headed south. The three-and-a-half hour journey quickly slid by; his mind was preoccupied by the previous night's events and his upcoming talk at the law school. Arriving at his apartment, he checked his messages and went through his mail. Then, climbing into bed, he set his alarm for eight the next morning. Awakening refreshed the next day, he headed for work.

His office was too hot. Though it was about fifteen degrees outside, the water-filled radiators were working overtime. And they were loud. They could be heard clanging and popping in rooms up and down the hall. One day the law school was going to have to fix them, he thought. They had probably not overhauled the old mansion's heating system since it was turned over to the university seventy years ago. Yet, despite its problems, he liked working in Flavelle House. Through generous, wide-paned windows you could see Trinity College's ivy-covered spires. The expanse of the backfield, Varsity Arena, and Philosopher's Walk spread out below. Inside, fifteen-foot ceilings gave a feeling of spaciousness, room to think and move. Even the linoleum flooring had character, with faux tile alternating in black and white squares.

If only it wasn't so hot. He would be lecturing in twenty minutes and was having a hard time concentrating on putting the finishing touches on his work. Bridge Period at the University of Toronto always created some excitement around the school. He felt great expectations in the air. He wanted to be well prepared. All first-year classes were suspended for a time, while students took lectures on special topics. They were usually issues of great concern to the legal profession. Subjects varied each year, and never failed to create a buzz around the place. Freed from the confines of black letter doctrine and an endless diet of cases, many students enjoyed grappling with the larger policy issues. They liked the diversity of opinion they heard during the week. This year's subject was 'Choices: Aboriginal Peoples, Canada, and the Law.' *Ultra Vires*, the law school's newspaper, had run a series of provocative articles about it a few days before. Judging from what he read, he knew it would be tough going in class today.

He hit the print button on his screen with five minutes to spare. Collecting his work from the tray, he made his way down to the lecture halls. Students crowded the corridors and lobby, cramming conversations between classes. He dodged and weaved his way to the lecture hall. At the door, his colleague stopped him. A sad expression held her face. Quietly, she took the young man aside, steering him into the corner. He wondered what was wrong.

'I've got some bad news,' she whispered. 'Catherine Wawanosh was found dead in her apartment this morning. Her roommate let us know a few minutes ago.' Resting her hand on his shoulder, she said, 'I'm so sorry to have to tell you like this.'

It took a moment for the young man to register what his colleague was saying. Catherine was one of his students. She was well known around the law school. He felt his heart and body go slack. He took a step sideways to steady himself against the wall. The world slowed its motion, his heart went quiet, and breath caught in his throat.

His colleague looked at him, gauging his reaction. 'Are you OK? Do you think we should cancel today?' she said. 'I know it's bad timing to tell you like this, but I thought you should know. They're all talking about it. They may be a bit distracted.'

The young man stood for a moment, trying to catch up to his thoughts, wondering what to do. The class was scheduled to start in a moment. He asked his colleague for a few more details about what happened. They conferred with one another for a minute or two, weighing whether they should proceed. After getting a sense of his colleague's views, the young man said, 'I think I can do it. The students are all here now, they are at least ready to hear us, and our guests for today are also up front waiting to begin. I think it's best if we go ahead with the lecture.'

Taking a deep breath, the young man left her side and entered the room. Bennett Lecture Hall was filled to capacity. A steady din of conversation pushed out at the walls. Walking down the aisle to the lectern up front, he saw that the other speakers sat quietly in place. Shaking their hands and saying hello, he asked if they were ready to begin. Professors Nag'anal'mot and Burrows nodded in agreement, and he approached the podium. Conversations lulled. He called the students to order and introduced the topic for the week.

Professor Burrows went first. At five-foot four, she was of slight build with long jet-black hair. Her glasses were too large for her face. Her clothes, while nicely tailored, did not draw undue attention. She didn't look like much of a force. Her quiet, steady voice might also have contributed to this impression, if you didn't pay attention to what she was

saying. But anyone listening to her words would never underestimate
her silent power. As a leading scholar on Aboriginal rights, her contributions were well respected. She adjusted the microphone, pulling it
down to her height. She began:

'With or Without You?[2] That is my question. Will we look inward or
outward in forming our futures? Aboriginal politics and scholarship is
built on this question. Should we reject Canada, or seek to strengthen
it? Aboriginal peoples have reason to lean towards rejection. We do not
have much to show for the loss of a continent, which seems somewhat
unfair. Living on small reservations and eking out a living, while traditional territories support millions, does not feel like a good trade. But I
was never a good judge of such things. You see, my great-great-grandfather was a chief who signed a treaty that supposedly gave away 1.5
million acres of land in southern Ontario, and I live a comfortable life.
Who can complain when you are a tenured law professor at a great
Canadian university?' Amused recognition rippled over the group. 'It
doesn't look like I got ripped off. I have a few nice beads and trinkets: a
mortgaged house in the suburbs, a loan for my Pontiac, a gold card. It
appears as though I got something out of the bargain.

'So what's the problem? Well, it's hard to explain, but I'll try.' She
shuffled through her notes and then stopped. Peering over her glasses,
she looked up at the students. 'It's like this: if you had something pre-
cious and you somehow lost it, you would wonder how that happened,
and why. You would deeply puzzle over this loss, even though you may
be doing fine by most people's measures. It would be difficult to forget
despite present circumstances, when you realize that the loss continues
to deeply harm others. Obscenely low employment and income rates
and indecently high mortality, incarceration, and poverty ratios signal
the persisting consequences of the past treatment of Aboriginal peoples. But this may not even be the worst of it.

'You may find the loss of a continent even more challenging to accept
if it occurred as a result of the very laws that should prevent such an
event. You may find this troubling, because this would concern more
than your own feelings. You may worry, because this loss has disturbing implications for our entire society. You might ask yourself: If the
law can dispossess me and those I love of those things which are of
most value to us, what is to stop this from happening to my neighbour?
If you then studied further and discovered that the law not only allows
for this dispossession, but also actually facilitates it in certain circumstances, you might fear for the general community. You might be con-

cerned about the tenuous nature of human dignity. You could worry about how easily rights purporting to protect us can be overturned. You might ask: Are we all on such shaky ground?'

Professor Burrows scanned the audience to gauge their reactions. They were like most of the classes she taught. Some looked simply bored, and others were nearly asleep. A small number were reading the paper, while some played solitaire on their laptop computers. Others were dutifully transcribing every word she said, preparing for their assignment later that week. A good number were actually listening, with pens down and eyes forward, trying to relate to what was being said. Removing her glasses and placing them in front of her, she went on.

'One only has to think of the recent history of Germany or China to appreciate the fragility of our rights and liberty. Only fifty years ago, Germany used the rule of law to displace and exterminate millions of its citizens. China presently uses the framework of law to dispossess its people. It controls how much they can possess and compels them to live in certain ways. It is troubling to think of the law's role in taking away people's fundamental human rights. Law, far from being a universal good, can also be a tool of great destructive force. Canadians are not used to thinking of their laws in this way, though we are not immune.

'Recently, I read two books that brought this message home. One was a work of fiction called *Stones from the River*, written by Ursula Hegi. The other was a non-fiction book entitled *Red China Blues* by Jan Wong. Both were thought-provoking pieces. Now, as an academic, I realize that you have to be careful about what you can glean from sources that are not painstakingly footnoted.[3] I also recognize that such works have their own objectives, biases, and partial truths, as do all academic works. However, these books do contain powerful points of view that help to further explore the delicate character of human dignity in different contexts. I think they provide some small insight that has implications for Aboriginal peoples and their relationship to Canada.

'*Stones from the River* is about a young German girl named Trudi, who grew up in the period prior to the Second World War. Trudi is a dwarf, a little person, and faces numerous challenges because she does not always fit comfortably into her society. She is ostracized, abused, and isolated because of her height. As she grows into a teenager during the Nazis' rise to power, she recognizes that certain others are placed in a category she has been in all her life: "different." The creation of categories of difference in Germany prior to the war was used as an excuse to legally ostracize, abuse, and isolate Jewish people in their country. This treatment undermined their rights and deprived them of their liberty, property, and even of their very lives. As Trudi witnessed the state-sponsored disappearance of many of her Jewish neighbours and friends, at the hands of other neighbours and friends, she took action. She harboured many individuals, and hid them from the authorities. What is poignant about the novel is how it portrays Jewish dispossession as being so orderly, so legal. Furthermore, it details how so many German people were complicit in this mistreatment.'[4] Professor Burrows took up her glasses and put them back on.

Momentarily searching her text, she found the passage she wanted to quote. She continued, 'In one compelling vignette that summarizes her environment, Hegi writes:

> It was six weeks after Christmas that Hilde first saw the yellow stars. They were made of cheap imitation silk and had to be worn by all Jews who were older than six on the left sides of their coats …The stars gave a different texture to the town because they marked the Jews as obviously as the brown uniforms identified the SA. You knew right away where someone belonged … In the bleak winter, those yellow stars often were the only color, and yet, many people pretended not to see them … It stunned Hilde how many people were Jewish, people she'd never expected to be Jewish, people with blonde hair and straight noses like hers. It was as though Jewishness were something deep within, something that could be pulled out of anyone with a new law and made evident with a yellow star.[5]

Professor Burrows let the words settle over the hall. Having read the text a few times now, she knew the depth of its meaning was not immediately apparent. And she realized the students would take the words in different ways as well, ranging from total disinterest to deep pain. Looking back up at the group, she couldn't help but think of the Jewish students she knew in the class. She wondered how many descended from families that had lived in Germany before the war. Then it occurred to her that there might be a few non-Jewish German descendants in the class as well. Quietly, she said, 'When you recognize that the identification and definition of Jewish people led to the loss of their life, liberty and property, you appreciate how law protects rights in certain instances, but in others can be a brutal instrument used to cause human suffering.

'Now let me switch countries and books. In Wong's *Red China Blues*, the point is also made that law can be a device of human affliction. The difference from Germany is that Chinese law used similarities, not differences, to bring down its citizens. Wong draws on her decades of experience living in Communist China to write her work. She describes how law helps to compel conformity and dispossess people of their lands, liberty, or life.[6] In moving terms, she writes about how the lawful collectivization of land has deprived many people of their homes. She describes the conditions of forced labour and imprisonment for people who do not comply with official party politics. She investigates the killing and execution of thousands of people in the name of martial law and legal order. I read Wong's book right after finishing *Stones from the River*. I did not choose to read the books because I believed there was any relationship between them. However, I was struck by their similarities. Wong described a society where conformity was enforced by an authoritarian state which relied upon the silence of many people to accomplish its purposes.

'The power of silence was especially noteworthy in Wong's investigation of the Tiananmen Square massacre. As a witness to the tragic events of 4 June 1989, she chronicled one of the few times in her Chinese experience where the power of silence between people broke down. She also saw how it was built back up again through legally sanctioned repression and intimidation. On that fateful night when people camped in the square, and millions filled the street to demand a "dialogue" with the government, they were met with "resolute and decisive measures" that denied open political questions and conversations.[7] Law and regulation were used to mobilize the state's resources, and thousands were killed in an effort to restore order. After these extraordinary measures, Wong describes how silence once again settled in among the people, to prevent them from challenging the situation they lived in.'

Professor Burrows leaned forward, resting her forearms on the stand. 'Now, what does this all have to do with Aboriginal peoples losing their land in North America? What does it have to do with our relationship with Canada? What does this have to do with choices? These books and my circumstances prompted me to ponder these questions. Aboriginal peoples in Canada do not live in a state that physically tries to exterminate them, with intent. Surely we must be grateful for that. This is no small accomplishment, when measured against the contemporary fate of peoples in other parts of the world. One thinks of the recent violent repression of Indigenous peoples in Guatemala, El Salvador, Colombia, and Peru, for example. Furthermore, I am reminded of the genocide

in Rwanda and Sudan, and the civil wars in Serbia and Kosovo. I recognize that things could be much worse for Aboriginal peoples here.
Yet, despite my deep-seeded gratitude for certain standards Aboriginal
peoples currently enjoy in North America, I remain exceedingly cautious. It seems to me that the experiences reflected in these books do
have something to remind us about human freedom, dignity, and respect. They contain important admonitions about the tenuous nature
of rights in our legal systems. Law can be either friend or foe to human
freedom. Nazi Germany and modern China remind me that law can
create categories, and silences, inimical to the flourishing of dignity and
respect. This insight has enormous resonance for Aboriginal peoples in
Canada today.

'On some occasions, Aboriginal peoples have been made legally different, just as surely as Jewish people were made different in Germany,
though each is admittedly unique in the consequences of this treatment.
By and large, law has not been their friend in fostering these differences. While the consequences of legal differentiation are not as oppressive
for Aboriginal people as they once were, the vestiges of these policies
remain.[8] In other words, Aboriginal peoples still live in tenuous legal
conditions, despite their changing circumstances. Aboriginal peoples
once owned and governed Canada. Now they are barely allowed to
govern themselves on the inadequate little parcels of land that have
been "reserved" for them. Their land cannot support them, and their
traditional governments are not recognized.

'What is incredible in all this treatment is that dispossession remains.
There have been very few constructive relationships built between Aboriginal peoples and the rest of Canada, when it comes to the scale of our
loss. State forces have been marshalled through law to deny Aboriginal
peoples their homelands and sanction the perpetuation of this condition. Like the situation of the Jews in Germany, or the general populace
in Communist China, the continuing repression in our midst generates
too little dialogue in the general population.

'In Canada, collective reflection about the fairness of Aboriginal peoples losing a continent only occurs in a context that does not support
asking foundational questions. In particular, our constitutional para-
digm for dealing with Aboriginal peoples is an important companion of
the more generalized silence on the point. For example, the difficulty in
reflecting on these basic issues is evident in the way courts have treated
questions about the justice of Canada's occupation of Aboriginal lands.
Silence is also apparent in legal challenges to Crown limitations on In-

digenous self-governance. In Canada, despite all their good efforts, the Supreme Court has still not treated Aboriginal losses in terms that ask the hardest questions. Legal issues do not address the fairness in the ownership and jurisdiction of the continent. Instead, Aboriginal peoples are told that the proper characterization for their "claims" is in terms of what was integral to their culture prior to European contact, or necessary to show the exclusivity of their possession of land prior to Crown assertions of sovereignty. In treaty cases, they are advised that the proper inquiry for proof of their rights involves scrutinizing the precise nature and scope of particular treaty clauses. There is no attempt to fully examine the broadest spirit and intent of treaties in terms of the wider ownership and jurisdiction of Canada. The courts' treatment of the justice of Aboriginal and treaty rights amounts to a silence that is just as dampening for Aboriginal peoples as that experienced by Jews in Nazi Germany or the general populace in Communist China.'

Professor Burrows stepped back from the microphone as she brought her talk to its conclusion, her quiet voice managed to reach the four corners of the hall. 'The comparison I have drawn might surprise people, and even seem somewhat unfair. However, I believe that the recharacterization of Aboriginal assertions to fit the presumed framework of law abets arbitrary rule over Aboriginal people. "The very essence of arbitrariness is to have one's status redefined by the state without an adequate explanation of its reasons for doing so."[9] Aboriginal peoples have had their status redefined by Canada without sound juridical reasons. There is nothing that could be more arbitrary than one nation taking half a continent from other nations, and then leaving them with next to nothing to show for it – all without an elementarily persuasive legal explanation. The Court has not effectively articulated by what legal right assertions of Crown sovereignty purport to grant underlying title to the Crown or displace Aboriginal governance.[10] The Crown's claim, that upon the "discovery" of North America it could enjoy title to land that was not its own, is wholly unsubstantiated by the physical reality at the time of their so-called assertions of sovereignty.[11] A supposed right by others to exercise dominion over Indigenous peoples does not accord with the factual circumstances at the time of contact.[12] At their core, the Crown's "vague" and "unintelligible" propositions concerning Aboriginal peoples lack legal cohesion.[13] In these circumstances, law becomes a tool for repression and not an instrument of freedom.

'With or without you? Should Aboriginal peoples work with Canadians in creating their future? There are many reasons to disengage. The relationship between Aboriginal peoples and the Crown is virtually one-sided and built on force. Consensual relationships are largely absent, and Aboriginal peoples are generally repressed. While there is no doubt that the situations in Nazi Germany and Communist China were and are different in so many respects from that faced by Aboriginal peoples, it is also true that Aboriginal peoples have also received arbitrary treatment in their relationship with the state. What is haunting in all three instances is that the law still sanctions such arbitrary treatment, even in the face of heartfelt apologies and many good intentions.'

Professor Burrows took up her glasses and returned to her seat. Polite applause scattered through the audience. She could tell that many were not convinced by her words. She thought some were even more sceptical than when she began. They may even be just plain bored. She knows from experience that her words can be hard to take; she has been in similar situations before. These thoughts passed through her mind as she watched the furrowed brows and tense conversations of the students sitting before her.

Professor Nag'anal'mot, seated next to her, had followed her speech with great interest. To him it was a perfect representation of the prevailing and misplaced orthodoxies in the field of Aboriginal rights today. So many flaws, he thought to himself. Comparisons between Canada and totalitarian states were simply inapt. No self-respecting academic would draw similarities between them. Assimilation did not count as genocide. Absorption of Aboriginal peoples into a free and democratic society is nowhere near being on par with communist indoctrination. In fact, being part of Canada was a benefit, not a burden, to Aboriginal peoples. True, there had been some harsh measures taken against them from time to time.They were too harsh, in fact, but these were in a different league compared to what Professor Burrows would have these students believe. All her discussion about being here first and losing land through unfair bargains was almost more than he could take. Why couldn't Aboriginal people be like more recent immigrant groups in this country and move into the mainstream economy? Assimilation was their best hope. They had to learn to transform themselves. It's what I did when I left my territory, he thought to himself. He was tired of the overblown rhetoric about Aboriginal rights in Canada. He looked forward to addressing the students. A short introduction was given, and he stood to address the group.

Professor Nag'anal'mot stepped to the microphone. At six-foot two with longish black hair, he looked every inch a professor. His oxford blue shirt, black tie, and tweed-hair jacket would put him on the cover of any college promotional. He had worked hard to get where he was today. It was not easy being an outsider in the academic establishment. At first, he felt he was unfairly excluded from the scholastic debate because of his views. Many thought he was too conservative, while others believed he was too radical. Some even accused him of being overly dogmatic. He wondered how critics could hold such contradictory views about him. For a while it meant that invitations to conferences and other such gatherings were slow in coming, but he persevered. He showed his independence at the events he did attend, and soon gained a solid reputation for marking out new territory. Some people called him a real setter – of trends, theories, and approaches.

Then, just as he was becoming well known in certain circles, his own department tried to restrain him. They tried to put him on a short leash to protect their name. His colleagues didn't want his views associated with theirs. Later, when the whole issue finally came to a head, he refused to be silenced by his Dean. So he spoke out forcefully in defence of his views, in defiance of those who wanted him neutered, his ideas tempered. He thought academia was becoming too sterile, that political correctness threatened to overrun freedom of speech and expression in the academy today.

'Today I want to speak to you about the non-Aboriginal orthodoxy in this country,' he began. 'Its guides are free markets, individual responsibility for personal choice, limited government, and social progress. These are the values that direct people's actions in contemporary Canadian society. Adherence to these precepts is what makes us a prosperous country in the world today. We depart from these principles at our own peril. Any attempt by governments to unduly interfere with the markets by creating preferential benefits for certain groups is inappropriate. For example, the provision of unearned transfer payments to Aboriginal people reduces their competitiveness by making them reliant on government handouts. It creates perverse incentives to stay in locations where employment is scarce, and the cost of living is relatively high. Furthermore, the transfer of money gets funnelled into too few hands when administered by the collective, through chief and council. Such funds usually end up only benefiting community elites. Rivals are unfairly shut out by the inappropriate distribution of unearned favours. It's all about personal discretion and whim, with no accountability to other band members or Canadians at large. This system fosters laziness, nepotism, and corruption. Canada is not built on such structures. It is a competitive marketplace that successfully interacts with other economies in the world because it fosters the entrepreneurial pursuit of individual self-interest.

'Let's take Professor Burrows' worries about losing a continent. I remain unconvinced. She did not so much lose a continent as gain a whole new world. Let me play devil's advocate for a moment. Suppose Europeans never came to this country. What would her people be doing today? They may still be living in the Stone Age. By and large, alone they did not have the technology, agricultural resources, disease resistance, ecological contiguousness, socio-political organization, or population size to develop large-scale markets capable of successfully competing with Europeans.[14] Europeans simply had too many natural advantages over them. Even if Europeans had operated at a distance and never occupied Indian lands, so-called First Nations would have been "toast." Europeans were simply too advanced. They would have triumphed over the Indians in everything that brings power and influence in this world: commerce, politics, war, arts, science, et cetera

'While we can have sympathy for the hunter-gatherers who were displaced by such superior forces, it was nevertheless because of these factors that their loss of the continent was both appropriate and inevitable. In fact, the arrival of Europeans can even be considered a net gain for Aboriginal peoples. They now live in the most prosperous part of the world, and have many opportunities to partake in the powerful advantages flowing from European civilization. While there is no doubt that Aboriginal peoples have been cruelly and insensitively treated from time to time, and have been subject to unwise laws and policies, it is also true that they are better off now than they would be had Europeans never came.'

Professor Nag'anal'mot paused to let the students write these points in their notes. He knew that some would consider his message heretical. But he also knew the majority would silently approve; they were law students, after all. And despite what their teachers may tell them, he knew that if they thought about it, they would realize they were firmly committed to the underlying principles he was espousing. He knew most of them were firmly committed to selling their legal training on the free market, through individual choice, with limited government interference in their career choice and earning power. He also knew that many of them believed they would see personal and societal development and progress throughout their lifetimes. Even if the students admitted that the past pursuit of these principles caused the so-called dispossession of Aboriginal peoples, and were inimical to what Professor Burrows expressed, he knew he was right.

He went on. 'The problem with the law relative to Aboriginal peoples in Canada is that the Constitution and *Charter* have legalized politics to such a degree that these principles, which promote prosperity, are threatened. Representative government is the best way to preserve the principles upon which Canada is based. Following the will of the majority ensures that elites and special interest groups do not improperly capture the market. While there is a need to protect the minority's civil liberties against the undue pressure of the majority, these rights are best secured through the protection of speech, association, expression, and worship, et cetera, as individuals under the *Charter* – or better yet, through our Parliament. The way the courts in Canada have defined Aboriginal rights, however, has departed from this model. They have usurped the role of the legislatures, and created uncertainty through their opinions. As a result, Canadians are in danger of entrenching an inefficient property regime under the guise of Aboriginal title through section 35 of the Constitution.

'Take the Court's *Delgamuukw* decision, for instance. It states Aboriginal title is communal and inalienable, except to the Crown. It noted Aboriginal title was not necessarily subject to exclusive control. These are misguided principles. Property should be individually owned, freely transferable, and subject to exclusive control to be truly efficient. Subjecting so-called Aboriginal lands to communal control reduces their economic value; it ensures they will be less productively used. When land is communal, no one takes final responsibility for its use. This leads to exploitation, overuse, and environmental degradation. It is known as the tragedy of the commons. Furthermore, restrictions on the alienability of property under Aboriginal title will narrow the market in which these lands can be exchanged, further reducing their value. If Aboriginal land can only be sold to the Crown, this gives the Crown a monopoly over these lands, and can lead to uncompetitive treatment by the government. Finally, the notion that Aboriginal lands can have a shared exclusivity casts a cloud over the average person's title. If an Aboriginal group is successful in proving their title under *Delgamuukw*, this could undermine other well-settled property interests in this country, making other properties potentially subject to Aboriginal title claims. The Court has made a tremendous mistake defining title in this way. It undermines generally accepted property principles in Canada, something a majority in Parliament would never do.

'Yet proponents of Aboriginal rights would have us set policy in this country in this way – through the will of the minority. The assertion of the so-called inherent right to Aboriginal self-government is one example. If claims to this power were taken seriously, we would have less than 5 per cent of the population exercising control over vast areas of the country. They would assert these rights on no other grounds except the fact that their ancestors were here first. To base government on principles of heredity, not individual choice and majority will, is contrary to Western democratic principles. It is wrong. In fact, it is racist to build governments on such a foundation. Furthermore, to claim that Aboriginal sovereignty is inherent is to engage in historical revisionism of the worst kind. At the time of first contact, Aboriginal peoples did not govern themselves in the way we use the word today. They were too low on the scale of social organization. They did not have effective control of their territories. Their law-making powers were extremely limited. They lived more by custom and habit than by the rule of law and order. There was also very little continuity in their societal associations. Warfare, disease, scarcity and inter-tribal conflict constantly altered their living arrangements. Then the arrival of Europeans, conquest, and Western superiority broke whatever vestiges remained of their low-level social order. So let us not talk of inherent sovereignty for Aboriginal peoples in Canada. It is an historical fiction and contrary to the civilizing influences of democratic governance.'

Catching movement out of the corner of his eye, Professor Nag'anal'mot distractedly brushed away a fly at the edge of the lectern. The small, black dot took flight and headed out over the audience before turning back and circling his head. After a few passes, he managed to knock it out of the air with the back of his hand. With this gesture he paused before barking out his final conclusion. 'All this talk of Aboriginal rights in Canada has got to stop. It is counter-productive, even dangerous, because it threatens the very foundations of this country. I cannot feel sorry for Professor Burrows' mortgage, car loan, and gold card. She should focus on how good she has it here, living in a free and democratic country like Canada. There is no use dwelling on the past. Aboriginal peoples in Canada will continue to be held back until they realize their future lies in assimilation with the rest of the country. Their governments are black holes of welfare dependency and political corruption. Their claims to title and governance are counter-productive and costly; they raise unrealistic expectations for the future. If Professor Burrows is concerned about totalitarianism, she should consider what Canada would look like under Aboriginal rule.'

Professor Nag'anal'mot finished. As he left the podium he tripped slightly, causing him to awkwardly lift his leg against its side to maintain his balance. Returning to his seat, he felt good to have marked out the ground he wanted to cover. Applause and silence mingled in the room, reflecting the mixed reception he expected. Then the students became talkative with one another after his speech; a murmur of voices enveloped the group. While he thought the students were generally supportive, he could tell his view was not universal. Listening to the din, a few derisive howls could be heard above the generalized chatter of the group.

Sitting at the front, their speeches now finished, Professors Burrows and Nag'anal'mot relaxed into their chairs. They exchanged a few words with each other as the third speaker approached the podium. At five-foot ten with no real distinguishing features, the young man had nowhere near the presence of the other two speakers. Dark hair, dark eyes, and an average build did not set him apart in any obvious way from the students in the room. In fact, he could have just as easily been sitting in their place without anyone suspecting he was a professor. As he prepared to speak, thoughts of his visit to the cave passed through his mind. Scrutinizing the contours of the room, he wondered how he could communicate what he learned from his trip home this past weekend. It would be hard without breaching his promise to his grandparents to keep those things sacred. Yet Nokomis had also encouraged him to integrate what he learned into his teaching. He was supposed to pass them on and help their traditions live today. To resolve the dilemma, he resolved to talk about his experiences indirectly. He searched the hall for insight while introducing his text.

He began, 'Stories provide perspective for judgment. Their setting, characters, plot, themes, and language can confirm or challenge our deepest understanding of the world around us. Their structure and substance can corroborate or contradict our perception of the issues they raise. If well told, stories may even prompt both reactions. Humans have the capacity to support, reject, or simultaneously entertain divergent responses to the ideas and circumstances they encounter. Stories can reveal a range of choice in structuring thoughts, behaviour, and relationships.

'You have just heard two very interesting stories from Professors Burrows and Nag'anal'mot. Though divergent in thesis and structure, they are well-known tropes in Indigenous–Canadian relations. Professor Burrows' account is of Indigenous peoples as victims suffering at the hands of the Canadian state. She would have us consider the losses Indigenous peoples endured in their encounters with other Canadians, and the danger this presents to the country today. On the other hand, Professor Nag'anal'mot's account is of Indigenous peoples as beneficiaries, receiving many advantages from their interaction with those who have come to this country. He wants to direct our attention to the net gains in comfort, security, and well-being that colonization created. Both accounts are representative of the themes that have accompanied discussion of this topic on this continent for the past five hundred years. They have battled with one another for pre-eminence over the centuries. At times "Indigenous peoples as victims" has received the weight of public attention, while at others "Indigenous peoples as beneficiaries" has carried the day. There is some explanatory power in each narrative, but they are both problematic. They are troubling because they are incomplete. Despite the differences in these stories, they are similarly deficient in one significant respect. They largely portray Indigenous peoples as passive objects in their relationship with others. They depict them as people who are acted upon, not those who are much given to action.

'Yet Indigenous peoples were active agents in their history. They made their own decisions in the face of the circumstances they encountered. The events and ideas they confronted, while greatly challenging, were not fixed and immovable. They could sometimes influence the development or implementation of policies and decisions aimed at them, or they could choose from a range of options in responding to them when they had little input. Their decisions and actions made a difference in the real world. They could either improve or aggravate their situation through their own actions. The same observation can be applied to Indigenous peoples today.

'Indigenous peoples in Canada continue to use their stories and exercise their agency in response to their ever-changing circumstances. In this way they actively resist interment in the country's deep layers of federalism. Three examples help illustrate this point. In 1999, a new territory arose in Canada's North, governed by and for the Inuit people who make up the majority in the region. Called Nunavut, meaning "our land," the area covers almost one-third of Canada and was created through the negotiation, vision, and hard work of Inuit leaders who wanted to determine their own place in the North. In addition to governing the entire territory, the Inuit were able to secure exclusive title to wide expanses of land, exclusive harvesting rights on lands and waters throughout the Arctic, control and participation on land use boards throughout the region, royalty payments for non-Inuit resource use, preferential employment status for government jobs in the territory, and a strong place in Canada's federal structure.[15]

'From a legal perspective, one of the most exciting aspects of the new territory's activity is the Akitsiraq law school. Akitsiraq is a legal education program run by the University of Victoria in British Columbia to assist the residents of Nunavut to articulate their ancient laws and present-day values in contemporary terms. I have taught there. The program strives to be attentive to legal pluralism in the North, and to integrate traditional Inuit knowledge with the requirements of the territory's governing constitutional and legislative provisions. Students receive all their classes in Iqaluit, the capital of Nunavut, and at the end of four years they receive a law degree from the University of Victoria. Inuit language and stories form an important part of this education as Elders, community leaders, and students interact with southern legal academics like myself to ensure that Inuit law fits the needs of the new territory's residents. As such, the Akitsiraq initiative facilitates the articulation and development of legal processes and reasoning appropriate to Inuit norms and needs.[16] Law is most successful when it expresses the normative order of the people whom it serves.

'Another initiative that demonstrates the efflorescence of Indigenous peoples in Canada comes from the Nisga'a people of north-western British Columbia. The Nisga'a historically governed themselves by reference to the *Ayook*, an ancient legal code that has guided their social, economic, and political relationships from "time of memory." The stories, ceremonies, and feasts central to the *Ayook* are at the heart of efforts to revitalize their legal traditions. Historically, the Nisga'a never entered into treaties with Canada, and they have consistently asserted an exclusive right to relate to the lands and resources throughout their traditional territories by reference to the *Ayook*. After initiating the *Calder* case before the Supreme Court, and gaining recognition of the justiciability of their position, the Nisga'a entered into a two-decade-long negotiation that culminated in a comprehensive treaty with the Canadian government in 1999. The agreement is an ambitious one. It provides for collective Nisga'a ownership of approximately 2,000 square kilometres of land in the Nass Valley watershed in north-western British Columbia.[17] The treaty covers such diverse issues as land titles, minerals, water, forests, fisheries, wildlife, governance, the administration of justice, fiscal relations (including taxation), cultural property, and dispute resolution. Many of these provisions provide significant benefits for Nisga'a people that are far greater than anything contemplated under the current *Indian Act*.[18] Of particular importance is the agreement's reference to the *Ayook* as a source of Nisga'a law and the creation of Nisga'a courts to determine its meaning in the context of the new treaty. This institution will help Nisga'a stories to rise to the surface and perforate the cover of Canadian legal fictions that have denied them rights in their traditional territories.

'Finally, on my reserve, the community's leadership successfully negotiated a co-management agreement to take responsibility for the fisheries in Lake Huron.[19] This represents a re-emergence of Anishinabek law that had been supressed for a century by the operation of provincial laws. The accord enables the people of the reserve to catch, consume, and sell the whitefish, herring, and trout found in waters surrounding our traditional territories. It sets out a process and protocol for the conservation and allocation of fish. It is considered a breakthrough for our people, because of the importance of this resource for our past and future sustenance. This development is a significant step in a protracted struggle to live according to our traditional economies, and exercise a measure of self-determination over their care. Many of our traditional stories speak about our historical concern for the fish. Archaeological evidence and oral tradition also indicate a reliance on these beings for food and trade. Treaties signed between 1836 and 1854, and a Proclamation from Queen Victoria herself in 1847, promised perpetual access to this resource for livelihood purposes. However, with non-Native settlement in our territories from 1860 onwards, and increasing pressure on the fishery for non-Native purposes, our ancient relationship with this resource was marginalized. In recent years we have had to overcome litigation challenges in the courts and resist direct action by non-Native fishers, who deny a separate role for us in the fishery.[20]

'For example, in the early 1990s my uncle, who was chief at the time, avoided a criminal conviction by successfully invoking an existing treaty right allowing him to fish for commercial purposes.[21] Later, in 1996, two of our fishermen survived violent personal attacks and the burning and sinking of their boats in protest over the exercise of their fishing rights. One still wears a scar on his cheek from the confrontation. Yet, despite these confrontations, and others that will no doubt arise in the future, the agreement between Canada, Ontario, and our Nation to share, monitor, and resolve disputes through a negotiated protocol is a hopeful sign. It reveals the potential for change that exists when First Nations in Canada bring their law out from under the shadows of the courts.'

The young man paused for a moment, thinking about his vision of the first hill. He thought of those lifeless corpses at its base, and reflected on the small bodies working their way up over rocks and spring scrub. With images of those first few feeble, halting steps in mind, he went on. 'First Nations and Indigenous communities are not the only entities climbing against steep challenges within the Canadian legal culture. Individuals, who have also sunk under the weight of much abuse, are also pressing their way forward. Residential schools were a particularly poignant cause of displacement for many individual Aboriginal people.[22] Taking an unfortunate page from the U.S. experience with Indian residential schools,[23] they received unqualified support from the prominent churches and federal government of the day to use these schools as a "solution to that problem, designated the Indian question."[24] Often forcibly taken from their homes, children were stripped of their clothes, shorn of their hair, and made to feel ashamed of their language and culture. The schools were viewed as a tool to assist the government in "civilizing" Native people by removing them from their community's influence. They were, in the words of one prominent graduate, "the laboratory and production line of the colonial system."[25] They created "an all-encompassing environment of re-socialization" for people caught within its grasp.[26] Tales of emotional, sexual, and other physical abuse pour out of residential school survivors' mouths. They spill across newspaper headlines in the TRC process. They threatened to overwhelm Canada's legal system before the class action settlement was finalized. Former students report that children had pins stuck through their tongues for speaking their languages.[27] They were deprived of food or personal liberty "to keep them in line," being subject to "frequent whippings" for bedwetting, running away, or even looking at another in "the wrong way," and were chained and "beaten black" and "bleeding" for violating the behavioural code of the schools.[28] In response to these abuses, over 10,000 lawsuits were filed on behalf of individual plaintiffs in the country. This represented only the tip of the iceberg for the over 100,000 students who may have experienced harm while in the so-called care of such institutions.[29]

'It is virtually impossible to live in any Canadian Indigenous community and not be affected by, or know someone who has not been affected by, the legacy of residential schools. Residential schools operated for over one hundred years, and although only 10 per cent of the current Indian population attended, their devastating influence is felt in every corner of Indian Country. While some may claim certain benefits from their residential school experience,[30] and many even made a game out of transforming the structures and ideologies imposed on them in such places,[31] numerous others have borne the overwhelming burdens of Canada's "help" in sending them to such institutions. While Canada's out-of-court settlement for survivors of these government-owned, church-run schools is important, the fallout from this experience cannot be contained by offers of monetary compensation.[32] The government's action probably helped certain churches in Canada avoid bankruptcy, but the inter-generational rupture in the passage of traditions is something that is exceedingly difficult to repair.

'I have lost many members of my family to suicide, alcoholism, and other dysfunctional behaviour, which was the result of the residential school breach. I, along with numerous others, am no doubt presently shaped by these influences and relationships. Healing from the fractures caused by these schools is a painful process that certainly requires money – but also involves the building of social, political, economic, psychological, and other processes that require plain old creative thinking and hard work.

'And yet, despite these almost overwhelming odds, many Indigenous people in Canada are up to this task. They are even further strengthened if they receive the multifaceted support necessary to bridge this past. In fact, residential school survivors are often the very people creating and sustaining the key strategies and stories resisting potential encroachments in their communities. Their efforts are impressive. I am also continually heartened and frequently inspired by the children of residential school survivors that I see coming into university to pursue their objectives in education. In my short time teaching, I have witnessed hundreds of Aboriginal people create a better world for themselves, their families, and (sometimes) whole communities. Their exercise of a measure of self-determination and choice is also enabling small pockets of people to create their own stories in their relationship with Canada. This process has to spread.

'Yet education alone is not the panacea that will magically allow Aboriginal peoples to author their own destiny. It must be recognized that no one truly has the kind of power that would enable them to write the story of their life free of outside influences and pressures. We all face social, political, legal, economic, and spiritual contexts that constrain the degree to which we can truly do what we want.[33] I have seen many people fail or give up in the face of the challenges they encounter. Nevertheless, the conditions in which we find ourselves are not fixed or immovable. They are subject to change and movement by a series of individual and collective actions over time and place. Indigenous peoples must once again take a greater part in influencing and defining the social, political, legal, economic, and spiritual contexts against which the stories of their lives are worked out. Canada is a work in progress, and Indian agency must be respected as an important element in the continued construction of the country. In the legal context, this means that Indigenous issues must find greater prominence in the multifaceted interactions they have with individuals, institutions, and ideologies that influence the unfolding of their world.'

In saying this, the young man was conscious of his need to draw on his recent experiences from the reserve the previous weekend. He hoped to try and fold everything he had learned over the past few days into his final statement: his dream, the walk around the lake, his reflections on the Indian Agent's house, his conversation with his Mishomis and his dream about baby eagles, and the scrolls Nokomis showed him in the cave. Then, continuing his message, he said:

'Law in Canada does not just orient our relationships to one another on a horizontal axis. It does more than merely mediate individual actions on an even plane. Law also has a vertical orientation that builds relationships hierarchically and thereby forges how we interact with each other. As such, those interested in law as it relates to Indigenous peoples must be attentive to its underlying aggregation of power and principle to understand its influence on their legal status. They must scale these heights and plumb these depths to appreciate the problems that Indigenous peoples experience in raising certain legal arguments and receiving appropriate remedies. In Canada, the law has often layered itself over pre-existing Indigenous legal landscapes, concealing this previous presence. Despite numerous attempts to extinguish these laws, Indigenous legal order continues to bubble through the cracks of its overlying cover.

'When Indigenous normative perspectives emerge, at least one of three outcomes can occur. Indigenous law could settle over its former mantle and become the dominant stratum in the process, it could melt the crust that formerly suppressed it and mingle to form a new surface, or Indigenous legal norms could get scattered by prevailing winds that are just too strong to counter. In Canada, all three processes have occurred at different times and in different places.

'For most of Canada's history, Indigenous peoples' law has been scattered by the prevailing order. It was believed to be insubstantial in comparison with the developing common law and constitutional structures.[34] It is only in recent years that Indigenous jurisprudence has started to form the dominant layer in certain legal fields, such as witnessed in the case of *R. v. Sparrow* through the entrenchment of Aboriginal rights in section 35(1) of Canada's patriated Constitution of 1982. In cases like *Sparrow*, Aboriginal law broke through the hard surface of colonial rule and reformed itself on top of the newer, non-Indigenous order. Despite the attractiveness of this approach for Indigenous peoples, it does not seem to be a sustainable way for preserving Aboriginal norms over the long term, because of the court's concern with the non-constitutional interests of non-Aboriginal people who may be affected by Aboriginal rights. Thus, the court has developed elaborate juridical structures that allow federal and provincial governments to legally justify the infringement of Aboriginal rights if they adversely affect non-Aboriginal people.

'Therefore, perhaps the most promising development for the maintenance and extension of Indigenous stories comes at those moments when Indigenous law's elements mingle with the land and those of the non-Indigenous jurisprudential order. The fluidity of legal categories can lead to the development of inter-societal practices that depend on accumulated legal strata to make them effective. In the realm of formal legal ordering, the court has observed that Canadian law dealing with Aboriginal rights is "inter-societal" and "bridges two legal systems."[35] As such, the Supreme Court of Canada has recognized that "the only fair and just reconciliation [between the two systems] is ... one that takes account of the aboriginal perspective while at the same time taking into account the perspective of the common law." As they observed, "a morally and politically defensible conception of aboriginal rights will incorporate both legal perspectives."[36]

'Furthermore, in law's extended spaces beyond the rise of the courts, the negotiation of treaties, land claims, fisheries agreements, and the pursuit of individual healing in an explicitly multicultural society can liquefy even the hardest rules that seem to prevent the emergence of

Indigenous law. Inter-societal law can be created "on the ground" between people and groups. In these settings, people can work out the narrative of their legal relationships in a way that is much more consistent with their preferred account of the world. They can exercise a degree of choice that is lacking when their norms and values are not reflected in the country's dominant legal institutions. In such supportive surroundings, Anishinabek tradition is elevated and enlarged. It further grows as it looks beyond its own cultural horizons and points outside of itself to answer questions that lie in the present and future. Indigenous stories are strongest when their authenticity relies on how well they meet the challenges of the contemporary era. They are the most relevant when they prompt consideration of how they might apply today. Ancient legends and recent narratives combine with stories from the common law, legislative assemblies, negotiation tables, and individual experiences to compose the chronicle that casts Canada in its current form.

'Perhaps one of my favourite stories illustrating this point was told to me by my Grandpa Jonah when I was a young boy. It was the kind of account I would hear over and over again, in the small cabin he built. The story has relevance for the themes of this Bridge Period, but before relating it I need to give you some context.

'The most prominent features on my reserve are three Palaeozoic-era escarpments, *ani-geeshk-aubikauh*, that dominate the reservation's western horizon. A fourth one lies just off the reserve. Built on a shale and dolomite base, these limestone cliffs are part of the larger Niagara escarpment that runs for over 500 kilometres up the backbone of Ontario, between Lake Ontario and Lake Huron. Formed over 250 million years ago as ancient coral reefs in warm tropical seas, they evidence the endurance of the land's earliest inhabitants. In their time they have seen dinosaurs and glaciers come and go. They stood as silent witnesses as the Anishinabek came to occupy this portion of the earth. They now stand in frozen stillness for a large part of the year and communicate the land's prior use, and a much warmer past. In their presence, though we are the first peoples of the area, we are continually reminded of our late arrival on the scene. We are forced to be cognizant of the prior environment and pre-existing conditions and structures.

'Now to the story. When Grandpa Jonah was about seventeen years old, he liked to spend his summers walking the length and breadth of the 16,000 square acre reserve. He would often leave his home early in the morning, and go off in a different direction each day. He returned home most nights long after the sun went down. On these adventures, he discovered the mysteries and beauties of the land that had caused my great-great grandfather to choose this as their permanent home some fifty years earlier. He saw the healing blue clays of Nochemow-aning at Hope Bay, the dry, flat lands of "the prairie" near Sydney Bay, the long, grey, fossil-strewn beaches of "the cape," and the forested up-lands that looked out over Hay, White Cloud, and Griffith Islands in Georgian Bay. He would also spend hours hiking along the foot and crown of the escarpments, exploring the various caves and sinkholes that had formed in the porous limestone.

'One day his journey led him into some caves in one of the bluffs that line the Saugeen Peninsula. Far north of the reserve, near what is now the Bruce Peninsula National Park, he found the discovery of a lifetime. Climbing in through the dark recesses of stone, he found himself in a natural cave. When his eyes adjusted to the light, he discovered pot-tery, bones, and artifacts from another time. He sat there for a while, wondering about the significance of his discovery and thinking about the people who had left these things there. When he finally emerged from the cave, he excitedly went running home to tell his family what he had found. Everyone listened with great interest, and over the next few days they set out to look for the site he had stumbled upon earlier. They looked and looked. They couldn't find anything. Unfortunately, in my grandfather's excitement the day before, he had forgotten to take note of where the cave was located. He returned many times that year, searching for the chamber that had brought so much excitement that one summer day. He continued that search throughout his life. It never ended.

'When Mishomis told this story, I believe he did so with a mixture of humour and deep purpose. One of the strengths of Anishinabek story-telling is that the participants can draw their own conclusions about its relevance for the issues they receive. In Anishinabek traditions, stories might possess multiple meanings, encouraging interpretive scope for the various people involved in their recounting. They are best related without the burden of explicit commentary. I am going to depart from that tradition for a moment, and give you my views. Though grandpa never said so, I think that on one level the story was his way of poking fun at himself and his skills in the bush. Everyone knew he was capa-ble and extremely competent in living off the land; in fact, he spent almost four years alone in the bush when he was in his late fifties. Yet despite his skills, he told the story to let people know that he could be just as foolish as the next person when orientating himself alone on the land.

'On another level, however, I believe the story had a deeper purpose. I think he wanted to warn us not to overestimate our confidence and knowledge about the land around us. He wanted to kindle a reverence and excitement about the secrets the land still held. A lot of his stories conveyed this theme. He was aware there was much we could learn from that which was hidden by the rocks, soil, grass, and trees that piled one upon another throughout our territory. We can't properly exercise our agency or make the best choices without remembering the land.

'And so it is for the current generation of people living at home. So it is for us living in Canada. Anishinabek stories are relevant to the study of law. They give us knowledge of the earth that is impossible to get from other sources. We continue to occupy a physical and jurispruden-tial world that is made up of intermixed layers of ancient and recent origin. The interdependence of these elements for the diversity of life on the land cannot be over-emphasized. To look just on the surface, and think that what you see from horizon to horizon is all that is needed to survive, is to misunderstand your place on the ground which you stand. To scale its heights – to learn its lessons – one must be alive to the underlying structures that support the visible and not-so-visible world around you. As my grandfather taught in exploring his terrain, it is not hard to get lost. However, the sheer nature of the stories found in both rock and human realm can uncover objects that can guide us to a more appropriate existence on the land, today and in the future. It is my hope that stories told in an old log cabin might once again direct legal jour-neys in the promising place that is now Canada.'

When he finished his lecture, the young man sat down. It marked the end of their session today, and the students noisily chattered and gath-ered their books, preparing to file out into the hall. Collecting his notes and thanking his colleagues, the young man watched the students climb the steps and crowd at the doors. Some hurried to make their way out, pushing and bumping others as they moved forward. Others patiently waited, talking with one another about the class or the events of the day. He saw one student inadvertently trip as she climbed the stairs. Two students nearby steadied her, and with embarrassed thanks she made her way forward. He spotted one of the Aboriginal law students near the door. She was crying. He watched as she looked back into the hall, surveying the room, before heading out into the building beyond.

PART TWO: NEEBIN

Individuals: The Second Hill

PAUGUK[1]

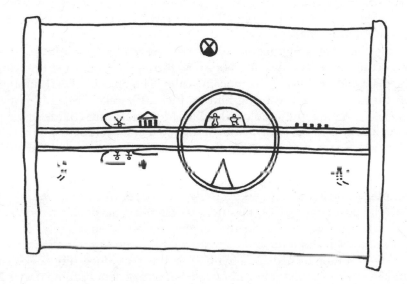

The light poured through the window at Nag'anal'mot's bedside. It was five o'clock in the morning. He couldn't believe the sun was already rising; it seemed to him like it just went down. As his vision cleared, he glanced over at the calendar: 21 June, Aboriginal Day. It was the longest day of the year. Of course, that explained the annoying light. Neebin is ascendant. Beebon is in retreat. Summer and winter have fought like this since the beginning.

Sitting up in bed, he gathered the cushions around his neck for support. Looking over the room, he saw the tale he'd been trying to complete laying on the blanket beside him. He has been working on it for months. It raised his ire a little to be reminded of it, before he was even fully awake. The tale bothered him more than he cared to admit. It felt disjointed, and he couldn't figure out whether he really had the right ending. Nag'anal'mot knew he needed to be more disciplined. For example, he couldn't really remember doing much with it when he came home last night. But there it was on his bed; right next to his old bones. He looked at the disorder around him and realized he must have attended another wild party last night, though he couldn't remember the details.

As he looked closer, he spied another book sticking out from under his blankets: *Guns, Germs, and Steel* by Jared Diamond. The Pulitzer Prize seal emblazoned on the front cover caught the rising sun, momentarily blinding him. He thought it was funny how well-written science fiction could have that effect.

Nag'anal'mot continued to be mesmerized by the light until another object caught his eye. A white stone flew through the window, breaking the glass and shattering the morning calm. The object hurtled through the air towards him, causing him to duck. It barely missed him and crashed onto the night table at his bedside. It left tiny chards of glass scattered around the floor, across his blanket, and beside the pillow. He was lucky he wasn't hurt. He nosed his head higher to get a closer look.

It was a skull, made of out rock.

He wondered who had launched it through his window. He was tempted to pick it up and take it back to whoever threw it.

Could it be from one of the students? He titled his head sideways as he listened for voices. He heard the whispered echo of laughter fading as the wind picked it up and blew the small sound out of range.

Nag'anal'mot turned his attention to the rock once more. Vacant, sunken eyes above a hollowed-out jaw stared back at him in silence. It reminded him of someone he knew, and caused an idea to form in his mind. He would teach them – and he was going to have some fun doing it, too. He thought the reserve needed enlivening; there would be no power in life without contradiction and ambiguity. The people needed to know who they were, and opposition helped. With that realization, Nag'anal'mot smiled, which then turned into a yawn – tongue fully extended, nearly dislocating his jaw.

Further along the shore, down the road from Nag'anal'mot, the young man stepped from his car into another world. He was home for a couple of months, while school was out for the season. Eight lanes of Highway 410 carried him out of Toronto into what was now called the southern Ontario countryside. He drove north along Highway 10 through Brampton, Orangeville, and Shelburne. Two hours into his journey he passed the village of Markdale and remembered that his great-great-grandfather had once carried a dying man eighty kilometres out of the bush to that place. The once-dying man was grateful, and Great-great-grandfather later received a medal from Queen Victoria in honour of his aid. Owen Sound was the next town he passed through. It used to be *Wadi-weediwon*. Then he thought to himself, it actually still is. His great-great-grandfather moved away from the site because of the treaties he had signed with Queen Victoria's representatives. Fifty minutes later the young man was home and passing the sign, 'Welcome to Cape Croker Indian Reserve, home of the Chippewas of Nawash First Nation.'

Neyaashiiniigmiing. The shale-covered ground beneath his feet felt warm, breathing in the afterglow of the evening sun. The young man wondered what stories the rocks would reveal tonight. Beside the house, with his back to the road, he looked beyond the old bathtub and rusted pots to the bay. A few people were pulling in their fishing nets for the evening. He thought of how the bay had witnessed this activity for centuries. As he scanned the horizon, he noted the white specks of seagulls scattering over the lake. Their voices carried across the water and merged with the waves on the shore. As he looked towards the house, his mother appeared at the window and waved him inside. Climbing up to the deck, he noticed the old tool bench was still resting under the porch from the summer before. It was just where he had left it when he helped install her new floor.

Opening his mother's door, the young man stepped into another world once more.

'Did you see that old porcupine at the door?' she asked him. 'It's a good sign. We hit it last night when we were on our way back from Wiarton. Nearly lost it, though. Donalda was passing us going the other way when we struck it. She slammed on her brakes when she saw what happened and came storming back, claiming she was the one who ran it over. Well, there was no way that she hit it, the poor little thing was clearly in our lane; you could see it had rolled in the direction we were travelling. We just about had to file a land claim to get the poor thing from her. She only backed down when she saw it lift its nose and decided that she would let us put it out of its misery. Good thing those *kaugook* are so hard of seeing. I would have hated its last memory to be of me swinging that tire iron. Anyway, we'll have lots of quills this summer. I'm hoping you can get me some birch bark soon. I want to make some quill boxes, along with a few brooches and other things this year.'

She walked across the kitchen and gave her son a hug. 'You'll get some bark for me, won't you?' she asked. Nodding agreement, the young man took off his shoes and placed them on the mat at the door.

Then, looking at his mother, he said, 'So I saw you have more rocks on the picnic table outside. Are you planning on opening your own jewellery store?' Every time he visited, there were more small stones gathered on the bench, sitting haphazardly amongst a few old plastic toys from his childhood. 'You know, the table's beginning to look a little like a miniature theme park, with my weathered plastic dinosaurs and soldiers spread over the site.'

'Aren't they beautiful?' she said. 'The stones, I mean. I find them when I'm walking along the shore. They catch the light in such interesting ways in the water, and they are so different when they dry off. I thought others would enjoy them, too, but mostly I just like to see them when I go outside. They are living in our language, you know: *asiin*. They have an agency all their own. I wanted to show them they were appreciated – that their beauty was noticed. So I put them on the picnic table for everyone to see. They have so much to teach us about life and our place here on the earth. I think they communicate that quite well, don't you?'

His mother was a large, attractive woman with a rounded nose, high cheekbones, and a warm smile. Known as 'The Queen' around the reserve for the large white Cadillac she drove, along with her faux ocelot hat, she was definitely a unique character. She had her father's philosophical bent, and her mother's openness to the world. She was not afraid to speak to anyone, at anytime, about anything. It wasn't that she was pushy. She was just curious, and loved to learn more about people and the world around her.

His mother went back to cleaning the fish at the sink and the man followed, plunging his hands into the gore. They worked in silence for a few minutes, sawing heads, fins, and tails away from the small bodies. 'So tell me about the end of term,' she asked. 'What about that Wawanosh girl from Saugeen who died unexpectedly a couple of months back? You were teaching her, right? What happened? Since the funeral, people have been pretty tight-lipped about it over there.'

Lifting a spine from its corpse in the sink, the young man thought of how troubling her death had been. He had known Catherine as a young girl. She was about ten years his junior. He had seen her at events that brought the reserves together from time to time. She was from Saugeen, Cape's sister reserve, on the other side of the peninsula, along the sandy eastern shores of Lake Huron. Her family had moved to the reserve from further south about a generation ago. He knew from the family name that her ancestors had signed treaties in what is now called the Windsor/Sarnia area in the 1840s and 1850s. What the young man remembered most about her from those earlier days was her love of baseball. Every once in a while the two reserves would have a face-off over a friendly game. She was a fierce competitor and took her baseball seriously.

'I don't know the details, mother,' the man said. 'She was in her first year, and was doing very well by all accounts. She was certainly very bright, and I enjoyed getting to know her better. She participated frequently, and would often come to speak to me after class about various issues. Funny thing about her, though, was that she took up opposing positions to just about everything anyone said. It was as if she was just begging for people to disagree with her, to pick a fight. I've seen lots of students like that over the years. I guess I know a few Native professors like that, too. Frankly, they scare me. It's intimidating to be with someone who is bright and contrary, especially when you're not always sure about your position yourself. It acts you on edge and creates unhealthy contention. Well, that's the way she was, a provocateur. If I didn't know better, I'd say that she purposely took this role upon herself like a cloak, until it became a part of who she was.

'You know, I see all sorts of students from reserves in different parts of the country. I think I've probably taught five hundred or more since I began teaching. Most are there to really do something with their lives; they want to make a difference. As a group, they do not fit the stereotype people have of law students, of only being there to get rich. The Aboriginal students seem to gravitate towards issues of social justice. They want to change the world. Of course, some want to makes lots of money, too, and I can't blame them for trying. Well, I thought Catherine fit into the social justice personality type, though with an edge. At first, students would welcome her participation, because she seemed to have a unique point of view. It was also clear she was very perceptive and bright. I think her sabre-rattling attracted admiration and interest in the beginning. But when this went on and on, in class after class, the other students began to tire of it. There comes a point when they just want to know what the law is, and don't want to fight endlessly over its implications. Students have exams and jobs that will depend on this information, even if they are interested in justice. A few weeks into the term, I noticed that some students would begin to roll their eyes when Catherine spoke. I could tell from the body language of the students that the class was growing hostile. I tried to do what I could to keep it a positive learning environment, but this became increasingly difficult as time wore on.

'Well, the unspoken tension must have got to her. I'm sure she couldn't help but notice the fact that she was becoming the subject of others' animosity. While she seemed to feed on this in class because it gave her new angles to work with, I could also see it bothered her. We had a few conversations about it in my office. I tried to help. She saw how self-generated contention could become self-centred, and disrespectful when done for its own sake. That's why I was as shocked as the next person when I heard that she took her own life; she had seemed so sure, and self-confident.'

The young man's mother gasped as the detail registered. 'Suicide?' she whispered. The news came as a shock to her. She dropped her knife in the sink and turned to look at her son. 'No one told me it was suicide.'

Tears formed in her eyes as she looked at her son. Water from the tap swirled blood down the drain and filled the silence.

She turned and embraced him once again. She hung tightly onto him for a few minutes. When she finally spoke, she said, 'I had no idea that's how Catherine died. I never dreamed she took her own life. She must have been awfully hurt to take that step; a cry for help to which no one could respond.' She picked up the knife and turned it over in her hands, reflecting the light overhead. Then, wiping her face with the back of her hand, she said, 'It does confirm something I've been wondering about these past few months, though – Pauguk has returned.'

The young man had heard about Pauguk when he was a little boy, but it had been some time since anyone mentioned his return. They both spent the next few minutes quietly working as his mother regained her composure. When they had finished gutting and filleting the fish, they cleaned up around the sink. The young man wiped the countertops and table while his mother wrapped the fish in foil and placed it in the oven. When she was finally able to speak again, she mouthed the word silently to her son: 'Pauguk.'

Sitting down at the table, she motioned for her son to join her. 'Let me explain,' she said. 'In the early spring when the birds returned, I noticed a species I'd never seen before. I only caught fleeting glimpses of it, so I was never quite sure what it was. You know how eagerly I look forward to the changing songs in the woods after the long winter. The call of the blue jay gives way to a hundred other songs. Well, this spring on my walks round the reserve I sensed that something was different. Every so often I would come across places where the trees were silent, when they would normally be filled with life: *sisigwad*. The muting of forest voices felt unnatural. I would stop, look around, and listen closely, searching for clues. Once in a while, ever so faintly, I thought I heard sounds like ice on the wind. It was chilling to hear such a high-pitched wail. It sounded like someone suffering tormented anguish. But I could never hold onto the sound for very long, and thought my ears might be playing tricks on me. So I would continue on my way, focusing my attention and enjoying the wind-song when it returned.

'Then one day, out on the prairie, a blur of motion flashed across my path. I followed its arc until I saw it come to rest on a jagged outcropping of stone behind some trees. Slowly I edged towards it, as quiet as I could be. Just as I came around the bushes, it was off again, rising through the air. Its bleached whiteness stood out against the blue sky. Almost chalk-like in colour, it was thin and bony. From where I stood it looked like a flying skeleton.'

The young man looked at his mother, wondering where all this was going. For as long as he could remember, she never went in through the front door when explaining something. He watched as she straightened the placemat in front of her, tracing the south-western design with her fingers. The mat lay beside a stack of dishevelled papers and magazines that had sat there for ages. The room was filled with such objects, saved for a rainy day. She left them there for a time when she felt they might be needed. There were books on the floor, dolls on the couch, baskets on the end tables, and eight-track tapes near the window. It wasn't that the place was dirty; in fact, she typically dusted and vacuumed every week. It was just that her idea of cleaning was different from most. If everything in the room wasn't visible, the place didn't feel organized to her. She was simply not a linear person, everything in her life connected in a thousand branches. While it worked for her, he sometimes got lost in it all and needed a little help. Prompting her along, he asked, 'How does this relate to Catherine?'

Picking up a magazine beside her, she absently flipped through its pages. 'You see, when Catherine Wawanosh married Richard a couple of years ago, people said his brother Paul was very jealous of their relationship. I even heard they had a serious altercation over her a while back. I never put much credence in it at the time. You know how gossip can be around here – it's not pretty. Anyway, if there was any truth to the rumours, I thought things would blow over. But then a trusted friend told me something disturbing about Paul a few months back. When I saw that thing over the prairie, near where they used to live, I began to fear for them.

'When the boys were younger, you would never see them apart: down at the dock, up by Lennox's store, or over by the ball field – all the places the kids hang out. They were like a pair of vines, intertwined at the root. Paul looked up to his brother, and followed him wherever he went. They would share the same space through their journeys. I'll always remember that time they collected tadpoles all summer down in front of mom's house. They filled jars and jars full of the little creatures. There were hardly any frogs there the next year. Then there was that summer they gathered all those crayfish, and put them in their mother's washtub. When she went out to do a load of washing, she was almost knocked out by the smell. The boys were like that all through their childhood and teens. They were the best friends you'd ever see.

'When Richard went off to college, he still kept in close touch. Paul even finished his last year of high school in the city so he could live at his brother's place. Then, when Richard was graduating, he got serious with Catherine Wawanosh. For the first time in his life, Paul found himself without his brother's company. He was like a lost puppy.'

'I remember that time,' the young man said. 'Paul even showed up in my office once or twice, asking if I'd seen his brother. Of course, I had seen Richard a time or two with Catherine, but for some reason I didn't tell him. I didn't have a good feeling about the way Paul asked me about them. He seemed obsessed and a little agitated. I didn't feel like it was my job to report on his brother and friend. I didn't think about it too much after that, though.'

'Well, you may not know the half of it,' his mother said. 'When Richard got married, Paul actually left town. He transferred to another university to finish his undergrad. I think he went out West to Saskatoon and enrolled as an exchange student. Did he mention that to you? You must have seen him just as he returned. He was actually gone for a whole year; it was probably the longest time he ever spent apart from his brother. Some people said Paul left because he was also in love with Catherine, and that was the cause of his split with Richard.'

The young man couldn't say the news surprised him, not after Paul's behaviour in his office. But hearing someone speak it aloud still made him feel awful. He tried to imagine the thoughts that went through Paul's mind to cause him to leave his brother's company. Paul hadn't mentioned his time in Saskatchewan when they visited together. Perhaps there was something to the bad feelings he had experienced that day. He wondered if Paul had been hiding something. But then again, he never could keep track of the people on the reserve; they always scattered all over the place. Back and forth, home and away, it happened dozens of times in their lives. But if Paul was in love with Catherine, it must have been a terrible time for the three of them. If it was true, he could see why Paul would not be anxious to divulge his love for her.

His mother continued, 'When the two boys died around the same time, that's when people really started to talk.'

Now it was her son's turn to be shocked.

'I didn't know they were *both* dead,' the young man said. 'I only knew about Richard's passing, and Catherine's, of course.'

Again, blood rushed to the young man's stomach as the world imperceptibly shifted beneath him – just as it had when he had heard about Catherine's death at the school. He was glad he was sitting down; the tightness in his chest was painful.

Seeing the look on his face, his mother reached over and put her hand on his arm. 'I'm sorry ... I thought you knew,' she said tenderly. 'I forget that you don't hear everything that happens at home when you're in the city. We buried them in the first three weeks of April; their three deaths were only a week apart ... Catherine died the week in between the other two, though, like I said, I didn't know how she had died.'

Again, the shock of the whole thing washed over the young man. He had been away for most of the last month, but he thought that someone would have at least mentioned Paul's death.

Catherine's death must have affected him more deeply than he realized. It seemed to have clouded his thinking. Her death had hit him pretty hard. He had never lost a student before. And having it follow so closely on the heels of Richard's death had compounded his pain. He wondered when it would ever end. Whole generations of people stopped in their tracks. Death was too frequent a visitor to this place.

As they sat silently for a few minutes, the smell of baked fish began to fill the room. Pushing back her chair, the young man's mother rose, turned off the oven, and checked their meal. Taking it out of the foil, she put portions of whitefish on their plates. As she was doing this, the man's thoughts filled with his dream and his vision of the second hill. People in their youth, struggling to climb, were pushed down and trampled before reaching the top, others suddenly vanishing. Nearly every time he phoned home, his mother would tell him about someone who had died. He wondered if she had mentioned Paul's death to him before. Just as with Catherine, he remembered the boys from his youth. They were approximately Catherine's age, only they lived on his reserve, so he saw them around a lot more when they younger. He knew their mother, aunts, uncles, and cousins better, too. Perhaps his mother had forgotten to tell him, or maybe she had simply been too weary when it all happened. It was hard to keep track of so much death.

When his mother spoke again, she continued, 'The way it unfolded was all so tragic. You may remember that Richard and Paul had gotten together at the end of term. According to their mother, there was a big party down at Catherine and Richard's place. Everyone seemed happy to welcome the younger brother home. They all wanted to know about his adventures. People said it was a good celebration; there was some drinking, but nothing got really out of hand. Unfortunately, in the middle of the night, Richard and Paul took a trip up to the roof of the building to take in the sights. People said there was a good view of CN Tower and the lake from there. They were gone for quite a while.

'Then, at first light, Paul came back down to the apartment in a sombre mood. He could hardly speak. He said his brother had accidentally fallen, and was lying on the ground below. Of course, when they got to him he was dead. Everyone's pain broke loose at the realization.

'The funny thing about it, though, was that Paul didn't seem as upset as he should have been. According to his cousins, he just seemed a little agitated by what happened.

'Then, when Paul tried to comfort Catherine – saying it was OK, they could be together now, that he would take care of her – she broke away from him in a dead run. People got a little suspicious, and wondered how he could be so callous at a time like that. It was as if he was only thinking about himself.

'I don't know much from there. As you know, Catherine died a week later, and no one has said much about it since. Like I said, people around the reserve have been pretty quiet about her death. I wasn't even sure how Catherine died until you told me. I just assumed something happened because of the shock of losing Richard, or that her grief caused an accident. I even wondered if she became careless in her state, and fell victim to some unfortunate circumstance.'

The young man's mother paused for a moment, and poured herself a glass of water from the jug on the table. When she was finished, she pushed one of the glasses towards her son. She was always trying to get everyone to drink more water. It was her belief that it soothed a lot of pain and remedied most problems. There were few things as sacred as water in her view of the world. When she finished drinking, she continued to speak.

'As for Paul, it turns out he died the week after Catherine: three deaths, three weeks in a row. First Richard, then Catherine, then Paul. It seems Paul drove off a cliff, rolled down a hill, and drowned in the river over by Sauble Falls. It took them some time to recover the body, so they weren't even sure if he was dead at first. His parents held out hope that he had escaped and made his way downstream. But they eventually found his body waterlogged at the river's edge. That's why his funeral was after Catherine's. It's so sad to think of them putting two sons in the ground in the same month, with their daughter-in-law as well.'

When she finished, the young man took a drink of his water and said, 'I don't remember any of this, mother – at least about Paul's death. I knew about Richard's and Catherine's deaths, of course, everyone was talking about them at the funeral, but I can't believe I didn't know any thing about Paul dying. Did you tell me about him already? I really can't remember.'

'I thought I did,' his mother replied, 'but sometimes my memory is not as good as it once was. I usually tell you what I remember when you call. Maybe you were away when Paul was found.'

The young man suddenly recalled that he had left the country right after Catherine's funeral. He took his trip to Phoenix with guilty relief at the end of the term, trying to separate himself from all the sadness that hung around him. He purposely buried himself in other activities while he was away, to get his mind off his grief. He didn't even call home. That was probably when Paul died. No wonder I didn't know, he thought to himself.

Sitting there, picking at their fish, they passed a few more minutes in silence. Dusk was now falling, and the moon could be seen rising over the water out the back window. As they finished their meal, a hush seemed to fall over the world. The seagulls and crickets that had been their vocal companions all evening went quiet. Even the sound of the flies and June bugs bumping against the porch screens ceased. The change in the air was perceptible. The young man's mother brought the change in the surrounding atmosphere to his attention. She whispered, 'Do you hear that? It sounds like nothing. This is what I was telling you about. Pauguk.'

Putting their dishes in the sink and donning light coats, mother and son headed outside and walked down to the shore. It was deathly silent. On the other side of the peninsula, the fireworks would soon begin in celebration of Aboriginal Day.

Standing on the rocks by the beach, a thin whisper echoed over the waves. Barely noticeable at first, it mingled with the wind and trailed off into the night. As it got stronger, the man turned to his mother and leaned closer, 'Is this what you have been experiencing on your walks recently?'

She nodded in agreement, and they slowly started walking towards the source of the sound.

The moon's light caught the surf and exposed the contours of the beach, enabling them to safely make their way forward. The limestone heaped on the shore gave way with each step. After they walked about 200 yards they saw a long, white shadow scattered amongst the rocks in the water, a few feet ahead. As they drew closer, the stones sliding under their feet seemed to catch its attention, and it took off into the darkness, disappearing into the night.

With its departure the silent whisper ceased, and the crickets and frogs resumed their nightly chorus.

Mother and son looked at each other, and crept closer to where the shadow had rested. Wading into the water, the young man noticed a peculiar-looking rock at his feet. Rolling in the waves, the moon caught its pockmarked surface. It was oblong in shape and about six inches wide. There were two large cavities on its face, sunk deeply away from the moon's light. Reaching down and picking it up, he felt its significant weight. Holding it level with his eyes, he thought to himself that the rock looked exactly like a human skull. Showing his mother, she quietly said, 'Pauguk.'

As a young boy he had often heard the story of Pauguk during the long nights at his grandparents' place. He was a flying skeleton destined to dwell between earth and sky, banished from the land of the dead for his actions while living. Lust, greed, betrayal, and murder were among his many crimes. His lonely, lingering presence was a lesson to those who followed his course. Whenever sounds were heard that couldn't be explained, his Mishomis would say, 'That was Pauguk.' For some, Pauguk represented death itself, his voice a haunting reminder of the corruptibility and fragility of life.

As he thought about the evening's conversation with his mother, the young man could see how Pauguk was front and centre in the events she described.

He remembered how Basil told the story.[2] A long time ago, Pauguk had fallen in love with his brother's wife, and could not control his longing for her. After trying to overcome his obsession by leaving his village for a season, he came back, only to discover that his passion for her had grown even more intense. Scheming to get rid of his brother, Pauguk took him on a camping trip and pushed him to his death from the height of a tall cliff. When he returned home, people suspected him of foul play in his brother's death. They did not trust Pauguk's story. Then, when he tried to comfort his brother's wife, she shunned him, and in her stress took her own life. Finally, when he realized that both his brother and sister-in-law were gone, and that he was the cause of their demise, he went into hiding. In his journey, he encountered the spirit of his sister-in-law. Her ghostly visit caused him great shock, and led to his drowning. When Pauguk travelled from this life to the next, he was denied entrance to the land of the dead because of his actions. He was banished to live a life as a wanderer, a skeleton with no prospect of comfort or rest.

'Mother,' the young man said, 'I can see why you say Pauguk has returned, and why you were interested in what happened to Richard and Paul. The spirit of acquisitiveness, lust, and greed had taken hold of their relationship with each other, and with Catherine. It's a lot like Pauguk.

'But who knows what Paul really thought, and whether he coveted Catherine or brought harm to his brother? I don't think we'll ever know the answer, with them now all gone. I see Pauguk in a different light, beyond what we talked about tonight.'

The man rested the 'skull' on his knee as they found a couple of large rocks and sat on the shore, waiting for the fireworks to begin over the peninsula.

He turned to his mother and continued. 'I agree with you. But I also think Pauguk showed his face in another way, with what happened to Catherine this past spring.'

'What do you mean?' she responded. 'How have you seen Pauguk so far away from here? Does he travel to Toronto, too?' His mother always encouraged him to see the wider world through older Anishinabek eyes. She encouraged him to share how their ancient ways still swirled around them. It was obvious to her that the events and stories surrounding them were still very much connected to their living, enduring culture. She always expected her son to make these connections more explicit, no matter where he lived. He saw in her questions an invitation to follow through.

He continued: 'Last term did not end well. There was a lot of stress on the faculty and students at the end of term, during the time of the Bridge Period Lectures at the law school. It was one of the reasons I came home the weekend before it began. I had a lecture to prepare for the Bridge, and a big writing assignment for a law journal that was due. But that wasn't all. I had just found out that a number of our students had been accused of falsifying their academic records in their applications for summer jobs with big Toronto law firms. They were cheating.

'It was such a sad time for us around the school. People feel deeply about the law school, especially the teachers on faculty. They are very loyal to the school and what they want it to stand for: integrity, academic excellence, leadership development, and professional responsibility. In addition, they feel like they have received so much from their association with the school, and have dedicated themselves to passing it on. They work there to give something back to an institution that has helped them in so many ways. They want to pass it on. I'm not saying that faculty members aren't there for other reasons, such as money, prestige, and other worldly rewards; but you would be surprised at how committed most professors are to the institution. There is almost a sense of public trust you get from some of my colleagues.

'Well, when the allegations from the law firms began, that students were submitting false grades, people felt personally hurt, like a trust had been broken in many different ways. I can remember the day we discussed it in faculty council. There were a lot of long faces and sombre voices around the table. The dean was great; he showed real leadership that day. He led a full, open discussion about what had transpired, and what the options were if the allegations turned out to be true. Then he turned the floor over to us.

'It was quite a sincere outpouring. I saw my colleagues in a different light that day, despite the circumstances that had brought us together. I was proud of them. We approached the issue from many angles; it was very respectful and professional. People expressed the need to support the students, in order to ensure that no one was falsely accused. Fairness and due process was one of the hallmarks of the discussion, though some would disagree with my take on that question. Others spoke of the importance of understanding why the students had cheated, if it was indeed true, which good evidence led us to believe. There was also talk of our need to do some internal soul-searching, to see if we had somehow contributed to the matter. Some spoke of the sadness they felt for those who had not cheated. They even expressed concern for those who were subject to the investigation. Many talked about the stain this could create on the reputation of the school, and how it could lead others to paint everyone associated with the school with the same brush. These and other concerns were all put on the table that day. It was a very emotional meeting. After all, we had personally gotten to know these students over the past eight months, spending five days a week with them. These were real people we were talking about. We were devastated.

'I was personally hurt, too. You see, we give students practice exams halfway through the year to provide some feedback on how they are doing in their courses. The students take them seriously, but since they are only practice exams, no official transcripts are issued. Nevertheless, first-year students are anxious to get jobs, and want something to show prospective employers about their performance in school when they apply. It seems that over the past few years, some students had gotten in the habit of submitting these marks on their own accord, through written notes. They did this in January and February when they applied for summer jobs.

'The thing is, this year the firms got suspicious when they saw so many As and B+s showing up on the students' reports of their own marks. First they discussed this in their own firms. Then they spoke to friends from other firms. They wondered if we had changed our standards. Finally, they contacted the law school.

'Well, we had not changed our standards. When the law school looked into the concerns of the firms, they discovered that falsification of grades had occurred on a wider scale than anyone could believe. The school acquired copies of all the applications the firms received from our students.

'Of the one hundred and eighty students in our first-year class, about forty were investigated, and twenty-five were eventually found to have committed an infraction. It turns out that Catherine was among the number subject to the investigation.

'Like I said, I felt personally hurt. It seems she had applied to six different law firms, and had given them a list of grades that did not reflect what she received on her Christmas exams, including my course. After all our conversations through the year, I could hardly believe it. I thought she was different, not like the stereotype people have of law students. While I wanted to give her the benefit of the doubt, the evidence against her was pretty strong. I felt betrayed.

'So I came home that weekend to clear my mind. I had also been shaken by Richard's death a few days before. I needed some space. I never got to speak to Catherine about what happened – she died the weekend after I found out.'

As they were speaking, the celebrations behind them started. Mother and son both looked back across the peninsula at the bright fires in the air. With the moon at their backs, and the blazing display before them, they paused to watch the show unfold. The sky glowed in brilliant tones against the stars. Lights rose and fell like visitors from another world, growing with life in their ascension before falling, fading into the night, caught between earth and sky. As the last volley exploded and cascaded to earth, the young man spoke again.

'So mother, you were right. I guess Pauguk has never really left us. He takes many different forms. When I think of Catherine's competitive edge, and the pressure she must have put on herself to succeed, I see some of Pauguk in what she did.'

The young man's mother asked: 'Do you think she became Pauguk herself? Lusting after something just beyond her reach, overcome by greed, breaking trust and betraying those around her? Do you think she is still between worlds?'

'I don't know, mother. When I think of the promise her life held and how it ended so suddenly, I see the tragedies about which our ancestors warned, needlessly repeated again today. It reminds me of what you often say. Our traditions are alive today. They have continuing relevance. They have much to teach us about our walk through this world.

'It also reminds me that when our teachings are not followed, people get struck down. Our agency is enhanced when we travel through life applying the ideas from our best traditions. When we don't take guidance from these principles we can get lonely, lost, or hurt. It's like the dream I've been meaning to ask you about, where people are broken on their journey up the second hill of life. I think that's what happened to Pauguk, and to Catherine, too.'

AUD-WAUDJIMOOWIN[1]

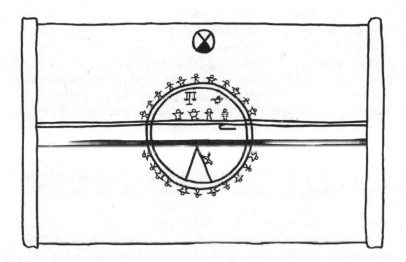

The sun rose bright the next morning, giving them an early start to their day. They had been visiting this place ever since he could remember. When he was a young boy, his mother would take them there to discover its hidden treasures. They would spend hours going through its stores, picking through abundance most ignored. When they returned home, their trunk was usually loaded with all the stuff they got; even their seats would be covered. At such times, they felt like the richest people in the world. They would go home and display their new acquisitions prominently throughout the house and in the yard. He would invite his friends to come over and play. They would have hours of fun with everything they had found. Nothing could have been better; in fact, he still had some of those things in his garage.

As his mother and sister walked over the site memories of those earlier days came flooding back.

'Do you remember those lamps we got here that one year?' his mother said. 'They were pure crystal, with the old oil wicks still intact. There were two of them, clear and luminous. They must have cost a fortune when they were new. And then there were dozens of those old glass hydro transformers, too, all different sizes, shapes, and colours. I displayed them for years on our windowsills; they caught the light so well.'

'I remember those,' his sister said. 'I think I was too young at the time to know what they were, but I used to take them onto the porch and play house. I pretended they were fancy glasses and cups for the imaginary banquets I held. I also remember the kitchen set we found here. An easy-bake oven, and a plastic sink and cupboard set. There were lots of dolls, too, and a few good books.'

Joining in, the young man said, 'You're right. There was some great stuff around here. I still have some of the Hot Wheels we got from our visits. Not only were there some rare cars, but there were also yards of plastic track and a turbo charger. I even unearthed a box of old hockey cards that was still in pretty good shape.'

'In some ways, it's hard to tell much was ever here,' his mother said. 'It used to be such a place of activity. Things piled up as far as the eye could see. Now, just a few old rusted objects protrude from the soil. They must have bulldozed the land when they closed it down, and laid a new layer of soil over top.'

As they stood there, a flock of seagulls settled onto the field. Grazing on crickets and other bugs in the grass, the birds seemed oblivious to their presence. In silence they watched them feed for a few minutes, enjoying the sight and the cool breeze that blew across the field.

When their mother next spoke, she did so with a note of awe and respect they rarely heard her use. From her tone they both knew she had something important to tell them.

'Do you see that one seagull by that patch of milkweed over there?'

They searched for the object of her discovery. Pointing with her lips, she directed their eyes. 'There's about four or five of them just standing together, separated from the main group. See the one in the middle? Its eyes are red. I've been studying it. I can't be sure, but it looks like it doesn't have any colouring. I think it's pure white, an albino seagull.'

They all watched for a few more minutes as the birds jostled with one another and searched through the weeds. Every so often the wind would rearrange them, as their wings caught slight currents and they changed places in the field. After observing the bird from many angles, they were in agreement: it was an albino seagull.

They spoke for a while about its significance. His mother wanted to go tell the chief. She wanted to find her parents and show them, too. If she could arrange it, the young man thought his mother would call the newspaper. While the young man and his sister thought that a colourless bird was interesting, they felt their mother was getting a little carried away.

'It's not like you've just seen the calving of the prophesied great white buffalo,' the young man said, a little too sarcastically. He immediately felt a tinge of regret. It must have been the city in him; it was one reason he came home, to shed some of the cynicism that built up down there. There were legends throughout the West of a significant day when a white buffalo calf would be born. Many said the day it was born would be the day that power would begin to return to the Indians. To the man and his sister, standing on the site of the old dump, watching a red-eyed garbage-eater frolic in the breeze did not feel like a sign of great things to come.

Yet they had to admit that great changes could take place through seemingly insignificant beginnings. It had been about twenty years since they regularly visited dumps with their mother. Now they lived very different lives.

He had gone to Toronto, gotten married, received a law degree, and eventually started teaching.

She had moved to the States and completed her PhD. She remained single, and came back to the reserve to work as a family therapist. Her first job upon coming home was working at the women's crisis shelter. It was the job she had always wanted and planned for during her years away. She wanted to do something important back home, and now she had both the cultural and professional skills necessary to provide the service. Yet when she began working, she saw abuse heaped upon abuse. It entwined with the personal and professional relationships of the people who laboured around her. She lasted four months at her first job; she had to get out. She applied to work at other places on the reserve: the Health Centre, Child Welfare Services, and the Education Authority. No takers. Word travelled fast. If you stand up for yourself and don't play the game, you end up standing by yourself. After receiving four academic degrees, logging over 5,000 hours of clinical time, and training and supervising dozens of new therapists, she was unemployed. She was tossed by the wayside by those who had authority over her. It was not the first time she had experienced this treatment.

When she was born her heart had stopped, and oxygen to her brain was cut off. Her father had prayed all the way to the hospital that she would be OK. After receiving a complete blood transfusion her condition stabilized, as her heart restarted and she began breathing on her own. They said there had been damage. Her parents were told that she would never walk. They brought her home and hoped for the best, expecting a miracle in the face of despair. She was slow to speak, and didn't walk when the time came. For a long time it looked as though the predictions would come true. Nevertheless, her parents got her all the help they could. They put her legs in braces, tried different therapies, and exercised faith.

Then one day, she spoke, and in quick time developed a complex vocabulary. Next she took her first step, which led to others, until she was mobile on her own. She was strong-willed. Walking led to running, running to skipping, and skipping to riding bikes. Though she was very late in each stage of her development, by the time she started school she could physically do most things others could. True, she had a slight limp because one side of her body was slower than the other, but she was determined enough to not let these things stop her.

But when school began, despite the gains she had made at home, her teachers concluded she would not be a good student. They said she was too easily distracted, slow in reading, and had a hard time working with numbers. And despite her physical gains, they observed that her left hand gave her difficulties from time to time. So without adequate support she did poorly in school, barely scraping by from one year to the next. Even so, she worked hard and did what she could to succeed. In some ways these were long, lonely years. If not for the love of her family, she might have given up. When she got into high school, guidance counsellors streamed her into a vocational track. She continued to work hard, but had great difficulty getting good marks. This took a further toll on her self-esteem, and for a while she wondered what she would do with her life.

Then a miracle of sorts occurred. In grade eleven she was diagnosed as being dyslexic. The light went on for people around her, and they knew what they could do to help. Teachers trained her how to compensate for the weaknesses caused by her condition. They taught her how to read and write in ways that worked around her problem. Special accommodations were made when she wrote exams, giving her extra reading time. These measures worked. A year later she was on the honour role. Her grades were in the higher ranges, except in math, where she continued to struggle. She was academically reborn; now when she worked hard, it paid off. She got into college and received a BSc, and then went on to get an MSc.

By the time it was all finished, she had her PhD. Just as with her physical disabilities, she overcame academic challenges through some initial assistance, and then plain hard work.

Now that she was home, she was experiencing similar challenges all over again: people underestimating her, not giving her a chance, pre-judging her ability in advance of her performance. Tossing her aside, blocking her ascent. She knew she would prevail, but the way was going to be hard. The young man knew this from watching her over the years, and from his reflections on how people treated disability in society.

So looking at the seagull, he had to admit that there might be something to his mother's excitement. Everyone has the potential to make a difference.

As they stood there listening to their mother, a few dogs wandered through the field. He noticed that Nag'anal'mot was in their midst, surrounded by a pack of four or five black dogs. Seeing them, he re-called that there used to be lots of dogs here in earlier years, searching through the garbage, ripping open bags and checking inside. Though it was like trying to find a needle in a haystack, they had a good sense of smell. They were often rewarded for their efforts. Sometimes it was old vegetables, at others a can of half-finished tuna or a loaf of mouldy bread. They were always pulling something rotten through the hole in the side of their quarry.

After watching the dogs for a few moments, they saw the figure of a man wander into the clearing from the depths of the woods.

As he got closer, the young man noticed it was Alan, his cousin. Un-cle Jim's firstborn son.

When they were younger they used to play together quite a bit. They were about the same age and had similar interests: hockey, bicycles, cowboys and Indians. They had also enjoyed the same TV programs, especially Saturday morning cartoons. In fact, even now he found it hard to look at his cousin without thoughts of Touché Turtle and Quick Draw McGraw coming into his mind. But that had been twenty years ago. They had both changed a lot since then.

Alan stumbled towards them. He spoke, 'Captain, have you seen the Klingons? I saw them land over by Uncle Bob's place and was follow-ing them for a while. I was just about to catch them when I lost my tricorder. Do you know which way they went?'

Alan stood there with his hands in his pockets waiting for an answer, swaying in the breeze. He was a stick of a man, about six feet tall, with little muscle left on his body and a gaunt face. The healthy young boy they once knew had grown into a skeleton.

After reflecting for a moment, the young woman spoke, 'We haven't seen any Klingons recently, Alan, but they may be back at the base. We can take you there if you want.'

Alan thought for a second, slowly looking them over. After a minute's silence he said, 'I need help. I saw the cops over at Uncle Richard's, and watched them put Greg and Mark into the car. They were handcuffed. We just got some crack, and I think they were being arrested. I was out back when they came. I hid under the boat until they left. Then I ran into the bush. That was two days ago. I don't know what to do.'

The young man's mother approached her nephew and took off her sweater to drape it over Alan's shoulders. 'We wondered where you were. I thought you learned your lesson last time,' she said. 'That glue has made you stupid. Everyone's worried about you. The police are still searching, too. You can't go running off like that, without any thought. There's no use trying to run away from things you have to face up to. You could have been seriously hurt. What were you thinking?'

Alan was schizophrenic, among other things.

When he was in high school, he seriously damaged his brain by sniffing gas, glue, and anything else he could find to make him high. He went on a two-year binge that was totally self-destructive. It created a multitude of problems for him and those around him. He had difficulty focusing on things, and he often had a hard time distinguishing between fantasy and reality. It was often like that for too many people on the reserve, but his case was totally different because of how his addictions interacted with his mental illness. Alan's multiple personalities made it challenging for people to work with him. He had to live under constant supervision. Both of his aunts had looked after him from time to time. They shopped for groceries, paid his bills, and checked in on him to see that he was OK. Others took part also. It was a constant chore. He had been in trouble with the law before, too.

Last time it happened, he pled guilty to trafficking in drugs.[2] There was a big healing and sentencing circle in the community to deal with his crime. It was quite an important event, and gained some notoriety at the time. People spoke from different perspectives about the impact of his behaviour on their lives. A police officer testified how the young kids in school were using drugs because of their flow through the community. He said children as young as ten were using. To pay for them, these young people had a tendency to steal from their parents and those around them. Teachers also spoke about the effects of drugs on their students. Their grades went down, and they became disruptive. As time went on, their options and future choices became exceedingly narrow. One guidance counsellor said that a few students had even told her they wanted to be drug dealers when they grew up. She couldn't believe how sincere they were in this misguided notion. The discussion about Alan continued in this vein for some time. Participants talked about how the problem of drugs easily snowballed and wreaked havoc in the community.

The Crown prosecutor outlined the seriousness of Alan's offence in law, and recommended a harsh sentence. He cited examples of the range in time that people served in jail for similar actions. He requested that an example be set to those around him by sending him to jail for the maximum time.

Alan's own lawyer also agreed that there was a problem, but believed a prison term was not the answer. The *Criminal Code* had been recently amended to direct judges to consider the particular circumstances of Aboriginal people in sentencing. In a case called *Gladue,* the Supreme Court later said there were many background factors which figured prominently in the causation of crime by Aboriginal offenders: 'years of economic and social dislocation ... have translated into low incomes, high unemployment, lack of opportunities and options, lack of relevance of education, substance abuse, loneliness, and community fragmentation.'[3] The Court also admitted that Aboriginal people face racism, both in the form of systemic and direct discrimination. Alan's lawyer applied these arguments in Alan's case. He said the best way to deal with Alan's challenges was by placing him with people that could help him.

An employee of Community and Justice Services on the reserve had prepared a community assistance plan, and he pointed to the people that were willing to help him execute this plan to stay clean. He referred to the twelve or so people sitting in the circle who were willing to assist.

Alan's aunts, social workers, and counsellor also spoke on his behalf. They talked of their willingness to help him overcome his problem. Everyone had some hope. Alan also spoke that day. He expressed remorse for what he had done. While his mental impairment was obvious to everyone in attendance, there seemed to be willingness that day to turn the corner on how they treated him. There was a rededication from those in the circle to work with him. Most did not want him to go to jail. They had seen too many people come back to the reserve after their release from the prison system more dangerous, more sophisticated in the arts of criminality, and less connected to the help that could be received. He was placed in the community's care.

That was all in the past now. It seemed very clear that Alan had reoffended. Now it was most likely he would end up in jail. After all the help he had received, it looked as though his problems lay beyond the community's ability to solve them. Truth be told, his problems were likely beyond the ability of the state to resolve, too. All they would do is lock him up for a few years. With its head in the sand, the criminal justice system would not face the challenges Alan lived with. He would end up on a revolving track from jail to home. It would lead to an ever-increasing cycle of harm and self-destructive behaviour. It seemed hopeless.

Looking at his cousin, the young man wondered where their lives had taken such different turns. He wondered if it had to be that way.

Then, looking at his sister standing beside him, he understood that Alan's descent into hell hadn't been inevitable. The situation was too complex to ascribe simply to external factors, as important as they might be. At some point in their lives, people were usually more than helpless victims of the system. There was a range of decisions over which most people had control at one time or another, even if the range of choices was limited. Some people did better than others in exercising this power of decision-making. Despite the challenges his cousin and sister both faced, he knew choice and agency formed a part of the story. They each made different decisions at tough times in their lives – some good, some bad. Now they were both living with the consequences of these decisions. While he knew their decisions did not automatically give them control over many of the things that happened to them, he also knew that their decisions had some influence.

As they stood there looking at one another in the field, the young man's mother spoke. 'Come on Alan. We'll take you home and feed you supper before we call the police. You can get warm and have a good night's sleep. We'll invite Aunt Bertha, Gary, and a couple of your friends over, too. We'll have a good night. We still love you.'

Alan looked at his aunt and across at his cousins. 'Beam me up,' was all he could say.

They all piled into his mother's car and started for home.

Driving over the old roads brought thoughts of an earlier time to the man's mother. 'I should be sad,' she said, 'but I can't help but feeling rich today, though I can't quite say why.'

Then, looking at Alan through the rearview mirror, she said, 'You're going to have a tough time before this is all through, Alan, but we'll do what we can to help. We've picked up worse things than you at that dump.'

Speaking in a quiet tone to her daughter beside her, she said, 'Maybe it was seeing that seagull, I don't know, or maybe it's just being together as a family, even if it is only for a moment. You can always find such abundance in this place if you look hard enough. Anyway, whatever it is, I'm looking forward to having some people over tonight. I can't wait to share with them what we got at the dump today.'

ANIMIKEEK & MISHI-BIZHEU[1]

It started so innocently, with just a few distant echoes in the sky. Then the west winds picked up and pushed the clouds before them, hurrying them on their journey. The clouds resisted and fought back, catching on the horizon's edge. Anchored at a distance, they piled themselves high in the air as they prepared for the coming confrontation. Darkness fell an hour before the sun went down. *Animikeek*, the Thunderers, fled their nests in warning, to search out the Anishinabek and remind them of their duties. At the same moment, *Mishi-bizheu* prepared for the battle, rising from the depths, searching out those who forgot. His black form roiled across the water and the tempest was soon unleashed. Jagged forks of stone and light pierced the lake. The underwater beings fought back. The contest between them was violent. All across the peninsula the trees bowed, rocks sang out, and every living thing sought cover.

There had been a fierce storm last night.

But the sun rose clear that morning. The previous day's humidity had been washed from the air. Water flowed from the east today. It wound its way in streams through the bay in front of the cabin. The currents, turquoise in colour, shimmered in the summer sun. The contrast meant it would be warm enough to swim. He looked forward to this moment all year long. For four months the wind blew snow across the ice. For another four months the snow seemed submerged just below the surface. It wasn't visible, but its presence was definitely felt. Then for two months the water was warm enough for bathing. Finally, for two months you could actually linger, swim, and submerge yourself in the water's healing embrace.

Mishomis got ready and headed over the path. He picked his way across the rocks to the water's edge. The stones he had piled near the shore last summer were still in place. The previous season's ice had only moved them out a few feet from the land.

Wading into the bay, Mishomis felt the thrill of the new season. As the water reached his knees, he placed the tips of his fingers in the edges of the bay. The touch sent a rush of excitement up through his arms. As he walked further, he stood on his toes and the water flooded around his waist. He settled into its temperature. Then, checking to see that there were no boulders before him, he spread his arms and jumped.

He immediately found himself buried in another world.

It was prehistoric. Light wrinkled the lake's floor, bending the rocks with its touch. Shades of grey, olive, and indigo blended and mingled before fading into the distant veil of perpetual night. Crayfish, carp, minnows, and trout passed through weightless, watery curtains. Ancient life had been pressed into the stone floor below, fossilized, and sleeping through countless generations.

As he was swimming through the light, a murky shadow passed before him. Mishomis froze, and then scrambled to the surface, catching his breath. The uneven bottom made it difficult for him to gain his balance. When he finally steadied himself, he was afraid to move. A dark figure, ten feet long, lay submerged against the rocks a few feet away. Sharp, black plates were visible along its face and spine. Its long tail swayed in the current. For a few moments their gaze locked on one another, and Mishomis faced a cold stare of timeless acrimony.

From the shore, a black dog looked on in curiosity.

When the water creature finally moved, its back broke the surface and left a small whirlpool in its wake. Mishomis fought hard to resist the pull of the newly formed current. Just as its tail gripped his legs, he broke free. He slowly stumbled away, pushing through the water before pausing at a respectable distance. He silently sang his heart song as he watched the creature disappear below the waves.

Turning to make his way to the shore, Mishomis again came to a stop. A silver-grey salmon lay lifeless, floating on a forty-five-degree angle in the water column before him. Its head was severed, thrown back behind its gills. Entrails had been pulled from within its body; its stomach, heart, and intestines rose in a pillar from its throat and drifted in the current. Mishomis swallowed hard, and then made his way around the fish. Its unstaring eyes pressed deep into his soul. Leaving the sight behind, Mishomis scrambled from the water and onto the shore, the rocks under his feet resisting his every movement.

His blood raced through his ears as he gained the water's edge. Momentarily perched between two worlds, Mishomis looked back over his shoulder towards the bay. No sign of life was visible above the waves. Breathless, he awkwardly stepped onto the land and crumpled to the ground. Struggling to sit upright, he bruised his wrist on a large, grey stone. He paused for a moment, while the waves pulled incessantly at his feet.

Mishomis sat still for some time.

After regaining a degree of strength, he stood up and looked for a drier place to rest. Finding an upturned stump, where the stones on the beach met the tangle of the woods, Mishomis reclined in the arms of its twisted roots. His breathing returned to normal.

When he was settled, Mishomis surveyed the beach, foreshore, and bay. The escarpment's distant rock face glowed in the morning sun. A few blood-red clouds graced the sky. Their long, feathery tendrils tracked east to west, marking a path through the air, from the water to the bluff. After following the cloud's shifting formations for some moments, Mishomis noticed a small, dark shadow form at the path's base along the horizon. Moving quickly over the water, the shadow grew until it gained the shore about one thousand yards to the east of him. It surged over the rocky beach towards him at a significant speed. Looking up to its source, Mishomis saw what looked like a large bird pass between the earth and the sun, before disappearing over the escarpment a few seconds later.

Animikeek and *Mishi-bizheu* were still restless after last night's battle. The sky and water were very active today.

Just as the shadow disappeared, Mishomis heard the rocks clatter together behind him. With a shattering jolt, he sat upright against the stump. His heartbeat quickening, he turned to see that it was only the black dog sauntering onto the shore. It sat down beside him.

Nag'anal'mot looked at Mishomis before lowering his head to settle his chin onto his paws. Upon seeing that his visitor was only the familiar old dog, the old man relaxed. There was a long silence, rhythmically broken by the waves washing against the shore. Mishomis and the Nag'anal'mot looked out over the water for some time, watching *Mishi-bizheu* brood over its depths.

The dog's presence caused an ancient thought to rise in Mishomis' mind. He remembered the first time his grandmother had taught him about conflict. She had said contradiction was always alive in the world: *Beebon* and *Zeegwun*, *Animikeek* and *Mishi-bizheu*, light and dark, good and evil. His grandmother knew a thing or two about conflict. Her husband was Tecumseh's brother, and the two of them had fought together throughout the Ohio Valley before losing their lives in the War of 1812. His grandmother would tell him that conflict was always before them. She said the Trickster constantly taught them this truth. She laughed when she saw people trying to escape life's cycles and eliminate their conflicts. It caused her to wonder if anyone ever really listened closely to all those Nanabush stories.

So that he would not miss these lessons, Mishomis' grandmother taught him that he couldn't escape conflict and opposition. She did so by helping him memorize the storied universe that surrounded them. He was told how to pay attention to its constant clashes, contests, convergences, and countermoves. He hadn't always remembered what she told him. There were times when he had been impatient with life's contradictions. The worst periods were when he tried to deal with his challenges through the bottle. His addiction had become a shameful affront to his grandmother's teachings. He couldn't think of anything that took him further away from Anishinabek law. It was a breach of the worst kind, because it repudiated the mindfulness each Anishinabek teaching promoted. During each binge he lost consciousness of the balance his grandmother encouraged. Intoxication gave him the temporary impression that he had escaped the world's opposition, but each time he awoke from a stupor he felt further out of balance.

Mishomis knew his grandmother, Widow Sachoo, wouldn't have been happy with him during those dark days, had she lived to see them. It made him feel ashamed, and this eventually caused him to seek help. He had grown tired of the way his actions repudiated all she had told him. As he started recovering, he remembered a Nanabush story his grandmother had helped him memorize. It was about how attraction and resistance repel and intermingle with one another. It taught him how winter gave summer its definition. Then he recalled other stories: about how thunder and storms gave meaning to duty and peace, about how darkness was an important condition in appreciating light. The insights he gained from these sources turned his mind to other stories.

As he further refreshed his memory, he more clearly saw how his grandmother's lessons contained guidance about how to live a good life: *bimadiziwin*. This connection, in turn, brought the seven grandfather teachings and their counsel to his attention. He learned that without evil, there could be no such thing as goodness; that opposition was essential to understanding wisdom, love, respect, bravery, honesty, humility, and truth. These memories helped him resolve that he would stop drinking to drown his sorrows. He decided to face conflict. When Mishomis took this step, his learning intensified and deepened. His struggles taught him to more fully appreciate what were formerly only words in childhood stories – that opposition was an important part in making choices. Through his own experience, he came to know his power to make choices in the midst of the contradictions that defined his life. He sought wisdom in other places, too. He regularly participated in the AA program on the reserve, and learned from others at the church. Christianity had brought much harm to the community, but he also made peace with it and found much good. Ceremonies also helped him deal with his addiction. By following these teachings, he had lived alcohol-free through the last forty years of his life. It brought him a measure of serenity. He lived with the creed that conflict was not an enemy to be eliminated; it was a friend to be navigated.

Rehearsing these hard-won lessons in his mind, Mishomis once again thought of his grandson's dream of the Four Hills. He saw how so many gave up their journey because they didn't want to struggle. Some didn't even start to climb because of the effort involved in striving against the incline. Too many gave up their quest because they encountered resistance. Mishomis reflected on how this was especially true with young people. Their lack of experience was often what hurt them the most, just as it had harmed him. Adversity was frequently avoided at all costs, because youth could have trouble measuring their decisions against the future. They had not yet gained the understanding that comes from the practical applications of others' teachings. Therefore, it could be hard for them to understand how opposition could shape people for the better, especially if those struggling were patient, and sought meaning in their trials.

These thoughts also caused Mishomis to remember the scrolls in the hills. He thought of the caves in which his grandson had recently been learning. Just like the thunderers and underwater beings, there are many things beneath and around us to teach us about how to climb well, and deal with opposition and conflict. Sometimes these lessons are literally at our feet. They are buried in the water and rocks that surround us. In fact, he thought to himself, the water and rocks can be the very lessons themselves. In the Anishinabek view of the world, the laws of life are all around. Thinking of his grandmother, he reflected on how these laws were even embedded in the language that had been given to them.

As Mishomis looked out over the water, he thought about how the very words he pondered with divided the world between the animate and inanimate. Anishinabemowin classified the world according to those things which are living and those which are not. Mishomis often thought of the significance in these linguistic divisions. They conveyed a philosophy and world view which was embedded in the very structure of his conscious thought. This recollection caused Mishomis to test it by looking with new eyes at the rocks stretched out along the shore: *assiniinook*. They are not dead, he thought to himself. They are alive, animate. They were not passive objects to be acted upon. They had agency and a power of choice which they exercised every day. They were subjects and actively participated in the world. He knew they had much to teach him. He knew his English-speaking friends sometimes had a hard time understanding this. He wished they could speak his language and see the world through its prism. This might help them appreciate why we act the way we do.

With this thought, Mishomis remembered a conversation he once had with a local contractor. The man's company had contracted with the band to build roads around the Cape. His company had an excellent reputation for being fair and working hard. They were good people. However, one day he noticed the bulldozers and graders quarrying a gravel embankment next to the road in the woods near his cabin. It was a shock. He always assumed that certain areas of the reserve would remain untouched. He sometimes forgot that people from the outside did not see the world in the same way. The embankment was home to their ancestors. They had been buried there hundreds of years ago, in a row along the top of the ridge. The pits where their bones lay were still visible, if you knew what you were looking for. They were buried there because the ridge was an old shoreline from thousands of years ago, when the lake had a different shape. The dead still touched the waters of that other time, even though they rested in the present. The rocks were not to be disturbed because they were fulfilling a promise to protect the people's ancestors. They had their own agency in the matter, and they remained solid and firm in their duty. It was up to the Anishinabek to exercise their agency in a reciprocal manner, and protect the rocks while they fulfilled their duty. Mishomis had tried to explain all this to the contractor. They had a good conversation and went into some detail. They spoke of the ancestors and rocks still being involved in the affairs of the people of the reserve, about how they still taught them and were making choices. The contractor was a good man and agreed to quarry in another place, but Misihomis knew he was just being respectful of something he did not understand; he really did not see the point. If only they could have conversed in Anishinabemowin.

Without getting to this deeper level, Mishomis knew that many people did not see agency in its clearest terms. Even those who spoke the language did not usually recognize the choices that were available to them, or how others' choices impacted on them. Mishomis thought they needed to look around them, Anishinabe style. They needed to see clearly, *mau-mino-aubiwin*, and observe the world around them with more than their eyes. They also had to listen more carefully to the stories, and watch the earth. He thought again of the period in his own life when he had failed to follow this counsel. He had been too willing to think that fate carried his destiny. He often acted as if he had no say in the matter. He could remember having conversations about this with some of his own grandchildren in recent years. Some even believed that was the message of the trickster, that you were helpless in the face of contradiction, conflict, and opposition. He wished he could help them see things differently. While the trickster conveyed the seemingly contradictory complexity of opposition, he did not communicate hopelessness. He knew you could learn from what he did, both good and bad.

All the same, Mishomis had to acknowledge to himself that choice could be limited or constrained, sometimes severely, because of conflict and opposition. He thought of his great-granddaughter's autism and his grandson's addictions. A person's background, abilities, opportunities, and past choices could impact the scope of their future choices. The land also had a say. Furthermore, he knew that people could exercise their agency in ways that curtailed the choices of others. But despite these facts, and the tragic consequences sometimes associated with choice or circumstance, Mishomis remained strongly convinced that agency continued. He felt that the challenge was to try and enlarge its scope, collectively and individually. These forces were related to one another. He had always believed that people's background circumstances and opportunities had to be improved at a collective level. The condition people were born into would impact the scope of their agency, and thus steps had to be taken to ensure things improved so that future generations could expand their horizons. At the same time, he was convinced that it was also important for individuals to make good choices. It wasn't just about group rights. Individual freedoms could lead to a greater future range of choices, though nothing was guaranteed, because opposition would always remain a force.

In summarizing these thoughts, Mishomis spoke aloud the words: 'We are meant to be Anishinabe: *nish*, good, *nabe*, men. We can't always get what we want. We can't control others. But we can use our influence for the better.' Hearing these words, Nag'anal'mot loudly snorted.

The sound jolted Mishomis from his thoughts, and he looked down at the dog beside him and laughed. 'I forgot you were there old friend,' he said. Then, looking at him closer, he added: 'What I would give to know what you are thinking. You and your ancestors have been around this place for generations. You know about conflict. In fact, you have caused some of it yourself. You must have learned something from watching us all these years. What can you tell me about who we are and how we should live, old boy?'

When Mishomis finished speaking, Nag'anal'mot stood up. He circled the area in which he had been resting four times before returning to his previous state. At the sight of the dog's actions, Mishomis laughed aloud once again.

As he looked at the dog more closely, Mishomis noted how Nag'anal'mot seemed to mostly be present when his grandson was home on the reserve. In fact, Mishomis wondered if the young man was in the vicinity, given the dog's presence. As he thought of his grandson, Mishomis once more considered the young man's request to help him understand his dream about the hills. He thought to himself that he would have to find the best way to tell him more about choice and agency, and their scope. They talked about it often. Mishomis knew such teachings were important to the young man's dream. He reflected on how choice was especially significant in relation to the young people his grandson had seen on the second hill. He was sure there was something in this power that related to how law should work in society, too, though he was far from being a law professor. In his mind, he always felt law should be about respecting agency. People needed to function in systems where choice, not force, was pre-eminent. This was the ideal his grandmother had tried to teach him. He also knew this was not how Indians were treated by the law, though he didn't know all the details.

Holding this thought for a moment, Mishomis looked at the aftermath of the storm that lay around him. In it, he saw a parallel to the destruction caused by the government's unchecked power on the reserve. The *Indian Act* was a dreadful piece of legislation that was more about force than choice. In his earlier years, he had lived long enough around Indian Agents to know that they always tried to make choices for the people of the reserve. He remembered Tuffnell in particular. They used to call him names behind his back. They hated his domination, and the restrictions he represented and enforced. Mishomis thought that law should encourage Indian agency, not Indian Agents, or any other form of dictatorship. He was relieved when the Indian Agents were removed. He saw that Indian agency was partially restored, but that did not mean his people could do anything they wanted. The *Indian Act* still gave the Minister of Indian Affairs and his bureaucracy a great deal of control. It sometimes seemed like the Indian Agents remained; only now they were more distant. Yet, Mishomis thought, even if the *Indian Act* was removed, there would still be laws to follow. There were consequences attached to most choices that could not be escaped. He did not like how some people around the reserve sometimes spoke about self-government and Anishinabek control as if this power implied the absence of all constraint. This view couldn't have been further from the truth. Last night's violent battle would remind any thinking person of that. Anishinabek people were not without law. This law had a constant presence in their territory that pre-existed the Anishinabek nation and had survived the onslaught of Canadian parliamentary manipulation.

Mishomis remembered a teaching he once heard from some visitors to the reserve a few years back. Two young men had talked about agency in ways that reminded him of his grandmother's teachings. They said something like: 'Imagine seeing a sign on the shore that reads "Danger! Whirlpool. No Swimming Allowed." You might think this is a restriction – but is it? In spite of the sign, you still have many choices. You are free to walk along the beach and pick up fossils. You are free to watch the sunrise. You are free to go home. You are also free to ignore the sign and swim in the dangerous place. But once the whirlpool has you in its grasp and you are pulled under, you have very few choices. You can try to escape or call for help, but if no one comes to your rescue, you are likely to drown. Even though you are free to choose your course of action, you are not always free to choose the consequences of your actions.[2] Some consequences, whether good or bad, follow as a natural result of any choice we make.'

Mishomis liked what they said because it reminded him of his grandmother's teachings. There were natural laws that could not be ignored. He remembered that the Cree even have a word for this concept: *pashtahowin*. His Nehiyaw friend Jimmy once explained to him that this is a sacred word and means 'consequences for crossing the line.' He said that if someone does something that is not right, that transgression will eventually come back to them. If someone goes against the Creator's law, things will not go right for that person. Jimmy added that individual beings must make choices, but they can't always choose the consequences that follow. He was quite adamant that individuals must act, but they must also be responsible and accountable for their actions to the Creator and their fellow beings.

As the old man sat on the beach silently looking out over the water, Nag'anal'mot quietly lay by his side for some time, gathering his thoughts. The rhythm of the waves quieted his mind as they beat against the shore and pushed him more deeply into his subconscious. It was very restful. It was hard for him to believe that the day had started so furiously. The contrast with last night was profound. It got him thinking about what he could do to help. While he enjoyed a good fight as much as the next person, Nag'anal'mot did not want this world inundated by water. He had seen this happen before. Many strong forces threatened to flood the fragile reserve. Except for the three large escarpments, much of the land was barely above the waterline in many seasons. Furthermore, Nag'anal'mot had witnessed many lives taken by *Mishi-bizheu*'s force over the years. Boats sunk, nets cut, and children drowned. He wanted to extend the peace he enjoyed at that moment, and felt that some kind of balance needed to be restored. Maybe, he thought, some might even find deeper meaning in how that balance could be restored if he took the right actions. In the face of *Mishi-bizheu*'s destruction, Nag'anal'mot gave deep consideration to what he should do.

In time, Nag'anal'mot got up from his resting place and walked away from the old man. As he strolled down the shore, he started to bark. He went down to the water's edge and challenged the water beings to a contest. Nag'anal'mot stayed at the task for some time. At first the lake flattened out and its surface became mirror calm. Hay Island and King's Point were mirrored in the water and were joined to their aboveground twins in perfect, symmetrical balance. This prompted Nag'anal'mot to bark even more vigorously. He sought to engage with his foes with even greater energy as he ran back and forth along the beach. Seeing that Nag'anal'mot would not be easily beaten through their initial retreat, the manitous caused the waves to begin rolling to shore with some strength. As the black dog continued to provoke their wrath, the waves increased in intensity. An hour later, with Nag'anal'mot still in full fury, the waves crashed with wild ferocity against the rocks, sending water over the beach and beyond. Whirlpools formed in the rushing currents and dark clouds returned to the sky.

For over an hour Mishomis watched the scene with great interest. He stayed on the beach until the weather threatened his security. Eventually, Mishomis shook himself from his thoughts and the surrounding scene, and hurried home along the beach.

The barking continued. Hearing Nag'anal'mot's rage, *Mishi-bizheu* and his companions tried another tactic. They retreated to their underwater holes to throw the entire underground world into a state of terror. Safe in their caverns they twisted and writhed, throwing themselves with rage on Nag'anal'mot's efforts. The waves heightened and the water rolled white and ever more furious. The beings laughed at Nag'anal'mot and continued their assault, feeling safe from his challenge.

Some hours later, switching strategies, Nag'anal'mot transformed himself. He became very quiet. There were different ways to challenge conflict. He saw other choices he could make. With that thought he taunted no more and instead waited patiently, changed on the spot into an old, solid tree stump tossed about in the waves. He knew that opposition didn't always require a defiant stance. Stealth and patience could also be effective. Only the foolish missed these truths. Mindful of these complexities, Nag'anal'mot lay still in the midst of ancient, twisted roots that lay on their side and rocked back and forth in the surf. At eight feet around, the tangle in which he found himself was substantial.

After a few hours, in the face of Nag'anal'mot's silence, the winds and waves ceased. Since the conflict began, the shores had dramatically changed the margin of land at the water's edge.

At first, *Mishi-bizheu* and his companions surveyed their work from a distance, not knowing what to expect after having presided over such a fierce storm. They saw rocks, plants, and wood twisted and strewn through inland pools. The corpses of birds and fish rotted at the water's edge. The water beings were enthralled with their work. In fact, they couldn't leave it alone, and admired it from afar.

As they looked out on the shore from the bay, they kept watch for Nag'anal'mot. They could hear or see nothing. After some time, sensing no threat, they became bolder, wading into the shallows to witness the results of their labour. Their dark shadows passed close to the land. They saw that much was different.

In time, the manitous discovered the old stump. They had never seen such a large piece of wood in the area. It dwarfed the only other stump on the beach, which was in front of Mishomis' cabin. Marvelling at their power, *Mishi-bizheu* and his companions thought of the force it took to wash a stump of this age and size ashore. They were proud of their work. The creatures came closer and brushed up against the old roots. They pushed against its base, testing its weight, hoping to feel its ancient power.

At that moment, the ancient stump's expansive tendrils writhed in dark motion. A balance tipped, and the old stump rolled over. Uncoiling almost like snakes, the broad roots wrapped themselves around the black-plated beings. Choking and strangling, they tightened themselves round their giant prey. Though caught in surprise, *Mishi-bizheu's* companions fought back, thrashing in the surf, shattering rocks, and gouging deep holes in the shore. Yet the grip of the roots was firm, and the creatures lost strength the longer they were absent from water.

In time, the struggle abated. Quiet settled back onto the lake; the gentle lapping of waves resumed on the shore. A sodden mass of black flesh surrounded the old stump, from which Nag'anal'mot emerged. He stepped over splintered black plates onto the scarred beach.

Stopping at a short distance, Nag'anal'mot looked over the scene. He observed that the sun was now deep in the Western sky, having almost run its course for the day. The world around him was broken and torn, but peace and tranquillity surrounded him. A certain balance had been restored to the reserve. He had made choices. He had confronted conflict. Struggle had served a good purpose. Looking down the shore Nag'anal'mot saw Mishomis emerge from his cabin. The rocks tumbled and fell over one another in a staccato chorus as the old man made his way down to the shore, eventually setting himself beside Nag'anal'mot.

Searching the shoreline and beyond, Mishomis watched for signs of life. At a point in the distant water a black object moved, ever so slightly. Mishomis watched carefully to see if it was a trick of the light. When he couldn't be sure, he took some tobacco from his pocket and placed it on the water, uttering a quiet prayer.

W'PISHEBAUBEE-AUSHIH[1]

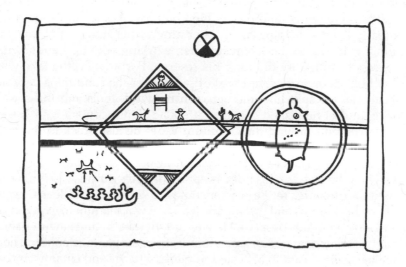

As he made his way alongside the canal, the stirring shadows of a new morning stretched lazily before him. They always chose this time of day to range over the land in search of a cool place to rest. It wouldn't be long before they would be forced to retreat. The harsh Phoenix sun would burn its way through the sky, withering almost everything before it. But for the moment the shadows relaxed, sprawling across the desert floor and quietly exploring the land's texture. Overhead, morning voices sang from the treetops as the young man headed towards the Superstitions, the mountains to the west of the city. The bird's harmonies gently transformed the din from a distant freeway, which slowly built as people crawled to work from distant suburbs. He passed a small colony of burrowing owls; the same ones he greeted every morning as he repeated his run. Despite his growing familiarity with the area, something felt a little different today. There was another feeling he couldn't quite place. He looked across the canal. There it was – the cause of his heightened sensitivity. Ten feet away Coyote loped along, matching his pace stride for stride. He was black. After a few moments, Coyote turned his head, looked at the young man and smiled. Then refocusing and facing forward, Coyote continued along the canal on its morning jog.

Later that morning, the young man was at the law school. It was Sandra Day O'Connor's new namesake. After ten years, he had finally decided to take his first sabbatical. He sold his house in Toronto, gathered up all his belongings, and drove. First he drove home, and spent July and early August helping his mother around her house at Neyaashiinigmiing. It had been a warm summer, working with his hands, with an excess of humidity draining his reserve. Fortunately, the lake was at her front door so he could cool off whenever the conditions became unbearable. He split his time between his work tools and the shore. During breaks he visited cousins, attended Band Council, and hiked the escarpments around the community. Yet he also stuck to the task at his mother's house. His efforts had produced a new room and more good memories. Then he got into his car again.

Leaving the reserve was not easy. It made life's purposes seem more distant and remote. Yet he was encouraged to travel and learn, especially by his parents and grandparents. They wanted him to experience the world beyond the reserve. He was taught that, in time, their lessons would become clearer if he saw them from other vantage points. Their teachings were meant to be tested in many settings and circumstances. It was one of the lessons of the Four Hills. He had been warned that too many people thought Anishinabek life ended at the borders of the reserve. Yet Mishomis was adamant that their ways were relevant beyond those artificial lines. Thinking about his grandfather's teachings, the young man decided to break from his Toronto routine, especially as a Canadian law professor. He wanted to climb higher. It sometimes felt so oppressive teaching the vestiges of British colonialism that haunted Canada.

So he drove south, down the east shore of Lake Huron, and on through Michigan, Indiana, Illinois, Missouri, Oklahoma, Texas, New Mexico, and Arizona. He took in the sights along the way: Dickson Mounds, Cahokia, Talehquah, Anadarko, Taos, Gallup, Window Rock, and Sedona. He came to a final stop in Phoenix, found a place in Mesa, and started work in Tempe.

It was late August. He was on research leave for a year. His new title was Visiting Professor and Acting Executive Director of the Indian Legal Program at the College of Law at Arizona State University (ASU). It was a 'look-see' visit. If he liked it here, and the people around the school liked him, he would stay.

The law school looked like it had tumbled to earth from geometry heaven. Angles piled upon angles and crashed against circles, squares, and rectangles. The effect was a postmodernist's delight. The Ross-Blakley Library was designed to look like a ship in the desert, with portholes, gangplanks, and bows resting on the surrounding rock piles. The older section of the school, Armstrong Hall, resembled another kind of ship. With its arcs, ascending lines, and rounded body, it looked like a spacecraft from the 1970s. Clad with taupe and coral walls, the effect was decidedly displaced. The palm trees, orange groves, bougainvillea, octillo, agave, saguaro, and prickly-pear cacti, surrounded by golf-course-grass fringes, highlighted its eclecticism. The law school was a mix of everywhere, yet distinctly Arizonian.

Things were different in the States. One of the reasons he came south was because it seemed like the Indians had it pretty good. For most of his life, the young man had the idea that life was better for them here. He often heard that many of the problems in his own country and back on the reserve did not exist here. His grandfather had worked in the States when he was a younger man and was friends with many powerful Native Americans: Iron Eyes Cody, Jim Thorpe, Big Tree, Will Rogers, and Bill Hazlett (who was his mother's godfather). Mishomis shared good stories about them over the years. He especially liked hearing about when Mishomis left Hollywood to travel the reservations in the south-western deserts. Some of his favourite tales were set around the Petrified Forest and Grand Canyon. His grandfather always spoke reverently about the red rocks of the southlands. Mishomis said they formed God's Cathedrals and were a sacred shrine to the Creator. He was told that the old man would sing to his children as they climbed these hills with them in his youth. When asked why he came south, he would respond: 'I wanted to see what was on the other side of the mountain.' To follow his grandfather's past, the young man tracked his memories to this land.

It was exciting being in the States. There were tribal courts, rich Indian casinos, big reservations, and legislative recognition of an inherent right to self-government – all supported by some powerful, high-level case law. While there were only just over two million Indians in the United States, they were situated in some very important spots. Arizona felt like the centre, with twenty-two tribes controlling 25 per cent of the state's land base. Indian individuals and issues were everywhere. The earth was alive with what most interested the young man. It felt wonderful.

The classes he was teaching were also very engaging. Fifty students were in his Federal Indian Law course, and another sixteen were taking a Comparative Indigenous Rights seminar. They were very bright, and earnestly engaged in their learning. They came from tribes all across the country, and were graduates of both Ivy League halls and humble tribal colleges. It seemed that each had big plans and wanted to make a difference in the world. A good number of students were enrolled in the Indian Legal Certificate Program, through which they took a pre-approved list of courses to receive special accreditation in the field. There were also very supportive colleagues, including an incredibly beautiful Pasqua-Yaqui woman who was the lead professor in the program. He was also getting to know an amazing Cheyenne woman who was the new program assistant. She was the most organized and effective administrator he had ever worked with. The young man also enjoyed the kindness and common-sense advice of the program secretary, a Leonard Cohen fan who loved to talk about Montreal. There were also a host of other activities to occupy his time, such as tribal court education gatherings, Indian Law conferences, Native American moot court contests, and a steady stream of guest speakers on various Indian Law topics. He was having fun getting to know some of the noted non-Indian professors who taught in his school. They were a welcoming group.

The young man found that as time passed he was also growing to appreciate the building. Once you got inside the law school, it had a unity and flow that was not apparent from the outside. There were large gathering spaces in lofted rotundas that lent themselves nicely to well-attended social, professional, and sacred assemblies. Indigenous art graced the walls, with the centrepiece being a twenty-by-twenty-foot image hanging from skylights in the central hall. The painting mirrored the message of his recurring dream, complete with four hills, climbing imagery, and other sacred symbols. While the picture was south-western in style, the young man found himself drawn to its imagery. There were even Holy Ones in the cardinal directions communicating to those who would listen. He couldn't help but gaze upwards when the Native Student group sold bannock beneath its bulk each week during lunch hour. He wondered if other people also saw themselves in the work.

As they visited after such events, the young man would often comment to the dean that he found so much that inspired him at the law school. She was so enthusiastic in building the Indian Law Program that he would come away from these meetings even more energized about its future prospects. The dean eventually introduced him to the university president, and he found himself wondering how it could get any better. It seemed like an embarrassment of riches regarding Indigenous legal education, since the president had even hired the former president of the Navajo Nation as his personal assistant. All in all, he thought the school responded exceedingly well to Indigenous issues. They had positively transformed their institution by hiring individuals who were moving these issues to the greatest heights on regional and national agendas. As far as the young man could see, he was about as close to Indian law school paradise as he could get.

So why did things feel unsettled?

It was only a few weeks into the term, and still late in the summer. But even this early he was finding that the Trickster was just as active in the United States as he was in Canada. Just this morning he had taught the *Lara* case.[2] At first glance it looked like a positive decision. The U.S. Supreme Court held that a section of a Congressional statute 'recognized and affirmed' an inherent sovereign power of a tribe that had previously appeared to have been extinguished. The Court said that Congress was constitutionally entitled to 'loosen' any restrictions previously placed on the bounds of inherent tribal authority. The case felt important for Canadian law. Aboriginal rights under section 35(1) of the *Constitution Act, 1982* are also 'recognized and affirmed' – the same phraseology used by Congress at issue in *Lara*. Could governments extend the scope of First Nations' inherent sovereignty by retracting the reach of Western laws? Was it possible that legislation could restore Indigenous political power by merely proclaiming government interference was at an end? If this was the implication, there was much in the case to celebrate. The Court seemed to be saying that Indigenous sovereignty could grow back as an inherent right, even after harsh and severe judicial pruning.

Yet, despite its promising result, the young man did not feel the *Lara* decision was built on an acceptable base. He was increasingly haunted by doubts about the wisdom of the American approach. Congress had absolute authority to restrict or relax tribal power. The Court said the Constitution granted Congress 'plenary and exclusive' powers to legislate with respect to Indian tribes through the Indian Commerce and

Treaty Clauses.[3] He always had trouble with this line of argument, be cause the Constitution did not give Congress an explicit grant of power over the Indians.[4] In fact, for many years for certain constitutional purposes, tribes were not considered subject to the laws of the United States.[5]

It was not good to have inherent sovereignty so dependent on Congress' plenary power. In Canada, the plenary authority of Parliament was limited by section 35(1) of the Constitution. He thought congressional power should be subject to the same limitations, but so far it was unconstrained. He thought that maybe Canada's best practices could be combined with those in the U.S. The U.S. enjoyed a broader base of recognized, inherent rights; this would be nice to see in Canada. In Canada, if Parliament wanted to narrow Aboriginal rights, it would have to meet a high justificatory standard. The Canadian approach to restricting federal power would be a huge gain for tribes in the U.S.

Despite the attractiveness of blending the best of Canadian and U.S. principles of Indigenous rights, he was learning that it would be hard to do this kind of jurisprudential mixing, at least explicitly. Political and legal differences between the countries would make it too difficult to authoritatively cite the other jurisdiction in their forums. Such challenges raised the value of stealth as a strategy in his mind. At the same time, other factors also made it difficult to advance Indigenous aspirations in each country. Indigenous individuals were not highly placed in either of the political or legal systems. Not many individuals had risen to places where they could exercise influential decision-making authority. He thought back to his dream of the four hills and his conversations with his grandmother and grandfather. His vision of the second hill reminded him that it was difficult for people to find footing on their chosen paths. Social pressures kept many people lingering at the base. They could easily be distracted even if they began their climb. Even if a person successfully got on the path, they could be kept back by others and trampled in a thoughtless rush. He also remembered that institutions did not always take well to innovation. Change was often very slow, especially within big bureaucracies. He did not see many institutions in the United States or Canada that had successfully transformed themselves to accommodate Indigenous actors.

Even if some success was achieved, his experiences working with the law also taught him that the best solutions always included troubling elements. This made it hard for some Indians to work within the system and still feel they could keep their self-respect. They would become

disenchanted with their quest, because they could not control the process or outcome. They wanted people to immediately accede to their
demands because they were convinced of the truth of their cause. He
thought of how arrogant it was for someone to want to compel another
to follow their ways and to force change, even if their intent and result
was perfectly right. There were some who had a hard time working
with people and concepts that weren't *pure* to their way of thinking.
Yet he felt that, in order to appropriately influence change, you had to
work with and persuade individuals who were not like you and did
not share your goals or outlook on life. Law as practised in Canada and
the United States sometimes required troubling associations and participation. This was even the case in most contemporary Indian communities he knew about. Their law and politics meant that you had
to work with those you did not agree with. Of course, he knew some
academics would vehemently disagree with him, and he was glad they
did. In all the contexts he was familiar with, from the reserve to the law
school, liberation intermingled with captivity. Charm seemed eternally
twinned with cunning. Decay found its way into regeneration; kindness lived beside mean tricks. This was essential to agency. It was impossible to escape the trickster in this life.

His thoughts were interrupted by a knock on the door. Professor
Murphy from the next office barged in. Red-faced, he asked: 'Have you
seen a dog run by?'

Not sure if he had heard him correctly, the man took a moment to
process the question. 'Pardon me ... did you say a dog?'

'Yes, it's been causing some excitement here for the past few minutes. We don't usually get this sort of thing in the law school. People
have been running all over the place trying to catch the mangy thing.
Dennis first saw it run out of the faculty lounge into the dean's office.
He followed to see whose it was. No one else was in the office, and it
had jumped on the photocopier. Copies were spewing out of the ma-
chine all over the place. He tried to coax the dog down, but it turned
on him before dashing out into the hall. The next thing you know there
was a commotion in room 159 where Trish was teaching. The creature
ran through the door and bolted to the front of the room, before notic-
ing Trish was standing in front of the class. At that point it ran out the
doors, and we've been chasing it ever since. I thought you might have
seen it.'

Professor Murphy stood in the doorframe catching his breath and
waiting for an answer. He mindlessly scratched his ear.

'I'm afraid I haven't seen anything in here,' the young man replied. 'I just returned from class a few minutes ago. The whole thing sounds very strange. I'll let you know if I see anything, though.'

'OK,' Professor Murphy said as he turned to leave. 'This is the first time I've ever seen anything like this around the school. It actually looked a little like a coyote. It really is quite amazing. I'm not sure how it got in here.'

The professor stepped into the hall, closing the door behind him. After his departure the room was almost silent, except for the hum of the fan in his laptop.

'That was odd,' the young man thought to himself. 'This is just like being home on the reserve. Are law schools everywhere just as chaotic?' He thought for a few minutes and arranged some papers on his desk before turning back to his writing. He was trying to figure out how the law might best address the conflict Indians always encountered. He was trying to mentally map the scope of choice possessed by individuals and institutions facing legal challenges. To answer these questions, he was writing about how Anishinabek law dealt with those who were your enemies. He worked for about fifteen minutes more when a paper slid under his door. He let it sit while he continued working.

An hour later, the young man stood up and stretched after hunching over his keyboard for too long. He was getting stiff, and his body needed a change of pace. Walking around the room, he came to the paper that had been slid under the door earlier. It was a couple of badly photocopied pages of a memo someone had written. He turned it over to see if there was a name on it. Nothing identified its author.

Walking back to his desk and taking a seat, he started reading.

MEMORANDUM

TO: Faculty, Staff, and Visitors
RE: How Dogs Were Created

'The Dog was created in Heaven itself, and sent down expressly for the Indians.'[6]

A giant was terrorizing the people. No one could leave the safety of their lodges because of the danger for those who travelled. Children would wander into the forest and never return. Hunters would not come back from their expeditions. Friends from other places never came back to visit.

Men and women of all ages who left the village suffered similar fates. They were never seen again.

A council was called for the village to discuss the problem. Everyone who could attend was there, from the eldest to the youngest. Each had a chance to speak. Many opinions were expressed about what was happening and how to stop it. Some wanted to ban any further travel outside the community. Others wanted to send out a party to confront their enemy and defeat him. Still others thought the fault lay within their community. They said that if people would return to their old ways and follow the good road, the tragedy would end. It seemed that there would be no end to the debate.

Late in the day the impasse was broken as a young woman, Zhawan, proposed an agreeable plan.

'Whatever is killing us must know where we live. How could we lose everyone who leaves this place if they did not know when each left? Our enemy must move in dark places just out of reach. It can't anticipate our every journey; it must watch us and plan each strike based on what it sees we are doing. There is only one way to stop this madness. I have a plan. Let's move, all at once. If we continue acting as we have done, surely whatever is killing us will go on until no one is left alive. If we wait, we'll all be lost, one by one. It's better to take action together. It might not be strong enough to face us as a group. If it does attack while we travel, it will have to deal with all of us at once. Let's take the whole village to the other side of the lake. We must go quickly and we must go together. If we have any hope of existence it's in a place far from here, away from our foe.'

A murmur of agreement rippled through the crowd. No one spoke in opposition.

The next couple of days were spent in making preparations. A destination was chosen for their new village. Food was stored, clothes mended, canoes repaired, and personal belongings packed. Other items were hidden away in pits, in case the people one day returned. Leaders were chosen for different purposes to conduct them safely once they left.

Next morning, as the birds began their songs, the people gathered everything into their canoes and set out through the bush. The twenty-minute journey along the stream to the lake took place in the twilight. Eyes watched them from the darkness behind the trees, but the people rushed on, not wanting a confrontation in the dense underbrush.

When they reached the open water, the sun has just cracked the horizon. Tobacco was placed in the waves, prayers offered, and a song sung as the boats pushed off. Gliding into the new day, they looked back at the woods that had been their home. The entire village took to the lake. Following the sun, they paddled all day. The sky was clear. No wind shaped their journey. They silently swept through the water as dark shapes swam below them, swirling in the murky green. Eyes scanned the horizon ahead watching for dangers, and a glimpse of land.

As night fell, food was taken from their packs and passed between them. Stars broke out overhead as they continued their course. Children slept as the adults took their turn at the paddle. All through the night they steered by the distant lights of the stories spread through the sky. Heaven's maps guided them to their new home.

As light dawned the next morning, new land was visible in the distance. It was a welcome discovery. Pulling closer they could see their destination. A large island lay off the mainland, guarding their new home. It was the place they had chosen, its distinctive limestone escarpments visible above the trees. They pulled nearer to their new home.

As they approached the shore, a crash was heard in the woods. The people looked up. Some of the larger trees behind the first row of green on the beach began falling. A cascade of broken trees came nearer to the shore as the people drew back into their boats. Suddenly, a large, black beast broke through into the clearing. Charging the boats, the animal stepped into the water amongst them. A hail of arrows, knives, rocks, and stones rained down upon it. They all worked together. Falling back from the crowd, the creature tumbled onto the shore. Rage and revenge gathered in the group and they fell upon it, striking blow after blow until it no longer moved. Blood gushed from many large wounds. Bones, muscle, and fur intermingled with the rocks at the water's edge. The enemy had been defeated; the people had won. They were safe to build their new home or to return to their old one.

Then, from the scraps of flesh and bone, movement stirred. Each separate piece gathered together, and a new creature arose. The people fell back, awaiting another onslaught from their foe. But nothing happened. The new beings, *animook*, were nothing like that from which they sprung. They came forward to the people with goodwill. With trust and open faces they playfully tumbled over one another, barking and yapping, inviting the children to join them in their play. They became the new people's best friends.

That is how dogs came to be.

When the young man finished reading the memo, he stood up and walked back to the door. Peering into the hall, he noticed how quiet things were. He went next door and knocked on Professor Murphy's door, but there was no answer. As he scanned the corridors he did not see a soul, though it was late afternoon. Only the Holy Ones praying under darkening skies were visible in the space above the rotunda.

He thought about the memo he had just read. Its message seemed targeted, even obvious to addressing the theme of his writing. At the same time, he saw a deeply hidden ironic twist, playing with the doctrine of discovery in the law. The story was double-edged. He wondered who could have wrote the memo and brought it here. He thought he had left all that stuff behind in Ontario. He wanted a new start, academic reflection in a new country, a more positive atmosphere away from home for a while. Who knew that he wanted a break from the fighting he always saw around him? Who knew what he was writing about? Now the young man saw that what he thought he had left behind on distant shores seemed to be here as well, just like the story in the memo. Similar concepts and choices faced him in Canada *and* the United States. He couldn't shake 'Indian' agency no matter where he went. There was no escaping the challenges Indigenous peoples encountered in North America. There was no escaping himself. Individuals had to struggle, himself included; problems were not easily left behind.

Wherever he went, he took himself with him. He would have to find a way to defeat his opponents. Despite his fears and their mutual differences, he would have to find a way to turn them into friends.

PART THREE: TIKWAUKIK

Institutions: The Third Hill

AUGOONAET-WAENDUMOOWIN[1]

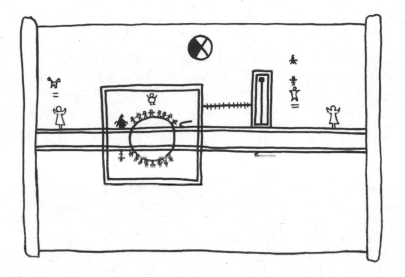

Nokomis awakes to find she is living inside someone's dream. As she adjusts to the new sensations, she finds herself looking out at the world through four-year-old eyes. The room blurs. Her eyes flick open, and then they fall shut. She is some young Ojibway boy sleeping in his bed, calico cat and bunny resting in his arms. The young boy's childhood friends Beatle and Cowboy are resting in the corner after a long day's play. They are dog tired. They are the little people: *maemaegawaehnses-siwuk*. Very few ever see these two guardians, except the young boy. Beatle and Cowboy remain a mystery to most everyone around. They live up the road, past Darlene's house in a large sinkhole at the top of the escarpment. It's called Cleaves Hill. Fall is an important time to the little people; food will be prepared and burned for them at the Feast of the Dead. They depend on their living relatives to remember them. Today they are restless.

Since the sun had risen, Beatle and Cowboy had swung on the swings, slid down the slide, and spun one another on the playground merry-go-round. Sometimes they wondered if that was all there was to life. Not that they were sad, it's just that they never expected play to be so monotonous, in a fun sort of way. Up and down, back and forth, round and round. Standing next to the teeter-totter, Beatle asked Cowboy if they should stop. Cowboy got a thoughtful look on his face, staring off into the trees. 'Well, if we stopped, what would we do?' he asked.

Beatle furrowed his brow in concentration, and kicked his feet in the dust. A swirl of games, activities, and adventures came into his mind. 'I guess we could go to work,' he said.

So the next moment, dressed in oversized three-piece suits, Beatle and Cowboy showed up at the Hudson's Bay headquarters at Bay and Yonge in downtown Toronto. A huge, forty-storey building stood before them. Entering the front door, the elevators doors stood before them, tall and intimidating.

'What should we do?' Cowboy asked timidly.

Bravely, Beatle cleared his throat and said, 'I don't know. Let's go up.' They pressed the button outside, and the doors opened.

Cowboy stuck his head inside. 'Looks OK from here.' They got in and pushed another button. Up they went, thirty-five storeys into the sky. When the little room stopped moving, the doors slid open. They stood before stately, marble-tiled halls. On the wall was a sign: Oatley Animook, Barristers and Solicitors.

Beatle put one foot out the door and tested the floor. 'Looks safe enough from here,' he said.

Cowboy wasn't convinced. 'Try pressing on it.'

Beatle got to his knees, made a fist, and pounded the floor. 'No problems here either; I think it's solid enough to walk on. Let's go.'

They stepped out in the hall. Beatle slipped. 'You always get the fun!' Cowboy whined. Then, mimicking Beatle's movements, Cowboy gently slid a few feet on the floor. 'That *was* kinda fun,' he said. He started running down the hall. Then he stopped in full flight, jamming his two feet together. He slid about fifteen feet. 'What a great place!' Cowboy exclaimed, looking back down the hall.

Beatle then looked into the boardroom standing empty before him, 'Come here!' he whispered loudly in Cowboy's direction. A huge mahogany table stood in the centre of the space, with eighteen chairs surrounding it. Beyond, on the other side of the window, a beautiful city was spread out below. They walked in, and Cowboy took a chair. Beatle followed and stood behind him. He leaned his hand on the back of

Cowboy's chair. It turned ever so slightly. 'Can you beat this?' Beatle crowed, and started spinning his friend.

When they tired of spinning in the chairs, they stopped, staring at the sky through the window, straight ahead. 'Seems like work's not all that different from play,' Beatle mused.

'Right!' Cowboy agreed. 'Up and down, back and forth, round and round. I guess that really is all there is to life. It's cyclical. Kind of monotonous, in a fun sort of way.'

'How do people get to spend every single day of their life here?' Cowboy wondered aloud. They wandered out of the boardroom into some of the offices. There was not much to distinguish one cell from another. Same size, same view, same desk, same phone, and same bookshelves. The cubicles in the middle were even more uniform. 'Must be some kind of cult,' Beatle observed. 'Let's see who they worship. It looks like they have lots of scriptures on those shelves.'

Beatle and Cowboy chose a random office and went to a shelf: Corporate Law, Commercial Law, Taxation Law, Secured Transactions, Creditor and Debtor, Banking Law, Leases, Franchises, Mortgages, Insurance Law, Bankruptcy and Insolvency, et cetera. The titles went on and on. 'Looks like they have lots of authorities in their liturgy. It must be pretty confusing to the uninitiated. I wonder where their church is?' Beatle asked. 'I'd like to learn what they believe. I haven't worshipped in a long time. Maybe there's a clue here. Let's keep looking. There's got to be something around here that would help us find it.' They looked on the desk, the windowsill, and the cabinet. Nothing. They looked under the chair and side table. Still nothing. Then, examining the wall, they noticed the official-looking script.

York University
Osgoode Hall Law School

The Chancellor and Senate of York University confer on

Barker Animook

Who has completed to the satisfaction of the Faculty of Law the requirements of the course of study approved by the statutes of the University the degree of

Juris Doctorate

And grant all the honours, rights and privileges that appertain to this degree.

In hushed tones, Beatle turned to Cowboy and said, 'That Osgoode Hall place must be where they learn their religion. Who knows what kind of rites and customs are taught there? It must be a spiritual place. I wonder who their priests are? It would be interesting to see who belongs to their congregation. Let's go find out.'

Cowboy and Beatle took the elevator back to the ground floor. They looked for the subway. Depositing a token and passing through turnstiles, they found themselves transported deep down into the earth. A map on the wall described where York University is located for them. After finding the proper platform and waiting for a few minutes, a big silver train rushed up to greet them. It disgorged its passengers, and then Cowboy and Beatle got on board. As they travelled, the train rocked back and forth. They stared at everyone in the face, but no one seemed to notice them. From Bloor-Yonge Station they travelled south, before eventually turning into Union Station near Lake Ontario. From that juncture they head north to Spadina, and on through a number of stations until they arrive at Downsview. The train was on one eternal round: it was cyclical. Stepping out of Downsview Station, Beatle and Cowboy caught a bus going north. An hour-and-a-half from the HBC building downtown, they finally found themselves at the Osgoode Hall Law School of York University.

Beatle and Cowboy found the campus was a forlorn-looking, windswept place, but they noticed that the fall leaves were beautiful. Red, yellow, orange, and green, they waved briskly in the wind swirling around the buildings. The September weather reminded them it was *tikwaukik*. As they walked around, they got lost a few times. They found that all the concrete and glass looked the same to them. After a few frustrating minutes, they found the law school. Osgoode sat in the midst of a small, secluded forest glade. 'They must love nature at this place,' Cowboy commented. A four-storey, reddish-brown brick box rose out of the woods, with the name of the law school emblazoned on the front.

Then Beatle noticed that there were no windows on most of the primary walls. 'Maybe the place is built to mimic a cave,' he said. 'The students must have to take special vows to live inside. The woods are probably here to tempt them, to see how faithful they'll be to their call.'

They read the commemorative plaque on the building's exterior. They learned that Osgoode Hall Law School has been graduating law students since 1889. It is one of the nation's most prestigious institutions, and its graduates have occupied many hallowed places in the country. A study of Osgoode's history was a study of the legal profession in Canada.[2] Before the law school opened, aspiring law students were simply required to article with a practising lawyer for three to five years, and write a series of examinations set by the Law Society in order to be called to the Bar. Once the law school opened, students' articles were supplemented by modest classes for a couple of hours a day. The Law Society completely controlled Osgoode, and would not grant universities the authority to issue law degrees preparatory to legal practice. In 1949 there was something of a rebellion at Osgoode, when the dean and some noted faculty members resigned because the Law Society would not reform its curriculum. Instruction was mostly in 'black letter law,' and narrow courses were taught, with very little attention paid to academic context. It was not until 1957 that the Law Society recognized the powers of the universities to issue degrees preparatory to articles and the Bar admission course. In 1968, the Law Society transferred Osgoode Hall to York University, and the law school moved from its downtown Toronto location to this place. They read that, while the pace of institutional change had been slow, Osgoode's move to York University signalled the beginning of real change.

Beatle and Cowboy liked the tone of the tract. They decided to peek inside the Osgoode building. With faces pressed against glass doors, Cowboy said, 'I can see how their training for the priesthood starts the day they arrive here.' The straight lines and corners seemed ever-receding.

'No doubt they want their adherents to get used to everything being standardized and uniform at a very early age,' Beatle replied. 'There are no distractions here; it's all very nice and sterile. Straight rows, high columns, hard surfaces, and re-circulated air. It's just like those ancient European cathedrals I heard about. The symbolism about their beliefs is built into the very form of their structures. In fact,' he continued, 'it's a lot like that office we just visited downtown.'

Emboldened, Cowboy and Beatle crossed themselves as they glided into the inner courts. In front of them they finally saw some external windows. Framed by stairs, they admired more concrete, glass, and brick. They saw a few skylights gracing the roof. 'Boy, these guys are serious about their vows, there's no life to be seen out there,' whispered Beatle. To the left was a giant moot courtroom, and to the right were the lecture halls. 'Let's wander upstairs; maybe we'll find a class we can attend.'

On the second level they found a series of seminar rooms. Most were full. They found a class with a few empty seats around a table, and made themselves comfortable amongst the other students.

A man walked to the front of the room. He was not quite six feet tall, of medium build, with brown hair and brown eyes. '*Ahnee. Gdinu-waendaugninaunik. Nigig nindoodem, Kegedonce ndizhikaaz, Neyaashiinig-ming nindonjiba.* Welcome to the Intensive Program in Lands, Resources, and First Nations Governments,' he began. 'I'm excited to be here to-day, and am glad you're thinking about enrolling in this course. If you decide to stay, you'll be the first group of students to participate in this new clinical program.'

The students in the class shifted in their seats as they settled into the first day of term. The professor told the students that sixteen people from across the country had enrolled in the course. More than half came from Osgoode, but others were from universities like Dalhousie, Manitoba, Saskatchewan, Toronto, Victoria, and Ottawa. There was also a good mix of Native and non-Native students. As Beatle and Cowboy looked around the room, they thought everyone seemed interested in the professor's words. It was amazing to see how they eagerly transferred everything the young man was saying onto their computer screens.

From the front of the class the professor continued: 'By way of in-troduction we'll do a few things today, and then I'll let you go early. Basically what I'll do is explain the course purpose, tell you how it'll be conducted, and let you know how you'll be evaluated.

'But before we do that, we'll offer a short prayer and introduce our-selves to one another.

'I've invited Lillian to be with us today. She'll offer the prayer. She's an Elder from Birch Island, and she'll be with us for most of the term to guide us through some Anishinabek teachings as we work with the legal issues in the course. I'll let Lillian begin.'

With the introduction finished, an older woman stood and slowly walked to the front of the class. She had light brown skin, short white hair, and heavily gathered wrinkles around her eyes and cheeks. Rest-ing her hands on the back of a chair, she steadied herself and began. '*Ahnee. Mukwa dodem.* I'm from the bear totem, Birch Island First Na-tion. I'm so glad to be with you today, and I look forward to getting to know you in the next few days. You're doing something important by showing interest in this class. I think you have the potential to make a real difference. Your professor invited me to spend the semester with you. I want to help you understand some of our old ways as you work through the ideas and experiences in this course.'

Lillian looked at the group around the circle and smiled. Then she raised her hands in front of her, level with her waist, and turned her palms upwards, continuing: 'I want to honour you. You'll be working with First Nations individuals and issues this fall. I also want you to know that our teachings are important for the legal profession. We've had a lot of lawyers who don't appreciate that fact. You can't effectively practise in our communities if you don't know who we are and what we believe. I was a nurse most of my life, and I saw most doctors fail miserably when they practised on our reserves. You can't help someone become healthier if you don't help to create self-sufficiency. Too many doctors just swooped in and out of our lives. They treated the symptoms and not the causes of illness. Sometimes that left us worse off. They weren't true healers. I hope you're not like that as lawyers. You need to understand us at a deeper level to provide legal advice that will resonate with our ideals. You need to help us get to the root of justice as we see it. We need to once again become self-sufficient in its administration. Please don't steal our decision-making ability with your fancy law school ideas. Help us restore our laws. Help us regenerate our internal regulations. This is a sacred task. I honour you for coming to this institution to learn about these issues.'

Lillian paused once again as she looked in the students' faces. Each person acknowledged her with their eyes as she attempted to gauge their understanding of what she said. When she was satisfied that everyone was actively listening, she lowered her hands once again and placed them on the back of her chair.

She continued: 'My role in this course will be to share some of our sacred teachings with you. From talking with your professor, he tells me that this course was built on the idea that our issues, individuals, institutions, and ideas matter. In keeping with this theme I'll talk to you about what we learn from the four directions. Your professor and I have been discussing how to introduce these themes to you. I understand he is also writing something about this which he may share with you later in the term – I think he said it has to do with the four hills of life.'

Lillian then asked the students to identify the four cardinal directions from where they were sitting in the room. The absence of windows made it difficult to immediately be sure. After a few minutes of laughter and conversation they eventually identified east, south, west, and north. Lillian continued:

'Our lives are cyclical. While we can also view and experience time as linear, many of our most important teachings orient us towards a life that stresses recurrence.[3] For the Anishinabek, the present and the past can almost be coextensive. This is often the case when the layered repetitions of similar events are brought into focus. These forms of movement can help us holistically understand our world. Spring turns into summer, fall gives way to winter, and the cycle begins over again. Babies grow into youth, youth mature and become adults, and adults persevere to become Elders, before the circle repeats itself.[4] Much of our cosmology is built on this pattern, and this fact significantly influences our legal traditions.[5] That's why it is important to take the time to learn about the circle. I have noticed that some other Indigenous peoples follow these cycles in understanding their world, too.[6] While some may criticize what I am teaching as too pan-Indian, I find these ideas consistent with our traditions. They help me to organize how I think about our ideas. Let me explain our view.'

Lillian then walked around the circle and stopped behind a chair at the direction the students had identified as being in the east. Standing there with her back against the brick wall to face the students she said, 'In the east, we learn about new beginnings. From this direction I have received teachings about knowledge, childhood, dependency, spring, tobacco, air, and issues which I will share with you this term. We often associate the colour yellow with this direction.' Lillian then walked one quarter of the way round the circle in a clockwise direction, and paused before speaking again. 'In this direction, the south, we learn about growth and development. It's from this direction that we learn about youth, semi-dependency, summer, cedar, earth and individuals. The south is connected with the colour red.' Lillian walked another quarter of the way around the room in the same direction as before and stopped once again. 'This is the west. From this direction we are taught about the power of reflection and maturity. Here we learn about adulthood, independence, fall, sage, fire, and institutions. Black is a symbol of the west.' Lillian then walked the last quarter of the circle and stopped at the place where she began speaking to the class in the first place. 'This is the north. It is the direction of wisdom and purity. As the weeks pass, it is from this direction that you'll learn about Elders, interdependency, winter, sweetgrass, water, and ideas. White will help us remember this direction.'

Lillian continued: 'When you're in law school and want to learn about Native people, you have to think about the law from our perspective. These teachings will be a start for you. Room has to be made to receive our issues, individuals, institutions, and ideas on their own terms. You need to be properly oriented. You have to use Indigenous laws to understand what we seek as we talk about justice. I hope I can help you appreciate this as the weeks go by. There will be more to say as the class develops; for now, however, I'll just ask for a volunteer to help me with the prayer to more formally begin.'

After Lillian's invitation, one of the students raised her hand to participate and she was invited to the front. 'Thanks for agreeing to help,' the Elder said to the student. Lillian consulted with the student for a moment in private before continuing: 'In Ojibway communities we often smudge before prayers are offered and events begin. We do this to focus our minds and invite help. I have asked for Diane's assistance because she will give everyone an opportunity to smudge. She will take this sweetgrass I'm going to light and walk around the circle and present it to each of you in turn. She will stop in front of you and hold the braid while fanning its small fire so that you can have a chance to wash yourself with its smoke. If you don't want to participate when it's your turn, just smile and keep your hands behind your body when she comes to you. She'll go to the next person without any problem. It's important that no one feels compulsion, that's one of our laws.

'If you do decide to participate in the smudge, you are invited to remove your watches and other jewellery. When Diane stops in front of you, take a handful of smoke in the cup of your hands as she waves the smoldering sweetgrass before you. Then take that smoke and wash it over yourselves four times. First, you will pass the smoke over the top of your head to remind you that your thoughts should be clean. Then with your second handful, you will pass the smoke over your ears, eyes, and mouth. This will help remind you to hear, see, and speak with respect and clarity. Third, you will pass the smoke over your heart to remind you that your motivations and desires should be good. Finally, with your fourth handful you'll pass the smoke over your body, legs, and feet. This is to help you remember to use your strength for the good of others. When you are finished smudging, Diane will pass the sweetgrass to the next person in the circle until she eventually comes back to me. She will go in the four directions: east, south, west, and north. Again, it's like the cycle of life, and this ceremony will remind everyone here of that journey. The smoke will drift to the ceiling and represent our thoughts ascending to the Creator. This should cause you to reflect that there are other directions of significance in our world view that have teachings attached to them. If you are perceptive, you might also pick up the vertical orientation of our world view from time to time, though I won't speak to you as much about these teachings this term.'

When Lillian finished speaking, the sweetgrass was lit and presented to the students. Almost everyone participated by receiving the medicine and washing themselves as she explained. Feeling uneasy, Beatle and Cowboy passed when the sweetgrass came before them. Having looked around the building before entering the classroom, they wondered if this law school could ever be made clean in the way the Elder described. They were starting to doubt this religion.

When the smudging was finished, Lillian offered a prayer, and then instructed the students in a few more teachings. She told them a bit more about the important foundations of Anishinabek law. The students then asked a few questions. Thanking them for their patience and time, she returned to her seat, along with the student helper.

At that point, the professor once again resumed his place before the students. He had the students around the table introduce themselves to one another before continuing. In line with the earlier instructions, the introductions went around the table in a clockwise pattern.

Reflecting on what they had seen in the classroom so far, Cowboy and Beatle noticed that the students had stood up and down, talked back and forth, and gone round and round.

After the students were finished with their introductions, the professor spoke. 'As I mentioned at the outset, the only other thing I want to do today for our first class is explain its purpose. We'll discuss how it will be conducted and how you will be evaluated should you decide to stay for the entire semester.

'First, I want to explain the purpose of this class. As you may know, there has been very little regard for Aboriginal issues in Canadian legal education and law. When I went to law school, very few courses dealt with Indigenous issues. There were only a few Indians in the classroom, and the institution was very slow in responding to our ideas. When I became a professor, I wanted this to change. As you heard in Lillian's remarks, I hope we can develop a learning environment where Indigenous knowledge is represented and respected. I want Aboriginal laws to form a vital part of the very structure of legal education. That is one of the reasons we started as we did this morning. It's why we will have an Elder with us throughout the course – to guide us on this learning cycle. Osgoode Hall Law School is innovative enough to support this program and recognize its value. When I was in Arizona, I realized that you didn't have to go to other places to participate in a positive environment. So I came back here, and with the support of the faculty I created this course. You'll notice the course description outlines our objectives as follows:

- To produce a new generation of Aboriginal and non-Aboriginal lawyers better able to address issues related to the partnership of Aboriginal peoples in confederation.
- To create a new clinical legal education program with significant multi-disciplinary and interdisciplinary features.
- To provide an accurate description of how current negotiations on lands, resources, and Aboriginal governments are currently conducted.
- To provide opportunities to acquire practical and theoretical information and skills on how to address legal issues relating to Aboriginal people in a more open and creative way, giving more emphasis to the historical, economic, cultural, linguistic, and spiritual differences that are not addressed in conventional law school classes.
- To provide a relevant legal education to students interested in both the legal (constitutional, formal, customary, and other) and important non-legal issues that arise in the fields of lands, resources, and Aboriginal governance.

'This program is somewhat unique in North America. It combines a rigorous academic experience with challenging field placements for an entire term, all in the context of Indigenous legal traditions. Some of you will be going to small, remote Indian reserves, while others will be placed in government offices and private law firms working on Indigenous issues. Some people will be working with international Indigenous organizations, while others will work with tribal councils, banks, and Indigenous economic development organizations. This semester, students will be placed in Canada, Mexico, the United States, Norway, New Zealand, Australia, Botswana, Switzerland, Guatemala, and Belize. If you are successful, a full fifteen credits will be awarded for your work. This is the only class you will be enrolled in for the whole semester, so work hard. This class will be your complete academic load. You will be doing land claims research, analysing new legislation, assisting in litigation preparation, attending negotiation sessions, drafting First Nations laws and constitutions, making presentations to chiefs, councils, and leaders, accompanying Crown attorneys on a fly-in circuit court, and so on.'

When the young man finished outlining the purposes of the course, he invited the students to ask questions. After a few minutes of conversation, he continued: 'Now, to let you know how the course will be conducted. There are four phases to the semester. The first phase will occur over these first two weeks. We will instruct you in both substantive law and clinical legal skills necessary to utilize the appropriate legal principles in your placements. We will use lectures, videos, class simulations, and problem-solving exercises. There is also a trip to a reserve and an opportunity to meet leading members of Indigenous communities. We have been invited to Six Nations. We also have invitations to go to Mjikaning, Cape Croker, and to organizations including the Chiefs of Ontario, if we have time.

'The second phase of the program will be your seven-week placement in the field. While you are involved with your externship we will make weekly phone calls to each one of you. We touch base frequently to answer any questions you might have and to ensure that things are going well. The class also has a Web-based component. You will also be in frequent email contact with one another, and I hope to set up a webpage and blog for our participation. The point is that we'll continue to have regular contact even while we are spread out across the country and in some cases across the earth. This will give you an opportunity to share what you are learning as you live in remote locations. You can also ask for assistance any time you need it. This will help ensure that the academic component of the program remains strong.

'In the third phase of the program you will come back to Osgoode for two weeks to consolidate your experiences and expand your knowledge in areas you've encountered in your placements. Each of you will submit a paper and make a two-hour oral presentation to the rest of the class based on your placement experiences. This will give you an opportunity to learn from other students and get a sense of what they are learning. It is hoped that you will learn somewhat vicariously through others' experiences, too.

'In the final phase of the course, you will complete legal research based on a topic you will choose in these first two weeks and work on during the term while in your placements. This will be a major legal research paper. I expect it will be well organized and researched, with an innovative thesis and a strong likelihood of publication.

'It is my hope that you will learn how to draw out law in creative ways to solve problems. I am not as concerned about teaching you common law doctrine. I assume you are familiar with that process from your prior law school experience. The importance of the issue-based approach in this course is particularly relevant in addressing the problems we encounter as Indigenous peoples within domestic and international legal contexts. The distinctive history, culture, and political situation of Indigenous peoples require distinctive approaches. Indigenous peoples' own laws play an important part in determining the applicable law in certain contexts. The course employs an approach that tries to assist you in respecting the laws of those nations.'

The professor paused once again to invite comments from the class about how the course would be conducted. Some students were worried about their travel arrangements, while others asked questions about their field supervisor's responsibilities and expectations. A few more details were explained before the young man continued his lesson outline. 'Third, and finally,' he said, 'I'll say a little bit about your evaluation. A variety of evaluative methods are used. Two papers are prepared during the term, a written presentation regarding your placement experience and a major legal research paper, for which letter grades are awarded. I will also prepare a written evaluation that will be permanently attached to your transcript based on comments I will receive from your placement sponsor, your presentation to the class, and the daily journal you will keep during your placement.

'Are there any questions about this aspect of the course?' the professor inquired.

The students were generally quiet as they looked at one another and the professor. 'Are there any final general questions before we end the class for today?' he asked, as he collected his books and papers together in front of him.

Once again, there was a general silence in the class. Sensing they might soon be dismissed, no one wanted to prolong their confinement when they could flee the building to enjoy the beautiful fall day outside. A general sense of comprehension and excitement permeated the room as the professor's question hung in the air.

When he saw that no one was speaking, Cowboy raised his hand. 'You're just like all the other religions out there. You're going to try to brainwash us in this course. I don't see how Lillian's teachings are going to make any difference outside these walls. We've seen all the bricks, concrete, glass, and steel that's out there. There's no place for that stuff in those buildings. Law firms will hate this stuff. Why should we even bother studying them? And while I think of it, I'm not sure I like the fact that you're importing "Western-based" law school stuff into Indigenous communities. At the end of these first two weeks, the students will know a little about Anishinabek law from you and Lillian, but they'll mostly be drawing on their two-and-a-half years of law school when they are in their placements. It's like a Trojan-horse facade of Indigenous law filled with common law warriors. They'll jump out of here and further infect our communities. It sounds like what you are doing is only another version of assimilation. How do we know we can trust you?'

Beatle laughed at his friend's analogies. Leaning in to speak in his ear, he whispered, 'What are you gonna do next, challenge him to a duel?'

Ignoring Beatle, Cowboy, in transformative mode and doing his best Nanabush impersonation, pressed on. 'The power that Indigenous peoples possess relative to Canada is so small that our communities are threatened whenever we engage with them on their terms. I am very suspicious of the approach you are taking in this class. Trying to integrate Indigenous and non-Indigenous law is completely misguided, even in a community context, as you propose to do in this program. Elders in a law school can't help us hold Canada at bay. Pretending they are this powerful will further erode our ways. These students will be submerged by the wider systems in which they work and live and our customs will be discarded. We need to develop law in our own communities, on our own terms. Forget law schools. In fact, forget Canada. Our energy should be poured into activities at home. What you are proposing is a waste of time and just ends up bolstering the status quo.'

Cowboy paused for a moment, before remembering some of the things he'd heard about that man who lives out West – the one who was critical of Indigenous legal education. Recalling the critique, he continued: 'For all your talk of trying to create a new generation of lawyers by being clinical, multi-disciplinary, practical, theoretical, and creative, I only see the "same old, same old." Your model of legal education was the one that existed before Osgoode Hall Law School ever came into existence: some practical experience under the supervision of lawyers, supplemented by a few classes. I can't see the innovation in that model. You can't forget that you are training lawyers in this place. They have a legal profession to enter through Bar admission courses, articling experiences, and long years of professional development. They have to work with mainstream parliamentary and legislative statutes. They have to work with English-derived, judge-made common law. Haven't you heard Audre Lord's statement, "You can't use the master's tools to destroy the master's house"? I hate to be rude, but I think you need a wake-up call. You need a guardian to speak up and tell you the sad truth of what you are doing. You are so out of touch with Indigenous communities and what needs to be done that I'm afraid I can't stay in this course. I just can't trust you.'

Beatle turned his head around and stared at Cowboy with a bemused look on his face. He silently mouthed the words 'Draw, outlaw,' as he pointed his finger and dropped his thumb at his friend.

Cowboy was not finished. Ignoring Beatle's covert taunts, he pushed back his chair from the table before he stood up, loudly scratching it across the floor. He scowled at the teacher and looked at the other students with disgust. Cowboy stood up, sat down, and stood up again. He walked around the table one time, and then another. Round and round, back and forth, up and down. Finally, Cowboy paused at the door and scanned the room again, before secretly smiling and winking at Beatle. Turning his back, Cowboy fled out the door with Beatle close on his heels.

The professor looked at the remaining students with embarrassment. Lillian looked down at the table, while everyone else stared at the floor. There was silence for a few minutes before the professor spoke.

Trying to act as if everything that had just happened was normal, he said, 'Well, it's good to get those concerns out on the table before we begin the course. It's too bad our friends left us, but I'd like to address what was said.

'I completely agree that there is a tremendous power imbalance that threatens Indigenous peoples whenever they engage with the systems that surround them. There are so many ways in which Indigenous issues, individuals, institutions, and ideas can be overwhelmed. What we do in this class will not be without its dangers. I know that, and I hope to teach you more clearly about those dangers, too. I want you to identify them with sharp eyes. There are substantial problems whenever you take systems and ideas that have been subordinated and try to make them work within existing systems. These problems are significant, and they are not overcome by merely believing that you will change the domineering system in the process. I will try to point out those dangers wherever they arise. I want us to be alive to the dynamics of power and force in Canadian law.

'In planning and teaching this course, I knew that we would face a sizeable challenge. It is a real struggle to scramble over the mass of challenges colonialism presents and help your communities rise in the process. Many people and institutions have given up trying to climb that hill. Most end up ignoring Indigenous issues, or they fall back onto themselves in an unhealthy, internecine jumble.' The third hill passed through the young man's thoughts as he said this.

'Is this an acceptable alternative – to turn our back on these challenges by turning in on ourselves? Should we just leave the common law as it is – without challenging its conceits? Should we ignore the powers around us that impact on our communities? I don't think so. People outside our communities exercise power over us without our participation. Canadian law is largely devoid of our views. It most often acts as if we are not even here – through the doctrines of discovery, Crown sovereignty, and constitutional law. We need to at least find ways to attenuate that force. I hope that Canada can eventually be made subject to our laws, too.'

As the professor lectured, he absent-mindedly wiped the allergies from his eyes. The student's earlier disruption and his own earnestness caused him to momentarily lose track of his ideas. As he talked, he stared at the open door, the ceiling, and the corners of the brick walls. He rarely paused to look anyone in the eye. It was as if he was lost in space and was only capable of focusing on the logic of the ideas he was developing. At that point, his subconscious thoughts told him that he was not having a good day. In this frame of mind, the professor continued.

'I agree with our dearly departed friend that we need to see the development of Indigenous laws and systems in our communities. I try to do that in my work when I'm not in the law school. However, strengthening our laws on their own terms does not mean we can't develop betters ways for both systems to live in proximity to one another. Part of what is necessary is to find ways that other systems can respectfully interact with ours, as Indigenous law continues to grow and develop. I hope this class becomes the means by which lawyers become multicultural, multilingual, and multi-juridical in legal terms. When you learn another language, you do not have to give up your own. It is true you may gain a new perspective on and understanding of your language once you learn another, but that does not mean that you have to forsake your own.

'I don't think this program is a waste of time. We are not merely bolstering the status quo. It might be considered radical to challenge and change the way individuals and legal institutions are organized. You create substantial change when people rethink the underlying principles against which they judge their laws. That is what I hope you will be doing in this class as you work in context. I hope you can see how communities can present issues from Indigenous perspectives with the respect and rigour we expect of you as Osgoode students. I am not interesting in seeing Canada or other counties remain places where Indigenous peoples continue to be disadvantaged.'

As they listened to the professor, the students lifted their eyes from the floor to consider what he was saying to them. They noticed that Lillian was nodding her approval beside him. The professor himself regained some of his composure and began to look at the students once again. Standing a little taller and focusing his gaze, he continued: 'I have a problem with the analogy we heard before our friend left the class. The notion that you can never use the master's tools to destroy the master's house has a nice ring to it, at one level. It does contain an appropriate caution. However, as I understand Anishinabek teachings, we are not interested in destroying Canada or its systems.

'Destruction is not our law. My great-great-grandfather did not want to break down others when he signed treaties. He promised and received promises of peace, friendship, and respect. I hope this course can teach us how to change and substantially reconfigure the forces Indigenous peoples encounter in our land. I believe it is necessary to do this peacefully to be fully consistent with Anishinabek law. Therefore, I don't like Ms Lord's analogy. It doesn't do justice, from my perspective. I want to focus on constructive transformation. I also don't like the analogy on another level. The metaphor doesn't have a factual basis. Of course you can use the master's tools to destroy the master's house, if that's your goal. You use hammers, crowbars, bulldozers, cement mixers, saws, and drills to build houses. These tools would be quite effective tools in destroying a house, if that was your wish.'

In saying these words the professor further brightened and recognized where he was going with his thoughts. Looking at Lillian and the students once again, he saw the promise of a brighter future, at least in his small corner of the world. It helps even if there are only a few more lawyers who are better prepared to provide culturally appropriate advice to Indigenous communities. A little leaven can have a great effect on the surrounding mass. This could help address some of the problems he was writing about and working on. With renewed confidence in what he was saying he continued:

'Finally, I think I need to address the point about this program not being very innovative. It is true that in one respect, this program looks like a throwback to the time when legal education was structured around clinical work with practitioners and supplemented by courses. But in most other ways it is very different.

'It is very misleading to describe this program as not being a significant institutional innovation. There has never been a time when Indigenous peoples have controlled any aspect of legal education in Canadian law schools. This course represents a break from that history. While I am teaching this course, it will be Indigenous controlled. I will be teaching from my perspective as an Anishinabek person. I am the first Indigenous person to have a full-time teaching position in this school, and to have tenure. This had already led to some limited institutional reform. I'm not sure an Anishinabek Elder has ever been involved in legal education here, either. I don't say that to boast, but to point out that the issues and individual before you represent true change at one level. Of course what we do is insufficient. Reform requires more than a course and Aboriginal faces. We have tried to make this program so much more. It is for these reasons that we will have an Elder in this class, providing Anishinabek perspectives throughout our time together. Over half of you as students are Indigenous. We will study other Indigenous legal systems and values. You will *not* spend most of your time reading black letter law, though it will form an important part of the course. You will learn Indigenous legal concerns and concepts, and how they interact with others. You will be placed with Indigenous leaders and lawyers around the world, and work on issues of concern to them and their communities. This is a far cry from conventional legal education. I think it deserves the label innovative.

'In the final analysis, I believe that our traditions are best preserved and facilitated if they answer our current questions. This is what I hope to encourage in this class. I hope you come to appreciate how tradition can be a living force with the Indigenous organizations and individuals you work with. And as far as trust goes, well, we all have to learn that. I don't expect you to trust me, at least not right away. I do hope you can learn from me.'

The professor finished and once again invited questions from the students. There was good engagement from the class, and a wide-ranging discussion ensued. Lillian also took time to respond and give her views on the importance of community and university education.

As the class wrapped up, Nokomis found herself shifting in her sleep. She had become so bored of the dream that she almost woke up. In her restlessness, the dream switched and she found herself in another world. Nokomis is no longer a young Ojibway boy. But she still seemed to be asleep.

She steps into a glade filled with soft light. A fine mist rises from the boughs overhead and reaches into the evening sky. The sun and moon are visible beyond the glen, sharing a moment together in their eternal round. In thanksgiving, Nokomis kneels in the clearing, a bed of pine needles cushioning her knees. The fragrance of the late fall gift takes her mind and returns her to a time when life here was new. She has felt that newness before, and knows it will always return. She gives thanks for it, and prays for the strength to welcome it when it does. But even as she does this, she can feel that Beebon is gaining ground. It is getting colder.

As Nokomis rises from her knees, a large black dog appears in the clearing. He clears his throat:

'Ahnee, Nokomis, Auneen aendodumun?'

Nokomis looks in surprise. 'What are *you* doing here? I think I know you. You're that trickster Nanaboozhoo.'

'Don't be so sure,' the dog says. 'I'm not always who you think I am.'

Nokomis considers this for a moment, then replies, 'You're just as elusive as those stories and storytellers of old; no one could ever quite be sure about them. Crossing the lines between human and animal, fact and fiction, they left you wondering what was real. And now you say you're not Nanaboozhoo. If you're not who I think you are, then who are you? How can I trust you?'

The dog yawns and cleans its paws. Looking up, he says, 'You can't trust me – that is what I'm here to tell you.'

'What kind of message is that?' Nokomis replies, her brow furrowed. 'That's not what I want to hear.'

The dog noses around in the needles, finds a small root, and picks it. He grinds it between his teeth and swallows. 'I'm not here to tell you what you want to hear. I'm here to tell you what you need to hear. Besides, you're jumping to conclusions. Just because I said you can't trust me, doesn't mean you can't trust others. The world is full of good beings – Anishinabe. That's what people should be – that's how your language describes them. I think most *are* good beings. Many can be trusted. But there are some who are tricksters. Good and bad, all mingled together, thinking of themselves and not the good of others. They can't be trusted – just like you can't trust me.'

Nokomis thought for a moment. 'But how am I to know the difference? How should I know who to trust?'

'That's easy,' said the dog, 'they won't ask you for anything that feels wrong. Watch for that. They won't force you. They'll leave it all up to you. You won't feel pressured. You'll feel free around them, like you can be yourself.'

Nokomis wondered if these words presented a trap. 'If I can't trust you, why should I take your advice? You might be trying to hurt me by telling me this.'

'Just because I said you shouldn't trust me, doesn't mean that everything I say is wrong,' the dog replied. 'You just need to learn for yourself. You must develop the power to distinguish. You must even learn from those who would trick you, and who would want to pressure you. You *can* learn from those you don't trust– just like you can learn from the one that just hurt you – from the ones that are hurting you. Learn, and be free.'

Nokomis smiled, 'You're right, Nanabush, I'm not going to trust you. You're too vain. But I am going to learn from you. I thank you.'

With those words, the dog disappeared into the forest. When Nokomis tried to see where he went, her vision was blocked by a large tree stump that stood where she last saw him. The dog was lost in the tangle of roots and branches in the woods.

Nokomis looked so hard for the dog in her dream that she woke herself up. Coming to herself once again, she saw the morning light stretching through the window bringing in a new day.

ASHAWA-MUNISSOOWIN[1]

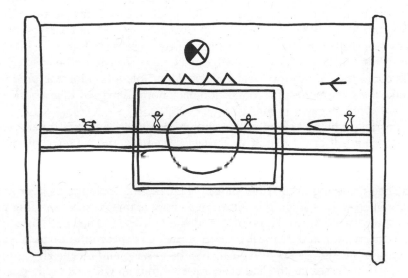

Everything was cancelled. The three-hour journey from the reserve to the airport had taken half a day because of the snow. Highway 10 from Chatsworth to Flesherton was a windstorm of white-outs and whirling fall leaves. It was the first blizzard of the year, though it was still early fall. No one had expected the weather to turn from one season to the next this early. When the young man drove through Orangeville and Brampton, he could barely see the cars ahead of him. He passed numerous accident scenes, where cars had slid off the road or ploughed into one another when visibility must have been non-existent. As they became buried under the accumulating snow, the damaged cars looked like icebergs piled along a cement river. He had barely made it back to Toronto. He turned in his rental car with only half an hour to spare before his scheduled flight. Never trust a schedule.

Now, with everything cancelled, he was sitting in the terminal with little hope of reaching Vancouver this evening. It was a little nerve-racking. He had to get back to UBC because he had a class first thing tomorrow morning. He had been teaching in Vancouver for a few years, but readily accepted invitations in Ontario to be closer to home. On days like this he wondered why he had relocated to the West. The travel could be brutal. It was definitely taking its toll right now.

It was the earliest he could remember it snowing around the southern Great Lakes. The snow was *augawauss-goonugauh*: 'the snow that forms an obstruction preventing passage.'[2] Its appearance was far too early. Before the winds swept in the storm, the leaves were still on the trees, and they were full of colour. After teaching for two weeks in Osgoode's Intensive Program, he had gone home to Cape Croker to visit for the weekend. He could not stay in the West for very long unless he took the time to make these moments of reconnection back home. He tried to get back to Ontario almost every month.

Last night he had stood on the shore outside his mother's house and watched a full moon rise. It was *waatebagaa-giizis*, the leaves changing colour moon. As the moon cast its first light over the water, the steady sound of a drum had reverberated down the shore. It was like hearing the heartbeat of grandmother moon. Then, after a few minutes, a group of women started singing in Anishinabemowin, their voices blending in unison with the drum. The sound made his spirit soar. They had sung for close to an hour, and their celebration rejuvenated all around them. There had been no sign of snow. The air had been crisp and clean. Though it was late in the season, he had even gone swimming with his mother and sister earlier in the day.

Now he sat in an airport. Hour after hour, Vancouver flights were posted on the board, and then cancelled. It was too much for some travellers. Their hopes had been raised and dashed one too many times. They gave up. He had been taught never to give up. Crowds thinned as afternoon turned into late evening, and people began to check into local hotels. He stayed by the gate. At 11:55 p.m. a flight was called, and he miraculously found himself checked in on it. The plane was loaded, de-iced, and cleared for Vancouver. He didn't like taking 'red eye' flights, but given the circumstances, he was glad he would get to his early morning commitments.

As the plane ascended, leaving Toronto behind, the young man reflected on his life and its connection to his Anishinabek ancestors. They had lived life in seasonal rounds. He saw a similar pattern in himself and amongst some of his uncles and cousins on the reserve. At least in that respect, Anishinabek law showed its resilience.

In ancient times, Anishinabek people had used different parts of their territory for different purposes, depending on the time of year. They would circulate throughout the land to enjoy its variety and secure their livelihood. In the fall, this time of year, individuals would have recently broken from their summer camps and dispersed into smaller, multi-family groups throughout the territory. They would live as extended families until the heavy snows began and would engage in hunting, fishing, and harvesting berries, nuts, fruit, and other seeds. In the winter, before the snow became too thick, families would once again divide from one another and further disperse throughout the land. Each would need sufficient territory to hunt, forage, and fish in this time of greater scarcity. They would be associated with one another in these family groups for three or four months. When the snow started to melt in mid-spring, people would gather themselves together again in larger, multi-family groups. They would congregate around large stands of maple trees, where they would tap the trees for their sap and make maple syrup. After this task was finished, people would then move to the heads of streams where returning fish would form a part of their diet. After a few weeks at the fish-run, the snow would have melted and late spring would be upon the land. People would move from the stream's headwaters and gather at its mouth. There, a large village would be set up for four to five months of social engagement, protection, and economic cooperation. The women would work together, tending to the material aspects of the community, while the men would go on extended hunting journeys for larger game. Then, in the fall, people would disperse from these bigger villages and begin their annual round all over again. Different streams, rivers, and lands might be chosen from year to year for village sites and settlements. People rotated across the land and would not always return to the same sites year after year, though over a decade or so the same sites would be utilized. In this way, people came to know all parts of the land as they cycled through it with order and purpose, access being regulated by kinship and dodem.

As the young man saw it, the ancient pattern remained, only the scope of the cycle had been expanded in these past generations. Large groups of people would come home to the reserve every summer, just as people gathered to central places in times past. Pow-wow weekend was the height; people pitched tents around family homes as these units consolidated their connections. In the fall, people would slowly start to disperse and do things in smaller family groups. This dispersion took place at the level of reserve, territory, province, and nation. From late October until April, people of the reserve would see less of one another, as they settled into smaller-scale social and economic engagements. People living in the territory and throughout the province and country would have even fewer contacts with the reserve in this period because of the scarcity of economic opportunity on the reserve. Today they had to range further afield than their ancestors to support themselves and their families. Yet, when spring came and the snows melted, the cycle starting spinning around them once again. People gathered in larger, multi-family groups to tap the sugar bushes and fish at the headwaters, before settling back home for a time in the summer. This was the routine he had fallen into. Simultaneously connected and separated from this ancient life pattern.

Now his annual round included the West Coast. Anishinabek territory had expanded to embrace a continent. Though *Neyaashiinigmiing* was still the central axis around which his life revolved, he lived like his grandfather and circled through North America. The Ojibway were sometimes accused of being opportunistic interlopers when it came to settling within other people's territories.[3] While his cousin Darlene had demonstrated that Anishinabek people had a continuity and time-depth in their home territory that was unmatched by other people,[4] the young man had to agree that the Ojibway knew how to expand. They were good at taking themselves with them when they travelled. This ability reminded him of the dog creation story that had been given to him in Arizona. The Anishinabek had learned how to survive and thrive beyond their traditional borders. He was grateful for this tradition.

The University of British Columbia had been a great place to teach after he left Osgoode Hall. As director of the First Nations Law Program, he got to work with Indigenous people from all over the province and across Canada. The First Nations Law Program had been going since 1975, when it was aimed at increasing the number of Aboriginal students in the law school. Bob Reid, Doug Sanders, and Michael Jackson were its early creators and champions. The program graduated more than 200 students in its first twenty years. Since he had become its first academic director, he sought to increase the program's substantive content. Stronger links were made with the profession practising Aboriginal law. Relationships were built with First Nations communities and governments. Seven courses dealing with different aspects of Indigenous legal issues were approved and placed in the curriculum, including First Nations and Economic Development, First Nations Self-Government, First Nations and Criminal Justice, International Indigenous Issues, and First Nations Legal Perspectives, among others. There were weekly brown bag lunches on Indigenous legal themes, and First Nations Conferences were offered along with a First Nations Awareness Week. An Academic and Cultural Support Program was initiated, as well as a graduate course offering in the field. He worked with the dean in his first few years to develop the program, fundraise, and pave the way for a First Nations Legal Clinic to operate in Vancouver's downtown east side, to serve the Aboriginal population there.

It felt good to be part of a university that had a strong, institution-wide commitment to First Nations educational issues. He loved his colleagues in the law school and their deeper involvement with ideas related to his field. He also enjoyed getting to work with Indigenous people in other faculties. It was a contrast from some former experiences. He would always remember a call he received one day from an Ontario university administrator consulting on First Nations employee issues. When the interview was nearly finished, out of curiosity, he asked how many calls she was going to make to First Nations employees on campus that day. She answered that he was the only one. A university that served over 40,000 students had only one Aboriginal employee: him. He was *the* Aboriginal community on campus. When he heard the disappointing news, he knew a change was needed.

Now at UBC, he witnessed the opening of the First Nations House of Learning in his second year on campus. It was spectacular. The long-house was a home away from home for many First Nations students and employees. The first time the young man's mother walked into the building, tears came into her eyes. She told him she could hardly believe a school would create something so beautiful for its students. It was a far cry from the residential schools and one-room school houses she had been forced to attend, and where she had been abused. The government singled out 'Indians' to attend such schools because of their so-called race. When Aboriginal children attended, they were taught that they were savage and inferior to those who had white skin. His mother had been punished for speaking Anishinabemowin. Her teachers spoke about her parents and leaders in derogatory ways. The most prominent lesson she learned as a young child was that non-Native people had special rights because of their ancestry. In everything she was taught, she felt that only non-Aboriginal people's practices, customs, or traditions were recognized and affirmed. Only non-Aboriginal people received preferential treatment, and only they enjoyed meaningful participation and input in her school experience.

Now, surrounded by the symbols in the longhouse, it was encouraging to see that education didn't have to be oppressive. It was possible to climb higher through education than his mother had been permitted. The young man hadn't seen anything like this in any university in Ontario. There was something special about the West. In these surroundings, he saw the power of reflection and maturity. The structure was a living symbol of the First Nations presence at the university. The cedar house posts in *Sty-Wet-Tan* (the Great Hall) were intricately carved with characters from up and down the coast. They communicated the life of the land and Indigenous people's ancient relationships with British Columbia. Their sweet, rich, earth-grown smell still permeated the air with their fragrance. The posts were important because they announced and commemorated the First Nations of British Columbia at the university.

The post at the south-east entrance of *Sty-Wet-Tan* was carved by Lyle Wilson, a Haisla artist. The pole was a symbol of Lyle's clan houses in Kitamaat Village, with a beaver facing outward, towards the hall, and an eagle facing inward, towards the building. In the next corner, the south-western house post was carved by Susan Point of the Musqueam First Nation, the traditional owners of UBC's endowment lands. Her work depicted a raven and a spindle-whorl. He liked the raven because, as the trickster, he reminded the young man of Nanabush. His presence always had to be accounted for in educational settings. In the next corner, the house posts at the Great Hall's north-west angle were made up of three human figures, a wolf, and a wolf pup. They were carved by Chief Walter Harris and his son Rodney, who were Gitskan artists from Kispiox. Chief Harris was a welcome visitor around the campus. He had even attended the young man's Native law classes on occasion, and told wonderful stories about Gitskan law. Chief Harris placed the human figures on his house post to represent university students, and their need to listen twice as much as they spoke. The fourth house post, in *Sty-Wet-Tan*'s north-east corner, was jointly carved by Stan Bevan, a Tahltan-Tlingit-Tsimshian artist, with Ken McNeil, a Tahltan-Tlingit-Nisga'a artist. Their pole portrayed a man and raven facing inward. It was meant to represent the unity of all people, because it created the impression that the faces were of one person. The young man liked that imagery, because he often saw different people even within his own being.

The longhouse was also a wonderful place to pause outside its walls. There was a waterfall flowing at the site because Chief Simon Baker (Khat-la-cha) had insisted its life should be represented here. Back home they would have called this *geek-idjiwun*, the stream flowing over the ledge. There was an adjoining library (Xwi7xwa), built in an Interior Salish pit house style, and a sweat lodge at the back of the building in a quiet, private space. The young man spent many hours participating in ceremonies on the site and tried to take this strength back to his life on the surrounding campus. It felt like a healthy environment, both physically and philosophically.

UBC's philosophy at that time was that there would be no centralized Native Studies program at the university, because Native Studies was to be integrated within every single academic unit on campus. The longhouse existed to knit the different units together, and provide a common meeting place across disciplines. Besides First Nations Law, there were programs in business, medicine, forestry, education, social work, engineering, arts and science, and many others. The thought was that people did not want to ghettoize Indigenous issues, but wanted them to be a vital part of inquiry across various fields of study. This model held great attraction for many people, and he was among its supporters. He had concerns about Native Studies when it became too inward-looking and did not connect to the circumstances in which Indigenous peoples lived today. It was not that he was against Native Studies programs; he just thought First Nations studies were better developed as separate programs once there was strength in the area in other faculties. Standing back from it all, he felt the institution had made solid progress incorporating Indigenous issues and individuals.

He was glad to be back at UBC after his time in Ontario. The snow he had weathered yesterday already felt like a distant memory. Now, as the young man prepared for class with only a restless night's sleep on the plane, his thoughts turned from the campus to his lecture notes. He was going to teach about racism and residential schools in his Indigenous Law class today.

The phone interrupted his preparation. It was Associate Dean Waugoosh. She said: 'When you are finished your class, could I speak with you? A matter of some importance has arisen, and I want to take care of it as quickly as possible.' Agreeing to meet when his class was over, an appointment was set and he went off to his lecture, which was uneventful.

When he was finished, the young man walked to the associate dean's office. At the appointed time, he knocked on the door and the secretary ushered him in. He was offered a seat and a drink as they sat across the table from one another.

'How have things been going this year?' she asked him. 'You are making important headway in your new job, and I want to make sure that you feel supported.'

After a few moments of small talk, Dean Waugoosh got to the point. 'I recently received an official written complaint from the provost's office that you may be violating the university's equity policy. It is alleged that you have been engaged in teaching racist hate speech in the classroom. Can you tell me anything about this?'

It took a second for the question to register. For a moment, the young man sat immobilized, unspeaking. Then, when he realized what she had said, momentary panic washed over him and his face flushed. Breathing shallowly, he tried to think of where such an accusation would come from. The fact that the associate dean was investigating, and didn't dismiss the complaint out of hand, must mean that it was serious. His mind ranged through his activities of the past year, but nothing came to mind. At length, he spoke. 'I'm sure there must be some mistake. I can't think of any instance where what I have said or done comes even close to what is alleged.'

Dean Waugoosh leaned back in her chair and removed her glasses. She glanced out the window and took a long pause. Eventually she said, 'Look, this hurts me as much as it does you. The institution has to take these things seriously. You know our rules. We have to ensure that the learning environment is not poisoned by racist, hateful speech. That's what a former student said you are doing. I just want to get to the bottom of things and clear the air, OK? I'm only doing my job.'

The dean turned her attention to a letter on the table between them. Picking it up and putting on her glasses, she said, 'I want to put some questions to you to sort a few things out. You don't have to answer them now, but I want you to think about them carefully.' She perused the letter, summarized its contents, and asked:

- 'In commenting on your reading materials, have you ever inappropriately singled out historical figures on the basis of race?
- Have you ever called the early settlers of this province "white"?
- Have you ever spoken in a derogatory way about the leaders of the early settlers in BC?
- Have you ever argued that Aboriginal people should have special rights because of their ancestry?
- Have you ever argued that only Aboriginal people should participate in certain practices, customs, or traditions?

• Do you give preferential treatment to Aboriginal students in your
  class by specifically looking for their participation and input?'

  Hearing the list of allegations, the young man could hardly believe
he was having an interview with his boss about these issues. He thought
of all his struggles in the classroom. He recalled some students' caustic
comments about Aboriginal people when they thought he wasn't listening. He remembered the stereotypical assumptions made by other
professors and students about Aboriginal beliefs and behaviours. He recalled the well-intentioned but inappropriately intrusive questions by a
colleague about his personal life as an Aboriginal person. He brought to
mind the dismissive treatment he felt from some students when he introduced Aboriginal issues in a 'mainstream' course. He tried to count
the number of Aboriginal students who had come to tears in his office
because they had been called racist names by other law students. He
wondered if any of them had ever had an official complaint launched
against them.
  As these thoughts passed through the young man's mind, the dean
continued, 'You can probably guess from this list of questions that it is
alleged that you treat people and issues in a discriminatorily differential manner, on the basis of race. The student states that you consistently make inappropriate distinctions between Aboriginal peoples and
others in your teaching. They say that you imply that so-called white
people have received improper benefits from land, resources, and governmental power in this province because of their race. They claim that
you argue that in certain circumstances, Aboriginal peoples should be
able to exclude others from certain historical activities on the basis of
their First Nations status. They say that you go out of your way to encourage Aboriginal students to participate in your class.'
  The associate dean finally looked up from the letter she held in her
hand. Looking him in the eye, she asked, 'What do you have to say
about these allegations?'
  A host of thoughts swirled through the young man's mind. Did he
say these things in the way they were framed by the writer? If he did,
he wondered when were they made, and what kind of context they
were made in. Even as he listened to the questions, it made him wonder what was racist and hateful about them. He had to learn more. The
young man took a deep breath before choosing his next words.
  'I may have said some of these things, but I believe they might have
been taken out of context. I was not teaching these issues in a racist

and hateful way. It is true, I have made distinctions between Aboriginal peoples and others in my class. These distinctions are a part of the law and historical experience in this province. It is legitimate to talk about them in that way. Early settlers referred to themselves as "white," and they were proud of this label. They thought it made them better than others, and gave them greater entitlements in law and politics as a result. They used these entitlements to displace or dispossess many Aboriginal peoples from their land and resources. You can read about this in a hundred documents; it is reproduced in the secondary literature and cases. Aboriginal peoples *do* have distinctive rights under section 35(1) of the Constitution, because of their ancestral connections. This entitles them to carry on certain practices, customs, and traditions that might not be available to other Canadians. Aboriginal peoples can also be singled out and other Canadians can be justifiably burdened by discriminatory laws if the government has a valid ameliorative purpose under section 15(2) of the *Charter*.[5] I teach about all these things, for sure. Acknowledging these facts does not make my comments racist. And finally, with regards to specifically singling out Aboriginal students for participation and input, I ask everyone to get involved in class discussion. On those rare occasions when Aboriginal students have not spoken for a prolonged period of time, I may ask questions that only they may be able to answer based on their community experience, such as living on a reserve or exercising one of the Aboriginal rights we are talking about. To my knowledge, though, the questions are always open-ended, and I do not ask anyone specifically to answer.'

As the young man further reflected on the questions, he thought more generally about the issues of racism, Indigenous peoples, and equality in the law school context. In his constitutional law class, he taught that the mere singling out of people on the basis of race was not necessarily discriminatory. In the case of *Law v. Canada (Minister of Employment and Immigration)*, Justice Iacobucci observed that 'true equality does not necessarily result from identical treatment.'[6] He said that formal distinctions in treatment will sometimes be necessary to accommodate differences between individuals, and thus produce equal treatment in a substantive sense. 'Correspondingly,' the judge continued, 'a law which applies uniformly to all may still violate a claimant's equality rights.'[7] Differential treatment does not always signal a denial of the equal benefit and protection of the law. Judgments about the fairness of differential treatment will always be contextualized; it will depend on the right at issue, a person's socio-economic status, and that of comparative groups. In *R. v. Andrews*, the court said that in approaching 'the ideal of full equality before and under the law ... the main considera-tion must be the impact of the law on the individual or the group con-cerned.'[8] As he rehearsed these principles in his mind, the young man wondered if his associate dean and the person making the allegations were aware of their application in what he was teaching.

While he was summarizing these thoughts, he linked them to his own teaching philosophy as he pondered what he would say next. Af-ter putting his ideas in order, he said, 'I have learned a lot about law schools since I started teaching. One of the main lessons is that you can't always teach to be popular. Of course, I don't try to get people to dislike me in my classes. In fact, I naturally want them to feel good about our time together. I try to treat people with respect and patience in my classes. However, when you teach, you sometimes have to chal-lenge people's ideas in order to help them learn. You want to help them entertain ideas with which they may not be familiar. Sometimes these challenges can be personally uncomfortable, intellectually confusing, or politically disagreeable.

'I think one of the hardest things for students in my classes is that they do not always know my political position on the cases and issues we discuss. It might surprise them to learn how deeply conservative I am. While I expect people to find some ambiguity in relation to my writing, I often get that criticism on my course evaluations, too – they say I need to be more forthright. I sense a good number of students want me to spoon-feed them answers to the tougher questions we dis-cuss. I try to avoid this approach, so that they can develop their own analytical skills. As such, I do not shy away from building and taking apart arguments from every perspective. Some people do not like it when I dissect arguments that are "politically correct" and leave them to work out matters for themselves with the tools I have provided. I try to encourage them to make their own choice in the matter. I want them to exercise their own agency. When I follow this approach and they have trouble making all the connections on their own, they are not hap-py. I have found this approach sometimes makes me unpopular. I am OK with that result, as long as they are learning. My real goal for them is not my friendship, though I accept and welcome that if it develops. What I want for them is independent, creative thought. Sometimes that requires submerging my own beliefs. Ambiguity is a big part of teach-ing law in an Anishinabek context, and I find it can be a useful learning tool, too. Thus, when I leave implications hanging in my classes, my students might ascribe to me an opinion I don't hold. Perhaps that is what happened.'

As the associate dean listened to the young man's statement, she gathered the papers with the complaint in front of her. After considering what he had said, she started to stand while saying:

'Well, I can see that you're sincere in your beliefs. From what you've said, it sounds like you haven't done anything wrong. You should watch yourself, though. You are not taking the easy way with your approach. What you are doing now might hurt you down the road. We want to support you and ensure that you get along well in your job. For your benefit, I am going to assign you a faculty mentor. They will be available to talk to you, should this sort of thing arise again. They'll probably attend your class from time to time to see that things are going well. I'll talk to the provost and recommend that nothing further be done about this complaint. Does this sound like a good plan to you?'

The young man didn't know what to say. How did such counsel impact on his agency and his right to choose how to conduct his classes? This event was so out of keeping with his positive experiences with the law school's amazing dean and other administrators. The associate dean was obviously trying to be as supportive, but he wondered about what she had done. First of all, the fact that he would even be called to her office like this, and have to listen to these allegations, would probably send a chill through his work. Why didn't she recognize that the allegations behind these complaints could not be characterized as racist except by someone who thought it was racist to acknowledge any distinctions between people on the basis of so-called race. He also wondered how supportive it was to have a more senior faculty member other than the associate dean know about this complaint and drop in on his classes. While he knew she was trying to help, it felt like he was being counselled to watch out, to warn him that others would be watching him closely to see that he didn't mess up.

As the dean escorted him to her door, he could not help but feel confused. Just before he stepped into the hall, the young man asked, 'Could I ask who made the complaint? Is that appropriate? Since they are no longer in my class, I can't see what harm it would be for me to know.'

The associate dean answered, 'Sure, I think I can tell you. I don't think there was a request for confidentiality in this matter. In fact, I think the student even wanted to arrange a mediated meeting with you.' She returned to her desk and picked up the papers she had been reading from. 'Here it is. It says here the student's name is Tom'lana'gan. Do you know him?'

MAEMAEGAWAHSESSIWUK[1]

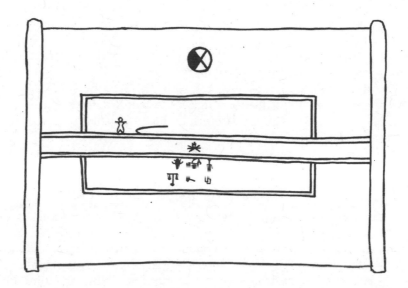

Inside the longhouse, a large fire blazes in the centre pit. The young fire-keeper adds another log every ten to fifteen minutes. The wood cracks, fractures, and sparks as the fire explosively consumes the surrounding air. Smoke slowly swirls and rises over the room, casting a heavy mantle over the proceedings before escaping through the roof into the black October night. Orange and yellow light ripples over the sandy floor. It spills onto benches and along the walls, spreading changing shadows on those gathered around the hall.

Back home it would be *binaakwe-giizis*: falling leaves moon. He is not sure what to call the moon in this part of the world, because the leaves wouldn't fall for another month.

He's in the Lekwammen Longhouse. Over sixty metres in length, it sits on the shores of the Songhees Reserve on southern Vancouver Island. The Songhees and Esquimalt First Nations are Coast Salish people descended from the Kakyaakan, Teechamitsa, Whyomilth, Kosampsom, Swenwhung, Chilcowitch, and Chekonein family groups. Their longhouse has been carefully placed, sitting on a peninsula where a narrow strip of land divides the waters. The houses were traditionally made by placing split cedar planks horizontally between two sets of poles, the planks held in place by cedar ropes that came from long cedar branches when the tree is grown in open spaces. Today, nails and cement are used to hold the structures together. The outer walls are painted brown; a tin roof with three charcoal-darkened tin chimneys covers the sprawling building.

For over 4,000 years the Lekwungen people have occupied the territory around Victoria. Their population was once in the thousands, but in the 1800s their numbers were tragically reduced by smallpox and other diseases. Historically, the Songhees Indian Reserve was originally located in Victoria's Inner Harbour, in the middle of their traditional territories. Their main village sites stood where the British Columbia Legislature now sits, at James Bay, and across the Inner Harbour on the west side of the bay. The Songhees now live in Esquimalt on Vancouver Island, five kilometres from Victoria, the capital of British Columbia.

Approximately 100 people are gathered in Lekwammen to celebrate Frank Calder's receipt of an honorary doctorate from the University of Victoria. The night also marks the beginning of the Calder Conference, a three-day event exploring Indigenous rights in Canada. Dr Calder is Nisga'a, from an area now known as north-west British Columbia, along the Nass River. In his eighty-eight years he has made many significant contributions to Indigenous rights in Canada. He was the first Canadian Indian elected to legislative office in the country, and he served for over twenty-five years in the British Columbia Legislature. He also served as a minister in the Canadian Parliament in the early 1970s. In the 1950s he founded the Nisga'a Tribal Council, and was eventually instrumental in bringing a case which bears his name to the Supreme Court of Canada. This landmark decision established that Aboriginal title exists in modern Canadian law. It was a breakthrough case and was the reason for the conference the University of Victoria was hosting, entitled Let Right Be Done. The *Calder* case provided the legal foundation on which the Nisga'a Treaty was ultimately negotiated, and provided a way for the BC treaty process to be started after 130 years of opposition by provincial and colonial authorities. The *Calder* case is nationally and internationally renowned, and has been influential in the settlement of land claims throughout Canada, as well as in the development of jurisprudence in Australia, South Africa, New Zealand, Malaysia, and other countries with Indigenous populations.

Dr Calder is at the centre of the hall. He is flanked by two witnesses and surrounded by Salish drummers and singers. As people arrive, they make their way to the fire to greet him and exchange a few words.

The master of ceremonies calls the event to order. People find seats on the benches at the sides of the hall as the drum begins to reverberate around the room. Joined by Salish voices, a traditional song is raised in tribute to Frank Calder's life and work. A series of songs follow to mark the host nation's relationship to this territory, and teach those present of valour, courage, patience, and fun. Then there is a traditional welcome to the land followed by good words from Nisga'a Elders, Frank's friends, and the conference coordinators.

When the ceremony is finished, people make their way to the adjoining kitchen for salmon and salad. Someone comes back to the fire pit and places a small piece of fish in the fire. Cowboy and Beatle linger around the flames chatting with their old friend Raven.

'This is some pretty good nish-shishin,' Beatle says to Raven. 'You sure know how to throw a good party on the West Coast. You could teach the Anishinabek a thing or two about how to do it right.'

Raven laughs. 'It's not so much that we know how to throw a party as it is an excuse to get rid of all this salmon. We just can't eat all the fish that comes through here ourselves; it's too much of a good thing. We have to dress up our dinners with all these fancy extras to get others to join us. It throws the authorities off our trail. If we didn't hold these events DFO might suspect the huge number of fish we catch are not for our personal community use. Can you imagine? We might be charged with the nefarious crime of fishing for commercial purposes if we didn't find ways to fence this stuff to people like you. Works pretty good, don't you think?'

Cowboy looked at the guests as they waded out of the kitchen with heaps of food on their plates.

Raven went on, looking at the man who earlier placed the salmon in the fire to feed the maemaegawahsessiwuk. 'I've seen your friend around Victoria these past few years. He's teaching at the university here now, isn't he? He seems to be enjoying himself.'

'We've known him from the day he was born,' Cowboy replies. 'He always enjoys himself, sometimes a bit too much. He wanders from place to place, here a while, there a while, before moving on. He's hard to pin down. Since he left home he's moved fifteen times in twenty years. The guy couldn't keep a job even if it was latched around his foot with a steel trap. He'd probably gnaw his leg off to stay in motion. It's as if he thinks someone is after him. You wouldn't know who that might be, would you?'

Raven laughs. 'Now why would you say that?'

They are silent for a few moments, and Raven continues. 'Do you remember the story they used to tell, the one about stealing fire?'

Cowboy thinks for a moment. 'You mean the one where the trickster is said to have changed into a rabbit to get close enough to a fire to steal some closely guarded flames so he could bring it back to his grand-mother, who was cold?'

'Yeah, that's the one – except I'm not so sure about the rabbit part of your story. Why do you think my feathers are all black?'

'Anyway, I think your friend there is taking that story too literally. He's getting awfully close to some dangerous things. He might get burned. Does he really think he can transform himself and the legal world around him just because he teaches in a law school? He should be more careful. Look at what he's doing, flirting with these powerful institutions. It's not as if you can come away and not be changed by interacting with them. Just this past year he became a lawyer, after arti-cling for a few months. He's also working with judges and giving con-ferences for them through the National Judicial Institute. He has even completed a contract with, of all things, the Department of Justice.'

Raven stands back and asks his two small guests, 'Just what does he think he is doing? Does he think *he's* the trickster? Transformation is hard. He should leave that job to the professionals. He is dealing with some very dangerous legal institutions. They are not to be fooled with.'

Beatle thinks of his friend's time at UVic law school. He has done a lot since leaving UBC. UVic provided an opportunity for him to become the first chair in Aboriginal law in any Canadian law school. He en-joyed a half-teaching load with some decent in-house research money. He had two other Aboriginal colleagues, and about thirty Indigenous law students were at the school each year. There was also a joint degree program in law and Indigenous governance, a supportive dean, and an Inuit law school that they ran in Iqaluit. Recently, the young man had accepted a six-month sabbatical in Australia. He had also been do-ing many things outside of his job, like working more closely with the country's legal institutions. He was busy. Beatle wondered if his friend was really spending his time in questionable, even dangerous, pursuits.

Did he really think he could change the country's legal institutions and not get hurt?

Beatle tried to catalogue the young man's activities in his mind. First of all, there was the legal profession. Last summer his friend had articled at a small, boutique law firm that practised constitutional law. Many of the lawyers at that firm were changing the law in Canada through their skill and arguments. While it was one of the leading firms in the country, what did he accomplish? Not much, in his opinion. Even though his friend had been a professor for fourteen years, he spent most of his time at the firm writing about obscure *Charter* rights issues. His opinions rarely found their way into pleadings, and the rare times that they did, they were not reflected in the court's judgments. Why should they be? They were actually of little relevance. He had also worked on a few Aboriginal rights cases. These were high-profile cases, but his ideas were way off the map and had little significance for the details of litigation. It looked like he was wasting his time. Even if he decided to devote his entire life to the practice of law and mastered all its detail, he would probably not make much of a difference. The profession was just too stratified and paper-bound to be open to the kinds of broad changes he was suggesting. Change had to come from elsewhere. Beatle wondered if the young man knew it was very unlikely that the profession would accommodate and incorporate Anishinabek ideas any time soon. It looked as though there was nothing of benefit his friend could steal from the Bar and bring back home to keep the fires of his people burning. He had to give Raven that one.

Then, Beatle thought, there was his work with the National Judicial Institute (NJI). The NJI was established in 1988 as an independent, non-profit organization to serve the Canadian judiciary, by planning, coordinating, and delivering judicial education dealing with the law, the craft of judging, and social context. One might think that he'd be able to make a contribution there. After all, the instruction took place in an academic-like setting, where judges would spend three days becoming better informed about Indigenous legal issues. You'd think he'd be at home in such a gathering. He had been doing this for ten years and had spoken to judges in every jurisdiction except Quebec and Prince Edward Island. The judiciary is at the apex of legal institutions in Canada. If you wanted to communicate most directly with those who made the most important decisions, it would seem like a Judicial Education Conference would be the place to go.

Thinking back on all this, Beatle knew that during the conferences the young man felt he was making some progress. Always the good professor, he purposely tried to stay away from giving his own opinions, because he thought the facts of Aboriginal history and the case law principles spoke of the need for justice all by themselves. At the time, his friend probably thought he might make a difference by getting this information before decision-makers. Then, a few months later, Beatle would see him leaf through the Law Reports and read the decision of a judge to which he had spoken. He saw that his young friend sometimes felt gratified by their decisions, but more often he was disappointed and saddened by them. Was he coming to realize that what he said probably didn't have much of an impact on the judiciary, for good or bad? Beatle thought the young man was kidding himself if he believed his short speeches could influence them in any way. He had to admit that Raven scored another one against his friend on this issue.

Finally, there was the Department of Justice. It had a high-sounding mission: to support the minister of justice in working to ensure that Canada is a just and law-abiding society with an accessible, efficient, and fair system of justice; to provide high-quality legal services and counsel to the government and to client departments and agencies; and to promote respect for rights and freedoms, the law, and the Constitution. Many people throughout this organization were honestly committed to achieving these objectives. With over 4,500 employees, it was the biggest law firm in the country. Of all the legal institutions with which his friend could deal with, the department probably enjoyed the most direct access and influence over the development of national legislation, law, and policy. It was the government's law firm. Recently, some of their biggest files had been around Aboriginal issues. It was taking about a quarter of the department's budget. Beatle thought of how this tempted his friend. The young man had been asked to conduct an Aboriginal cultural audit to provide a critical assessment of Aboriginal people's experience at justice, to identify systemic barriers they might encounter, and to acknowledge the best practices to assist in the development of a strategic plan to support the department's goals.

The man had flown across the country and visited eight Canadian cities to meet with over one hundred Aboriginal lawyers and a good number of their managers. His report turned up many positive findings. Aboriginal employees were found in growing numbers at most occupational levels. They were making a difference in management, administration, legislative drafting, policy, litigation, research, alternative dispute resolution, community outreach, and other aspects of departmental service to the public and government. It was heartening. At the same time, the audit turned up some troubling problems. These were heartbreaking. The report identified many barriers Aboriginal employees faced within the department, related to tokenism, racism, discrimination, inappropriate assumptions about employment preferences, negative perceptions about the department, the need for transparency in employment equity, inappropriate job classifications, exclusionary departmental culture and policy, isolation and alienation among Aboriginal employees, language and career development issues, and promotion concerns. There was a lot of anger expressed and tears shed by some of the Aboriginal people he interviewed.

Given these findings, his friend tried to draft a constructive report. It made a series of recommendations to assist in the development of a strategic plan to support the department in achieving its goals. Some of the recommendations included the following:

1 Developing a training program relating to the recruitment of Aboriginal peoples.
2 Overcoming negative departmental perceptions of justice by working with Aboriginal communities and developing relationships with Aboriginal leaders, individuals, and institutions.
3 Being clear with an Aboriginal employee when they are being hired under an employment equity program.
4 Creating an open classification category relating to Aboriginal employees that gives managers some discretion in describing jobs for those who work more directly with Aboriginal communities.
5 Rewarding collective accomplishment and team building for Aboriginal and other employees by noting, highlighting, and giving even higher profile to collective achievements.
6 Encouraging employees and managers to refamiliarize themselves with the Policy on the Prevention of Conflict and Harassment.
7 Utilizing Aboriginal methods of dispute resolution to settle conflict where appropriate.
8 Hiring a person with expertise in a variety of Aboriginal dispute resolution techniques in the Office of Conflict Management.
9 Creating greater Aboriginal awareness through a variety of methods.
10 Formalizing Department of Justice involvement with Aboriginal support mechanisms in other departments.
11 Developing the Advisory Committee on Aboriginal Peoples

(ACAP) as a vehicle to broaden Aboriginal support in the department.
12 Ensuring that managers are aware of Aboriginal language concerns.
13 Offering bilingual bonuses to Aboriginal employees who are required to use an Aboriginal language as part of their job.
14 Facilitating Aboriginal career advancement with a view to having
an Aboriginal Assistant Deputy Attorney General by the end of the
decade.

There had been a lot of consultation and follow-up in the department
after the report was produced. Some excellent people sat on committees
to implement its objectives. Nevertheless, Beatle wasn't very confident
these recommendations would really go to the heart of what his friend
was proposing. Working with government was about more than giving sound advice; it was also about dealing with power, and the young
man just wasn't prepared to play those games. It was hard to transform
entrenched institutions.

Recalling all this, Beatle thought to himself that maybe Raven was
right about the young man. It sounded like his friend was playing with
fire. Beatle thought of the advice and promptings he had tried to give
him over the years. Maybe the young man didn't listen to the little
people any more.

As Beatle ran these things through his mind, Frank Calder came to
the centre of the hall. As the guest of honour for the evening, it was
his turn to speak. Conversations around the room went quiet; the only
sound was the fire crackling in the centre of the room. Dr Calder stood
about five-foot four, and was wearing his Nisga'a button blanket with
a Killer Whale crest spread across the shoulders on his back. On his
head was a cedar bark wreath, and in his hand was a cedar staff with
different stories and clans carved along its length. He raised his arms
in welcome.

Dr Calder began.[2] 'I am very happy to be with you here this evening.
I would like to thank the Coast Salish people for their hospitality and
recognize their stewardship for the territory on which we are gathered.
I would like to thank those who cooked for us this evening, and those
who spoke and drummed and danced. It was beautiful. I would like
to thank the University of Victoria for organizing this conference for
which we are preparing. I would like to thank you for coming and cel-
ebrating with me here this evening. You are my witnesses about what
has happened here at this happy event. I thank you all.'

Dr Calder paused and looked around the four corners of the room, acknowledging with his eyes those in attendance. He smiled and continued, 'As we get ready for the conference tomorrow, I want to say a few words about why the *Calder* case has some importance to me.

'When I went to residential school at Colqulitza around Chilliwack, we had a motto that I have always tried to live by. It was "There is no Backward Step." These are good words, for those of us who believe it. I have held that idea in my mind since 1924. I have tried to remember it. I have tried to apply it. Now, seventy-nine years later, I have heard another motto in connection with the title of this conference: "Let Right Be Done." I also want to remember it. I intend to live by that saying, too. I have tried to live by it even before hearing it today. The *Calder* case is about letting right be done.

'What is right? The *Calder* case isn't just about the Nisga'a. It isn't just about Native people in this country. It's for the whole world. A very distinguished black man from the United States once said that when someone is on your back, holding you down in the gutter, the person on your back is in the gutter, too. That is true. I like the result of the case, a three to three decision. That is symbolic. It is about negotiating on an equal basis. The guy who is holding me down gets off my back and turns around and faces me, and we negotiate face to face. That is the case's result. That's what we did, and that's what we all can do. The Nisga'a negotiated a treaty. It's not perfect, but it lets us get on with building our people and our country. And it's for us, and it's for the whole country.

'I admire the people that are coming to Canada from all around the world. They are working hard. To our eyes, they seem to be leaving their culture, their language, and their ways of life behind. Why do they do this? They do it for one reason – to get a job so that they can live! That's as it should be. As Native people, we shouldn't be left behind. We should work and be prosperous in our own country. We should participate in the economy, get good jobs and build this country.'

Dr Calder shifts his stance and steps closer to the fire. He goes on, 'There is a word going around these days: "globalization." Some are afraid of it. When I went to school, I didn't lose anything. I kept my language. I kept my customs. I kept my chieftainship. I kept my identity. I did this because of my parents, God bless them. They told me to never forget who I was. We should not be afraid of getting involved with others. We can get involved with all those things out there, like lawyers, judges, and governments, and still be ourselves. Someone once asked me if I was afraid of doing the things I have done. I didn't even have to think about how to answer them. My grandparents had prepared me. They taught me. I knew what I had to do. I wasn't nervous when we visited our lawyers, Mr Berger and others, to fight for our land. When we went up to the Supreme Court, I wasn't intimidated by their judges. When I was elected, I wasn't afraid to be a member of the Legislature or Parliament. I didn't go backwards when we talked with the minister of Indian affairs and the prime minister about the issues in which we have been involved.

'Back home they called me the "Little Chief" because I am small. I like that, I can laugh. I may be small, but I have not backed down from what was right. Don't let anyone call themselves bigger than you because they are standing on your back. You shouldn't look down on others just because they are supposedly "little people." Sometimes they have something to say that is good and right. Sometimes the little people have a lot they can teach us.'

Dr Calder once again raises his hands in thanksgiving. The speech ends, and the guests stand and enthusiastically applaud. Drums join in the approval. The room breaks its formality and people visit in groups throughout the hall.

Raven scoffs and turns to leave.

By the fireside, the *maemaegawahsessiwuk*, Beatle and Cowboy, look on with interest, amusement, and approval.

ISKUGAEWIN[1]

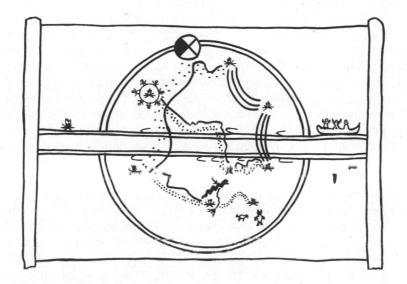

'So, did you learn much out West?' Mishomis asks his grandson. 'I heard you've been doing some travelling.'

The young man looks at his grandfather sitting across the boat from him, baiting a hook with some roe. He deftly winds it around the metal barb with his strong, sinuous fingers. His grandmother Nokomis is beside him, her line in the water. She has caught all the fish today.

The young man responds, 'Yeah, I've been out West: first I was in Australia, then New Zealand, and finally in Minnesota. It's been interesting. I spent about four months teaching for a semester in each place during a research leave. You can pick up a lot when you travel and make comparisons. I think our traditions can travel just as well as any others in the world. You always taught me that many of our laws had relevance beyond the reserve. I'm trying to see how far I can push that idea.'

The old man looks at his grandson and says, 'I've always wanted to go to Australia. Tell me, what did you learn?'

The young man gazes out over the bay to the escarpments beyond. 'When I think about my time "down under," I guess I feel pretty sad. Indigenous people aren't doing very well in that country. When I arrived there, I was shocked to discover that the average Aboriginal man lives twenty-four years less than a non-Aboriginal man. To give you a comparison, the difference in life expectancy between Indigenous and non-Indigenous people in Canada is about ten years less, which is still a cause for concern. In Australia though, the gap is getting worse, while at least in Canada the gap is steadily narrowing. People live longer in Bangladesh or sub-Saharan Africa, once AIDS is factored out, than Indigenous people do in Australia. What's ironic is that Australia is one of the most prosperous countries in the world. I couldn't imagine living in a community where all the Elders are gone, where people over the age of fifty-four are rare. That made me very sad.

'The country is very beautiful, though. When you walk off the plane, the first thing you notice is how different the songs are in the trees. There are parrots, budgies, lorikeets, cockatoos, cockatiels, kookaburras, and so on. Their colours are brilliant, and their voices are so different from anything you would hear over here. Even their crows seem to have a distinctive accent. There were other differences, too. At night, I loved to look up at the stars and see a whole different side of the universe. The Southern Cross is very distinctive. We also saw herds of kangaroos and wallabies in the grasslands. There were lots of lizards, spiders, and snakes when you walk around, too.'

'Did you see any dingoes?' Nokomis asks. 'I hear they have dogs there that are half-wild, half-tame.'

'I don't think I saw one, Nokomis, though you can never be quite sure. They are easily mistaken for other creatures.'

As they bob on light waves in the bay, the late fall wind gently rocks the boat. The leaves have long since fled from the trees, but the sun has been warm today. Some might call it Indian Summer.

'I heard an old story about a Dingo when I was in Canberra,' the young man says. 'It's a little like the way we tell things here. You interested in hearing it?'

'I always love a good yarn,' Mishomis says as he casts his line in the water. 'Do their stories have meanings like ours do? I'd be interested in hearing what they're like.'

'Their stories do have meaning, Mishomis, though I am not always sure I understand them at first. The one about the Dingo sticks in my mind though, probably because it sounded familiar. It's about fire. I think it has something to say about reclamation and regeneration.'

Mishomis focuses his eyes on the nearby shore. A large stump lies on its side with its tangled roots wildly grasping the air.

'So how does this story about the Dingo begin, grandson?' Mishomis asks.

The young man thinks back to the manuscript of the story sitting on his computer screen at home. He has been working on it for some time.

The Far West: Australia

Fire stalks the land, raging through bush, swamp, and desert. The whole continent is dry and virtually starved of its life-giving force. Fire snakes along the forest floor; one spark, and the gum bark kindles a relentless blaze. Green and blue eucalyptus trees burst into flame, their oils mingling in explosive fragrances. Fires twist and meander over wide tropical floodplains, through billabongs and swamps, heading underground if their path is obstructed from above. Desert fires thirst after small shrubs and foliage, stinging the red land as its crimson tails uncoil.

Fires can destroy and create, devastate and renew. They can be deliberately set to clean up the country and manage the land, or they can be used to decimate ecosystems and despoil life's sources. There can be cultural fires and wildfires. Cultural fires are set by the land's traditional owners; wildfires are those sparked by storms and other natural events. Many plants are fire-adapted, and thus actually depend on fire for the completion of their life cycle. Other plants are fire sensitive, and would suffer greatly if caught in a huge firestorm.[2] Indigenous Australians and Canadians know about fire. They have used it to cultivate their homelands for centuries.[3]

Indigenous Australians and Canadians know about another kind of fire, a heat so intense that it can burn both heart and home: colonialism. It has been used to destroy, devastate, and despoil. Like a wildfire it has swept across the land, damaging those caught in its path. It's time to reverse this trend, and seek for places where small, controlled, cultural fires can be set to regenerate the land and its people. A properly set fire can cause long-dormant fruits and seeds to germinate and take root in their natural habitat. Proper burning requires detailed knowledge of the terrain and a range of local factors such as prevailing winds, plant communities, and the fire history of particular places.[4]

Nanabush and Dingo stalk the land, and look for ways to steal fire. They head west, towards burning bright skies.

Remembering the gist of his writing, the young man summarizes the manuscript's beginning for his grandparents. He tells them about wild and cultural fires. He talks about colonialism and Nanabush and Dingo wanting to start fires. Upon hearing the idea, Nokomis smiles at his words: 'That's a good story, grandson; I think it starts well. Is there more? I'm also interested to hear more about where you visited.' Nokomis is reeling in a fish as she asks the question. She has caught another whitefish; it's her sixth one today.

Her grandson shakes his head at her, and smiles in disbelief. She could always out-fish everyone. Answering her question, he begins. 'Well, my trip started out in Canberra; I probably heard the beginning of the story there. I was the inaugural international visiting fellow at AIATSIS. I can't remember what the acronym stands for. I think its Australian Institute of Aboriginal and Torres Strait Islander Studies. There's a lot of people who visit the place; they are all Indigenous or work closely with Indigenous people and their issues. Through their work they tell stories, produce videos, write books, research land claims, record languages and songs, compile genealogies; all sorts of things. They are involved in some really fascinating stuff. It's a great institution. They should initiate something like AIATSIS in Canada. It was set up under a federal statute in the early 1960s to promote an understanding of Australian Indigenous cultures, past and present. They have a beautiful new building on the shores of Lake Burley-Griffith, right next to the Australian National Museum. Its library and archive house the world's most extensive collection of information about Australian Aboriginal and Torres Strait Islander peoples. I believe there are over one hundred people who work there. They are led by a council of important Indigenous leaders, and they make important contributions to keep Indigenous culture prominent in national life. Anyway, I'm pretty sure that the Dingo story came from someone who presented a seminar there one day. It's about a Dingo who chases a snake to try and steal fire.'

As he remembers the story's connection to AIATSIS, the work on his computer once again jumps into his mind.

Ngunawal Country

Nanabush and Dingo race through the land, twisting and turning, chasing after Serpent carrying fire in his mouth. They snake through Goulburn, Queanbeyan, Yass, Wee Jasper, and the Snowy Mountains before plunging through the earth at Yarrangobilly. They arrive in Canberra, the Australian Capital Territory. The surrounding hills are mostly barren, having been washed clean by flames. The only remaining vegetation is the fire-resistant native gum trees. The pine trees introduced to the area upon colonization have been burnt beyond regeneration. They will not be planted in the region again, because they are an excessive drain on the water table. They are inefficient users of the resources compared to the Indigenous trees. Their passing leaves huge, black scars on the land. Their corpse-like stumps and trunks make the land unusable and impenetrable.

Something drops in the water behind them, shattering its surface, and breaking the young man's concentration. Mishomis focuses his attention on a spot about fifteen feet off the boat's starboard side, watching the ripples spread outward. A moment passes in silence. Suddenly his pole twitches and then jerks and bends towards the water, and the line starts spooling off the reel. The three of them watch with interest. After a few seconds Nokomis says, 'Let it run,' just as Mishomis jams the reel. The line snaps, and the rod straightens. Mishomis looks up and Nokomis smiles at him. 'Glad to see you're feeding the fish,' she says.

Mishomis gives her a friendly scowl, and looks at his grandson. 'You were saying something about Dingo chasing a snake and trying to steal fire?'

The young man returns to his thoughts and gathers them together before he speaks aloud. 'A long time ago, there was a big ceremony going on in Australia's centre. All the animals were there: kangaroo, lizard, wombat, turtle, crocodile, hawk, echidna, koala, dingo, snake, and all the others. They were talking about some new white animals on the coast that had been killing them. They were talking about what to do. Some wanted to befriend them, share the land, and give them gifts. Others wanted to drive them back into the sea. They talked for days and days. No one slept. Eventually they arrived at a decision; they decided to give the newcomers fire. It was a compromise decision, because fire could be a blessing or a curse, depending on how it was used. They wanted to see how wise the newcomers would be with the land.

'At the very moment the decision was announced, the serpent sprung from the group and stole the fire around which they had gathered. It was their only fire. The serpent headed towards what is now Canberra and then worked his way to the East Coast by the sea. Dingo gave chase. They carved out the rivers and valleys through their journeys. After a while, they ended up in the area that became Sydney.'

As he is speaking, the young man feels a small tug on his line and pauses for a moment. The action does not repeat itself. At that point, Nokomis interjects, 'Isn't Sydney the place where you were based when you were in Australia?'

'That's where I was teaching, but I found myself all over the country,' the young man replies. 'Sydney was something of a home base, however. We lived in an inner city suburb called Newtown, but travelled extensively. I was actually a visiting professor at the University of New South Wales, or UNSW. It's a pretty good institution. I co-taught a course in Australian Indigenous Rights with my friend Garth, and got involved with some of the activities around the school. UNSW has focused on Indigenous issues for quite a few years, so there was a lot to do. They have a summer pre-law course for Indigenous students, a fledgling academic and cultural support program, an Aboriginal Law Reporter, and an Indigenous Law Bulletin. They also do some good work out in the communities through clinics, conferences, and seminars. For a long time, it was probably the best place for Indigenous people to study the law in the country. I think it might be in the process of being overtaken by another school, the University of Technology Sydney, where a bright young Indigenous woman teaches. There is a House of Learning at UTS called Jumbunna that coordinates research, publications, and course activities. I was very impressed. Like I said though, I used Sydney as a home base, and ended up travelling around the country.'

As he thinks about the schools, the young man once again loses himself in his thoughts. He absent-mindedly notes the few clouds that linger at the edge of the horizon. The water gently ripples in the late autumn breeze. The boat slowly circles, its stone anchor resting on the bottom of the bay. Nokomis and Mishomis let the young man's thoughts unwind for a few minutes as they drift in place. With the sun reflecting off the four escarpments lining the peninsula, they feel content to let the silence stretch on. The young man's thoughts return to his manuscript:

Cadigal Country

Nanabush and Dingo follow the serpent down the Hawkesbury, past the Blue Mountains, through Katoomba, down to Woy Woy. They turn and then wind their way along the coast before pausing at La Perouse. At Botany Bay, Nanabush has a word with Dingo. 'We can't chase this thing all over the countryside; I've got an idea. We have to make a plan. We're at a standstill. Let's see if we can work together to get that fire.'

Nanabush and Dingo whisper back and forth between one another for a few minutes. Serpent takes the moment to catch his breath, looking on from the airport near the back of the bay. When they are finished, Nanabush yells across the water, 'Ahnii snake, ginebig, you are pretty fast. Dingo and I are having a hard time catching you. We didn't think you'd be so wily. You are a worthy opponent. You've got something we want – that fire there in your mouth. We need it to make the fires of our people brighter. I've got a proposition for you. We could go around and around like this day after day, and all of us could get tired, or we can have a contest. If we just keep chasing you, we'll both get exhausted; that seems like a waste of time. Why don't we settle this another way? I propose a challenge, a test of skill, a wager, a bet. That seems to be the only thing fair to do, given that we are so evenly matched.'

The serpent does not move, nor does he make a sound. The fire burns brightly from the stick in his mouth.

After a few moments Nanabush calls out, 'Good, I see you're not racing off. I'll take that as agreement to our challenge. Here's what we're going to do. We're going to have a jumping contest. Whoever can leap the farthest wins the fire. The winner gets all it represents. We'll jump north, and see where we land. But there's just one thing. We need to level the playing field. It's obvious that we're different from one another. We can't act as if these differences don't matter. Dingo and I have legs and you don't. Even though you are so much longer than us and have a great spring in your coils, we think our legs are an advantage. That's not fair, because it makes us unequal. Just to show you our good faith, we'll jump from here. We'll give you a break; you can get a head start and jump from the Parramatta River.'

The snake looks on with passive black eyes and nods its agreement.

Nanabush and Dingo smile. They transform themselves. Kangaroo legs protrude from their torsos. They jump.

Serpent makes his way to the Paramatta, past Coogee, Bondi, and on to the Opera House, and the Quays. He perches on the Harbour Bridge, tightly coils himself, and springs northward.

After a few long, lazy minutes, Mishomis breaks the silence: 'So, where did you find yourself while you were in Australia?' he asks. Upon hearing the question, the young man pushes his fingers through the tackle box searching for his favourite bait, a twisted trickster to fool the fish. He takes a red-and-white-striped lure from the tray, and ties it around the end of his line. He looks up at his grandparents and resumes the conversation. 'My first real trip outside the Canberra-Sydney corridor was to Brisbane. I was invited to speak at the University of Queensland. I have a former graduate student who teaches in the law school there. UQ is one of the sandstone schools in Australia, kind of like the Ivy League schools in the U.S. The entire university is centred on a large quadrangle, surrounded by ornately carved sandstone buildings. It rests on the banks of the Brisbane River.

'I also visited the Aboriginal and Torres Strait Islanders Studies Unit when I was in Brisbane. It's part of the university, and has been a centre of excellence in Aboriginal and Torres Strait Islander issues for over twenty years. The unit maintains a committed system of personal and academic support for Indigenous students. They provide over thirty interdisciplinary courses dealing with Indigenous issues. They offer an access program, a double major in Indigenous studies, and they help facilitate student access to ATAS (Aboriginal tutorial assistance scheme) and ABSTUDY (government funding Aboriginal educational assistance scheme). They publish the Australian Journal of Indigenous Education, and other occasional monographs and papers.

'The unit's course coordinator is a wonderful man. He made sure I ate some traditional food while I was there. I think his daughter spent the better part of the day finding some mud crabs for me. It was delicious. He also showed me where Rainbow Serpent lay on the university grounds. Rainbow Serpent created the land in their dreamtime. It was a great honour to hear of their genesis. I also met the deputy director of the unit. She works at the highest levels of the Reconciliation Movement in the country. Both the coordinator and director are also AIATSIS council directors. They are the type of people who really drive Indigenous issues in Australia, and it was great to meet them. I enjoyed their hospitality.

'There were some awkward moments in Queensland, though. One night, after one of my talks, we went to a private restaurant. The evening had attracted an eclectic crowd of judges, lawyers, academics, Indigenous community activists, and Aboriginal community people. But when we gathered to socialize, the event was very racially stratified. There was a palpable divide – black people visited and sat on one side of the room, and white people did the same on the other. The divide may have also been a class thing. It made me very sad. You could see some of the troubles the country encounters reflected in our little dinner.

'It wasn't long again before I was on the road, but the image of that evening has never left me. I was about to encounter even more serious divides.' Recalling the tension, the young man's thoughts once again turn to his work.

Yuggera/Waka Waka Country

A large shadow darkens and passes over the Brisbane River. Nanabush and Dingo land at the base of Mount Coot-tha, pushing the slope higher with their powerful legs. Serpent lands at the airport, a few miles to the north. Nanabush and Dingo are infuriated, having lost their wager. Their tricks did not give them the advantage they hoped for. They scramble down the river to the sea. They find Serpent sunning himself on the runway, fire stick clasped firmly between his jaws. He sleepily basks in its warmth. They look on in jealousy.

'Well, you won that one all right,' Nanabush calls out to his opponent in a jaunty tone, trying to hide his annoyance. 'You've got some powerful muscles along that skinny spine of yours; I'll give you that. I underestimated you. Your difference was probably not the disadvantage we thought it was. We shouldn't have given you that head start, don't you think? I bet you couldn't have beaten us otherwise.'

Dingo and Nanabush confer with each other for a few moments. A firetruck's siren wails in the distance, drawing closer as they speak. When they are finished, Nanabush calls out across the runways.

'Serpent, ginebig, let's try that one more time. Once again we'll see who can jump the farthest north, but this time no one gets a head start. The standards will be the same; there'll be no differences between us. It was probably unfair before, unequal. Let's be equal. What do you say?'

Serpent opens one eye and gazes down the landing strip. He slowly nods his head in the affirmative.

Nanabush and Dingo smile. Nanabush transforms himself into a snake and Dingo jumps on his back. They coil, spring and jump; a split second later serpent follows.

Thinking of his grandfather's question about his travels, the young man can't stop his earlier writings from occupying his mind. From where they are floating, the old Indian Agent's house is clearly visible through the trees on one side of the bay, the leaves long having given up their cover. The remains of his great-grandfather's house are in full view on the other side of the water. Floating in the divide, caught between their pull, the young man looks at his grandparents. He continues his conversation.

'Like I said, when I left Brisbane I encountered even more severe separation and segregation than in Queensland. I went to Darwin in the Northern Territory, a very humid place with lots of beautiful, tropical flowers. They had Aboriginal reserves there, somewhat like we do back here. In Darwin, the poor people lived on the reserves and the rich people lived everywhere else. Actually it's wasn't quite that bad; there are some middle-class people in Darwin who are Indigenous. In fact, there seemed to be a decent number of them. But from what I could see, for every well-off Indigenous person in town, there were two or more that were homeless. There were a lot of "blackfellas," as they call themselves, homeless in the public parks. There were signs on the public lawns from the local Aboriginal council proclaiming Larrikia protocols. These protocols basically asked the park dwellers to move on, saying it wasn't respectful of Larrikia law for them to loiter on their land without permission, which I guess it wasn't. Something felt wrong about the whole thing though, middle-class and poor Aboriginal people, asking even poorer Aboriginal people to move along, so that the "whitefellas" could enjoy public spaces in peace.

'Well, after walking around downtown, I went up to the university to give a speech. It was a funny place. They were focusing on building a strong business studies program, which is great in and of itself. What was not so great is that this development seemed to be occurring at the same time they were de-emphasizing Indigenous Studies. At least that's the impression I got from the people I visited with who taught there. I could be wrong, but there they were, in the centre of one of the most densely populated Indigenous places in Australia, and the university was changing its name to someone associated with Social Darwinism. It was losing some of the nation's best Indigenous scholars. It seemed like a misdirected institutional vision to me. I think you could develop a good program in business studies while maintaining historical strengths in Indigenous studies. Anyway, I am getting distracted. I was telling you the story about the Dingo.'

The young man looks apologetically at his grandmother and grandfather. 'I am going off on a tangent. Sorry about that, I know you wanted to hear about Dingo.'

His grandmother looks back at him and smiles. 'Don't worry, grandson. From what you said, it sounds like you are telling us about Dingo. He seems to be every bit as cunning as Nanabush.'

Hearing his grandmother's reference to Nanabush sends the young man's mind back to his manuscript. He always felt the constant press of his writing when he was in the midst of a book. It was hard to leave the details alone, even when you were miles away from a keyboard.

Larrakia Country

Lush coastal rainforest gives way to dry bush and scrub. Broken mountains and scattered rocks turn into flat, dry plains of red sand and small shrubs. Taroom to Tambo, Mount Isa to Alice Springs, Dingo rides Nanabush, bouncing from place to place. Serpent flies before them, over Tennant Creek, Katherine, Batchelor, and Darwin, never touching the ground. For him, travelling through country is like travelling through time.[5]

Nanabush and Dingo land to the south of Serpent.

Nanabush is furious. Dingo dismounts and they confront their adversary.

'How did you do that?' he storms. 'You are not playing fair. There is no way you could jump all that way without touching down. What are you not telling us?'

Serpent wordlessly breathes out in response, the flames in his mouth flickering with each whisper. Nanabush and Dingo strain to hear.

'It's obvious that you are faster and stronger than us,' Nanabush responds. We are not really equal even if we try to be the same as you. You have tricked us. You can travel over the land and through the air much quicker than we could ever hope, even if we adopt your form. We need true equality. We need to understand your secrets; we need to be like you in more than just form. We need to do exactly what you do. Perhaps you can teach us how you do it; how do you cover the land as you do?'

They listen closely for a response, but are only met with silence. Serpent turns from his foes and races west, spreading flames from the stick in his mouth as he slides along the ground. His actions divide, separating the life from the land.

Leaving his writings again for a moment, the young man casts behind him. Being with his grandparents always reminds him of when he was young. Time seemed so slow back then, as if it would never end. Those long hours have stretched into years, bringing them to this place. He watches while Nokomis adjusts her scarf and Mishomis pulls his jacket more tightly around his neck. He sees the deep lines on their faces and notes their movements are getting slower. Time does not end, it weathers and changes. He feels glad he invited them out here today. Those long, slow days of youth have raced away. He treasures moments like these which suspend its rush.

Nokomis catches his eye and continues their conversation. 'It's funny how the trickster finds his way round the world. Life is full of charm and cunning, wisdom and foolishness, kindness and mean tricks. Australia seems no different.'

'That's true, Nokomis. Changes can come quickly, even though they're imperceptible at the time. When I was in Perth, I visited an old friend who used to teach in Saskatchewan. He went to Australia so full of hope. The *Mabo* case had just been released. It was a breakthrough decision. After two hundred years, Australian legal institutions finally recognized Indigenous land rights. The High Court held that it was unjust and racially discriminatory to perpetuate the idea that Australia had been *terra nullius* – empty land – when it was settled by convicts from Great Britain. They wrote that Native title finds its origins and content in the people's traditional laws, and could be protected in contemporary law. My friend has now been in Western Australia for over a decade, and has become almost completely disillusioned with the Australian legal establishment. He finds no equality in their law. Since 1992, things have gone mostly backward. He doesn't see much hope for the future. The Commonwealth Parliament has extinguished a broad range of Native title interests. The states are recalcitrant and block Native title at every step. The courts have made the proof of Native title exceedingly difficult. The same judgment that raised such high hopes contained germs of further dispossession for Indigenous peoples.

'I also found it interesting to hear him talk about his law school. He thinks too many students treat the place more like a country club than a serious educational institution. He finds some of his colleagues are inclined to put minimal hours into their teaching so that they can devote more of their time to consulting or practising law off the sides of their desks. The rest are more likely to golf and go to the beach than worry about the tough challenges facing the world. He doesn't know what to do. All the while, Indigenous rights are slowly being extinguished.'

Noonygar Country

Serpent twists through the Kimberleys, passing through Fitzroy Crossing to Broom. Winding along the coast, he slips past Dampier and Shark Bay. The Indian Ocean is bright and vast; wave after wave pounds at the beaches, washing sands over endless shores. Ships become more frequent the farther south he travels. He spies Rottnest Island and knows he is near his destination. Spotting Fremantle, he enters the Swan River and meanders along its length. Arriving at Perth, he sees glass and concrete towers mirror the blazing sun. Serpent settles into their reflections.

Nanabush and Dingo arrive exhausted. They are near their wits' end. Equality doesn't seem to work. They decide to take another approach.

Nanabush and Dingo transform themselves into lawyers and slither into the central business district. They meet with barristers in their chambers and consult with representatives at the Native Title Tribunal. They find a lot of support for their case; there seems to be a whole industry that will encourage their action. They do some research, sign some documents, and march down Adelaide Terrace. They launch a Native Title Claim at the registry office, claiming the fire in Serpent's mouth. Their argument is that fire belongs to Dingo and his people because he is part of a recognizable group that had associations with the fire in the territory of Australia prior to the arrival of others. Dingo claims further that he has traditional laws and customs relative to fire in Australia that give rise to his claim, and that he has continued to hold Native title to fire in Australia in accordance with these traditional laws and customs.

Serpent is compelled to stay in Perth while the matter is brought to trial.

When the matter comes before Federal Court, Dingo loses his case. The judge rules that Australia's territory is too large an area for him to make a recognizable claim. Dingo needs to be more precise and prove his rights over a particular bounded area. Without such precision, there is the risk that he could usurp the rights of other potential claimants. The Court also finds that while Dingo may have had traditional laws about fire in the past, he was unable to show that he still continued to hold fire in accordance with those traditional laws and customs. In particular, the Court finds that Dingo lost legal connection with fire in accordance with traditional laws when fire was stolen by Serpent.

Dingo and Nanabush understand the act they are complaining about, the stolen fire, is the very act which defeats their claim. They have to admit the cleverness of this logic. It goes round and round in circles; they couldn't have done a better job themselves.

With the judgment rendered, Serpent flees the witness box.

Casting off wigs and black robes, Nanabush and Dingo follow in hot pursuit.

The young man is roused from his thoughts as the boat lands with a thud. He kills the motor and jumps into the shallow water, pulling it onto the shore. Nokomis throws him a rope, and he ties it to a small stump just off the beach. He returns to steady the boat as his grandparents disembark. When they are safely ashore, he reaches into the boat and gathers an armful of fishing tackle. He makes a pile on the shore before returning for the fish. Eight *addikmaegoossuk*, all caught by his grandmother, are hauled out of the vessel. He hands them to his grandfather to prepare while he cleans out the boat.

Mishomis looks at the fish, holding one at arm's length as he considers the catch. 'These are very beautiful creatures: long body, large, silver-white scales, dark fins, and a greenish-blue back. *Addikmeg*, caribou of the sea, whitefish. They have fed our people for generations. We should be very grateful they have chosen to feed us tonight.' Mishomis takes out his knife and splits the belly of the first fish open. Separating flesh from the bone, he throws its guts in the water as the seagulls circle, screech, and dive.

'Did you eat any good fish when you were in Australia, grandson?' Mishomis asks.

'They had something called Barramundi, which I enjoyed. In fact, there was a number of fish that I really liked which I had never heard of before. I can't remember their names, though.'

Nokomis walks along the shore, gathering sticks to prepare a fire. When she is finished, a stack of old driftwood and twigs lie piled in a circle of stones.

'I do remember that we had this great dinner in Adelaide one evening, in South Australia,' the young man goes on. 'They served all kinds of fish. It was a feast. We were gathered at a hotel in a place called Glenelg on Holdfast Bay. I remember the place's name because Lord Glenelg was partly responsible for one of the treaties signed by great-great grandpa. Glenelg was a British Colonial Agent at the time, and had responsibility for Aboriginal affairs in the colonies. The world seemed like a smaller place when I was there on that beach. I considered how two groups of Indigenous peoples so far apart and on the opposite sides of the world could be joined by a common historical figure.'

Nokomis looks up from her work. 'What were you doing in Adelaide? Did you just travel the country to eat fish?'

'I was invited to give the Eddie Mabo Memorial Lecture at the Annual Native Title Conference. It was organized by AIATSIS and the Aboriginal Land Rights Movement in South Australia. I got to meet Eddie Mabo's wife; her husband was the one who brought the case. He passed away a few years ago, but she is still going strong. She is a very warm and dignified person. The Torres Strait Islander people have much of which they can be proud. I also met Aboriginal people from all over the continent at the conference. Each year it is held in a different part of the country, and someone gives a keynote speech to introduce the theme. That was my role. The conference is an important institution for land councils, communities, activists, governments, lawyers, academics, and others interested in Indigenous rights.

'The title of my talk was "Practical Recolonization." It was a twist on the government's attempt to force "Practical Reconciliation" on Indigenous peoples in Australia. I wanted to show how I thought the government's proposals for practical reconciliation really amounted to continued non-Indigenous colonization. I had been thinking of my recurring dreams about the four hills, and the speech was my attempt to discuss Indigenous agency in an Indigenous context. I hope they caught the gist of it. It can be difficult sometimes, working in another country like Australia. There are enough similarities to enjoy a level of comfort, but enough differences to prompt questions about your assumptions. You can't take things for granted. I always said speaking in Australia was a little like driving on the other side of the road there. You feel confident until you come to a corner and have to consciously remember which lane you should turn into. Your intuition sometimes fails you. It's like that when you try to take your experiences with Indigenous issues into another country.

'Anyway, the idea behind my talk was that Indigenous peoples should consider whether they wanted to resettle their country and re-inscribe their values over the sociopolitical landscape. Indigenous Australians actually own 18 per cent of the land base, although they are only 1 per cent of the population. This seems like a good result, unless you remember that their land is probably the most economically unproductive in the nation, and that they were once 100 per cent of the population and owned 100 per cent of the land base. The separation from their homelands and their loss of resources has had dramatic consequences for their ways of life, languages, and culture. I know the significance of having a strong connection to home, here at the Cape. I can't imagine how devastating it must be for some of those people not to enjoy that connection.

'I don't think Native title cases and legislation will re-establish their connections, from what I read and experienced. So my talk was meant to prompt some discussion about whether Indigenous peoples in Australia could undertake some kind of process of recolonization, practically speaking. Take direct action. Colonization has worked for non-Indigenous people, as they have created powerful systems and resettled on Indigenous lands to justify their lifestyles. I wondered if Indigenous peoples were interested in appropriating the language of equality in that country, or showing its hypocrisy, by arguing that they have a right to physically and intellectually recolonize the country, just like non-Indigenous people have tried to do and are doing. There were lots of twists and turns in my argument, and it's hard to remember the details. In the final analysis, my biggest goal was to try and bring a different perspective to their situation as an Indigenous person from another country. Sometimes another perspective can give you a fresh view on an issue. I'm not even sure how serious I was about the process I was advocating, though I was serious about the result. I believe in regeneration, and sometimes you have to turn up the heat to see this occur.

'It's like that story about the Dingo I was telling you about. Dingo wanted to steal fire for a purpose. I think Indigenous people should seek for places where small, controlled, cultural fires can be set to regenerate our lands and peoples. Properly set fires can cause a long-dormant idea to germinate and take root in its original habitat. Proper burning requires detailed knowledge of the terrain and a range of local factors, such as prevailing winds, communities, and the history of particular places. I think we should use that knowledge before we lose it.'

Mishomis guts the last fish and hauls them over the rocks. He places them on a makeshift rack Nokomis has built in the stone circle surrounding the fire pit. Nokomis reaches down and helps her husband arrange them on the green wood. When they are nearly finished, she turns to her husband and says, 'I think that we should eat the fish before we lose it. We'd better hurry up. Our grandson is speechifying again, and those seagulls out there are getting awfully bold, now that they have almost finished their meal. They might claim these fish for themselves if we're not careful. Discovery can be awfully hard to dispute.'

Kaurna Country

The wind is hot off the Indian Ocean. Dust rises in clouds and sweeps over the Nullarbor Plain, a broad, treeless expanse. Through Albany, Esperance, Eyre, and Ceduna, Serpent, Nanabush, and Dingo chase across the Great Australian Bight. Nanabush clips the serpent. A rough wound opens on the snake's back and washes blood of red, black, and yellow over his entire body. Serpent loses strength, and his long form crashes into the Spencer Gulf, washing the land to Lake Eyre. Serpent is injured, and crawls over the Flinder's Range. Weakened, he lays down in Adelaide at Encounter Bay, his body twisting behind the hills across the Murray-Darling watershed.

Nanabush and Dingo approach Serpent with caution. They stand in the water off the shore.

Nanabush calls out, 'Ginebig. I see I hurt you. I hope you are OK. I didn't mean to hurt you badly. It looks like you need some help.' Nanabush turns from Serpent and searches through his backback. Pulling out a string of bois blanc, twisted cedar rope, he holds it up to the snake. 'See this? It can help you. I once had a great cut across my backside, and I sewed it up with this.' Nanabush pulls it by the yard through his fingers to demonstrate its length. 'It was made by my grandmother, and will hold anything. Let me sew you up.'

Serpent watches Nanabush and Dingo. Uncontrollably his body writhes with the pain of the rough cut.

Nanabush comes closer.

'I will help you, just let me grab this stick you're holding to thread the rope. I promise you will feel better once you're sewn up.'

Serpent thrashes in place without strength to move further.

Nanabush touches the snake's tongue.

'There, it's all right, you'll see.'

Nanabush grabs the stick from the snake's mouth. The fire burns brightly on one end. With one deft move, Nanabush threads the rope and lifts the stick in the air. Then, plunging it through Serpent's back, he knits the skin together with a great pull. He repeats this action across the length of the gash, closing the wound.

When he is finished, he tosses the stick to Dingo. They take off along the coast.

With thoughts trailing from his writing – from southern Australia to his grandparents – the young man watches his grandfather build a fire. A fragile tendril of smoke curls over the wood, smudging the area before it. Dried leaves and needles mesh in a smouldering heap in the circle's centre. Mishomis leans over the glowing embers and cups his hands around his mouth. With short, focused puffs, he breathes life into the fire. As he steps back, flames burst from the mound and begin to consume the twisted wood. Nokomis, Mishomis, and their grandson sit around the fire, on the reserve, watching the blaze grow stronger.

Nokomis looks through the flames at her grandson. 'So how did that story about Dingo end? You never finished it. You told us about how all the animals had agreed to give fire to the newcomers to see how it would be used. Serpent stole the fire just as they made their decision, placed it is his mouth, and went chasing across the land. How does the story finish?'

'Oh yeah, I forgot to let you know how it turned out. Let me tell you how the story ends.'

Wurundjeri Country

Dingo passes through Kangaroo Island, Mildura, Swan Hills, the Twelve Apostles, and Geelong. He stops in Melbourne. He pants in great gasps along the shores of the Yarra River, trying to catch his breath. Nanabush is nowhere to be seen; he left him in the dust. Rainbow Serpent is not around; he lay dreaming, somewhere back on the land.

Dingo is mesmerized by the fire stick burning brightly in his paws. It is very hot, but there is no smoke. You can tell it is a powerful fire by the height of the flames, and the way its little wings break away from the main blaze.[6]

He wonders what to do next. He sees three choices.

He could fulfil the wishes of the council and give fire to the newcomers. Knowing what they know, would they renew or devastate the country? He is not confident they would treat the land well.

On the other hand, he could return the fire to his people. They could convene another council and decide a new course of action. Would they still be capable of gathering and making decisions? It was a long time since Serpent stole the fire.

Or he could act himself and use his own agency. In that case, he could place the torch against the hills to the north of the city. Dingo knows the prevailing winds, communities, and fire history in this place. He is a traditional owner and has a responsibility to take care of the land.

Should he run, return to council, or restore?

He makes a decision, takes the fire, and sets it against the wind. He watches it run. He can tell it's running towards the west from that little thing on the right. It's the land's traditional law, reignited. It will regenerate what has been wasted. He can see the fire leaning towards the left. The flame is lying down and quickly running.

PART FOUR: BEEBON

Ideas: The Fourth Hill

MAUZ-AUBINDUMOOWIN[1]

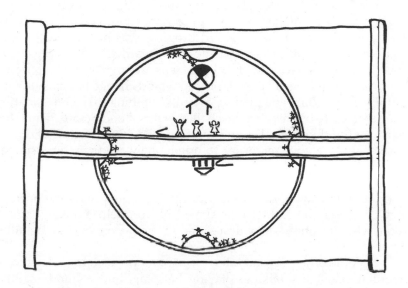

As night fell, the young man's thoughts once again returned to his recurring dream. He had the ability to return to a previous night's thoughts, if he focused his mind on them as his head touched his pillow. His mother and father had taught him that dreams were among the most important experiences he would have on this earth. They could provide guidance and direction, if properly remembered. As a result, for most of his young life, the first question his parents would ask him each morning was, 'What did you dream last night?' The reflections prompted by these repeated inquiries gave him the interest and discipline to hold a night's fading visions more clearly in his mind. He had taught himself how to learn from what he thought about when he was asleep. Now, as he fell into a deep sleep, a familiar dream pattern repeated itself. In this dream, he saw people scrambling up and down the faces of four rugged hills. When he looked closer, he noticed each hill seemed to have

different groups of people trying to scale its heights.[2] This often left him
feeling perplexed.

The first hill, to the east, was covered with very small people. Many
were weeping and crying; some were covered in blood, or lay lifeless
at the base. The foot of the hill where they were piled was shrouded
in darkness. The shadows and twisted heap made it hard to see how
many were gathered there in death, or life. A bit higher, other tiny bodies could be seen crawling over rocks and spring scrub, determinedly
edging their way higher over rough terrain. Knees were scraped and
hands were raw, but their upward progress was noticeable. At other
points, it was possible to see some totter forward on wobbly legs. They
make their way forward with halting steps and the tender help from a
few around them. Small bits of tobacco would change hands in thanks.
Some were laughing and playing, joyfully climbing to their destination.
They seemed to be enjoying the challenge that stood before them. They
learned from their mistakes and carefully watched those around them
to see how to go on. Yet, every so often, one would trip, or lose their
hold on the hill, and tumble and scrape to the bottom. Others would be
pushed down, and suffer a similar fate. A few had reached the top, and
stood in the yellow glow of the morning sun. Surveying the horizon,
they could see three other hills spread before them. Looking curious
about what lay ahead, they descended the slope, onward to the hill in
the south.

The people on the second hill were a lot more boisterous. They were
wrestling, excitedly talking, playing ball, tag, and a hundred other
games. The man thought he recognized a few faces from the first hill,
but they seemed somehow different now. Once again, a great throng
was gathered at the bottom. There was such a number that people kept
getting pushed down and trampled in the race to climb the hill. Their
close confines under the hot, humid sun made it look unbearable. The
numbers thinned as the hill rose. Scanning the hill, the man observed
a group chasing a young deer. The arrows they slung widely missed
their mark. Attempts to stalk and surprise the deer were hindered by
taunts and teasing as they chased it through the cedars. Many seemed
to have lost interest in what lay on the hilltop. Some suddenly disappeared from the hill, ending their journey in mid-stride. Others tired
of the chase, and headed out on their own. They could be seen quietly snaring rabbits, or pausing at certain fishing holes as they made
their way forward. They contended with deep canyons, sparse rivers,
and a jagged red landscape as they moved on. Their fight for survival

strengthened those behind them. The few who made the summit could once again be seen gazing at what lay ahead. They, too, made their way down and forward to the hill to the west.

On the third hill, a good-sized crowd surrounded the base. Though fewer in numbers than those at the foot of the first and second hills, they nevertheless managed to cover much of the available space at the bottom. Every once in a while, the man observed that some would break free of the group and start their climb upward. People could be seen walking together, supporting and helping each other over the black expanse of the endless, sage-covered hill. Others struck out alone, pressed onward, and built strength as they overcame the obstacles strewn on their path. At higher elevations, the man could sometimes hear violent fights and see alternating displays of anger and neglect, charm and cunning, kindness and mean tricks. These outbursts could become so loud they would wrack an entire section of the rise. Their strong words seemed perfectly blended with the vivid colours of the autumn flora. He saw that conflict caused some to eventually turn away from their partners. Others discovered companionship for the first time, or took up with another partner and made their journey onwards with renewed determination. Some pushed forward, knocking down others as they went, while still others would gently take the hand of a fallen comrade as they scrambled up the rough face of the hill. In thinning numbers, a few would eventually find themselves at the peak. Reflectively, they could be seen looking backward at the ground they had covered, and then turning their faces forward to the last hill in the distance.

The fourth hill to the north was very quiet, even at its base. It was peaceful. There were many fewer people here than at the foot of the other hills. Thick with snow, its stark white facade made it seem even calmer in its stillness. Its figures walked silently, slowly struggling against the deep gravity of the incline. The man saw that some collapsed without any apparent reason. Others fell, got up, fell again, and got up again, repeating this action as they fought their way forward. Individuals would watch helplessly as partners crumpled beside them, finally unable to move any further. When this happened there would be a long pause, as the stronger one knelt by the weaker and said tearful goodbyes, before ultimately standing again and bowing even more deeply at the gradient before them. Near the pinnacle of the northern hill, its upper reaches were dappled with sunlight. Strains of gentle laughter and quiet whispers filled the air. Sweetgrass smoke curled and blended with the breeze. The people standing on the crown of this last hill wore the lines and furrows of the terrain they crossed. The white of the stone-ashen sky seemed to adorn their heads, as if they had been purified through their experiences.

Then the dream faded.

Upon waking, as usual the young man wondered what it all meant. Looking up at the ceiling, he thought of the images he had seen. He pondered their significance. Try as he might, he couldn't figure it all out. Then he thought of his Nokomis and Mishomis again. They had spoken about this before, and he knew they were willing to help. In one swift motion, he swung his legs out of bed and rested his feet on the rough, wood-hewn floor. Pausing for a moment, his breath gathered in small clouds around him. The air seemed still, and he noticed a touch of frost on the windows. Winter had finally arrived. If I hurry, I can help them with their fire, he thought, and then I can ask them about my dream again. Scurrying around the cabin, he quickly dressed and made his way out the door, along the diamond-snow gravelled path. When he arrived at his grandparent's place, his Nokomis and Mishomis were just stirring from their night's sleep. The young man gathered a few small logs from their woodpile, split them, and let himself in. Crouching at the woodstove, he could see his Nokomis and Mishomis talking in the other room. As the fire crackled and grew in the stove, his grandparents joined him.

'*Ahnee*! Did you sleep well? *Kemauh*?'

'*Eha. Ahneesh ae-izhi-bimaudiziyin.*'

'*Onishishin*, but I had that dream that I don't really understand. *Ninihsitohtashiin.*'

'Do you want to share your dream again – *enahbundumowin*? Was it the same as before?'

'*Eha*. It seemed so real, but as usual, I can't really get the whole sense of it. It did seem unusually vivid last night, though.'

The young man followed his Nokomis and Mishomis to their table. Chrome and Arborite reflected the new day's sun streaming from the far window. Mishomis paused at the sink and stove to prepare a pot of tea over which they would visit. When they were all settled, the young man fiddled with the salt shaker for a few moments, gathering his thoughts. Giving him the time he needed, his Nokomis and Mishomis sat quietly, enjoying the warmth of the fire and sun starting to fill the room. Slowly, methodically, the young man then started explaining what he had seen in his dream the night before.

When he was finished, the old man and woman were still. Finally, Nokomis asked her grandson, 'What do you think it means?'

The young man tried to order his thoughts. 'I don't know. Part of it seems so obvious, but I think there must be more.'

After a moment's silence, Mishomis asked, 'What do you mean?'

'Well, as we have spoken about before, I know that many of our teachings are wrapped up in what I saw. The problem I'm having is that I can't fully imagine what they have to do with what's going on in my life. I'm so busy at work and home; I thought that coming up here would clear my head. Instead, I just feel more confused.'

His grandmother looked into her tea and said, 'Tell me what you are thinking.'

'Well, I always love coming home because there are so many good memories here. It feels like a place where I can get perspective on the world. Everywhere I turn, I recall people I have met, things I have been taught, and events that have made me who I am. The waters are so calming, too. And I know this sounds weird, but walking along the shores I literally feel the presence of our ancestors. They teach me that our family has lived here for so many generations that I can't help but feel a deep connection to this place. I think of them wherever I go. So I came up here again to feel this, to take this lens and look back on what I am doing. I needed to collect my thoughts because so much is going on.'

'Grandson,' his Nokomis said, 'your dream does indeed have much meaning. Perhaps you received the help you are seeking ... unless, of course,' she added with a smile and a poke in the ribs, 'you're eating funny mushrooms or something.' The young man smiled. As always, he was thankful for his grandmother; she knew he could get too serious. Her gentle teasing helped him relax. He was glad he'd put salt in their sugar shaker again last night.

After a moment's pause, his Mishomis added, 'I know you are struggling to write something worthwhile about Anishinabek law. Making our values more prominent could be an important development. It would be good to see if people would take our ideas more seriously. Do you think this has anything to do with your dream?'

The young man nodded, 'Maybe that's part of it. The dream's images seem to be wrapped up with the trajectory of Anishinabek law you taught me. I can't help but think of the caves out back as I ponder the dream. But I know there must be more. You've said dreams themselves can sometimes be a part of our law. I must have been thinking about all these things in relation to the book I am writing. I am also thinking about the development of an Indigenous law degree they are discussing at UVic. If properly advanced, the resurgence of Indigenous law could be one of the most important initiatives in legal education for Indigenous peoples in a long while.'[3]

'Why do you say that?' Mishomis asked. 'Tell me how you think it all fits together.'

'Well, to put it in perspective, I think the first real steps forward for Indigenous legal education came when politicians and courts started to take our issues more seriously. Cases like *Calder* in Canada,[4] *Mabo* in Australia,[5] and *Williams v. Lee* in the United States[6] really kick-started a wave of reform for law schools. The fact that our rights were regarded as more than just moral obligations and had legal weight to them was very significant.[7] People sat up and took notice; law professors slowly started to introduce these cases into their regular courses. Eventually, whole classes about Indigenous peoples and the law were created.[8] Of course, there was also resistance in certain schools. Some thought that those who addressed this issue were teaching soft law, or not teaching law at all.[9] Looking back, there were some pretty immature things said and done about the development of Indigenous issues as a legal subject, lots of bruised egos, and so on. I think we've edged past all that. Our rights are here to stay. Even here at home we have had a case or two enforcing our treaty rights and challenging government action.'

The young man paused for a moment as he reflected on the growing light being shed on Indigenous issues in the law. He thought of the cumulative impact of all the attention now devoted to them by the courts and politicians. He knew the U.S. Supreme Court spent a disproportionate amount of its time on Indian law issues.[10] He also thought of the over twenty-five Aboriginal rights cases decided by the Canadian Supreme Court in the last few years.[11] He knew he could go on and on: the rising importance of the Treaty of Waitangi in New Zealand,[12] the Declaration of the Rights of Indigenous Peoples,[13] the *Awas Tingni* case,[14] the development of the Sami Parliament,[15] et cetera. He knew many mistakes had been made as these issues developed, but he also saw that much had been learned.

Breaking into his thoughts, Nokomis said, 'I remember when we went to our burial grounds those people built their house on. That land was reserved under our treaty, but they went and built that house anyway. They even knew there was a treaty there but these contractors and politicians thought they could ignore it. That made me mad. It wasn't easy to cause all that fuss about it. I hate to stir things up, but I was glad we did. People realized if they didn't settle with us they would end up in court. That house is now gone and our ancestors can rest in peace.'

The young man remembered his grandparents' role at the occupation.[16] They had been so strong and supportive. He had visited the site since then, too. Standing amongst the maples and listening to the nearby stream, he remembered feeling that their strength somehow continued to mingle with their ancestors' power at that site. It was a quiet, sacred place. Looking at his grandparents, he could see they had aged since then. He didn't look forward to the day when he would have to lay them in the ground, even though he knew they would continue on.

'Like I was saying,' he went on, 'I think the fact these kinds of issues became a part of law was an important development. It had tremendous implications for legal education. Students, lawyers, and judges started learning and applying the principles from these cases. They could use them to change the way Indigenous peoples were treated.' Changing tone, he said, 'This was soon followed by another change in how legal education was carried out. It was a bit more boisterous than the first. People started to get more directly involved with what was happening, and this led to a few tussles. Deans, professors, and students realized they didn't know much about Indigenous peoples, even though they could quote the cases dealing with their issues chapter and verse. Some had never even met an Indigenous person. On further reflection, they also soon noticed that Indigenous people were under-represented in the legal profession, but over-represented in the criminal justice and child welfare systems.[17] This didn't strike them as being right.

'Slowly, a few law school admissions committees started seeking out Indigenous students for their applicant pool.[18] Some were admitted; other schools caught on. Competition, contention, and cooperation mingled in unequal parts. A few schools made great efforts to recruit and assist Indigenous students; others quickly lost interest, if they ever had any at all. Debates about affirmative action raged through some schools, while others slowly got on with the business of effectively training this new group. Insensitive taunts and aimless administrative wandering combined with structured, measurable progress. Through it all, the number of Indigenous lawyers slowly grew. Where there were about six or so Indigenous lawyers in Canada in 1973 there are now over one thousand legally trained Indigenous people in the profession in the country.[19] The same thing happened in the U.S., and is gradually gaining ground in places like Australia, New Zealand, and Norway.[20] Their presence has enriched the halls of those schools, and these graduates are making a significant difference to their communities and the broader public. Many more non-Indigenous students have also taken up an interest in our rights, too. Both groups work together to create a better future. Their ascension really marks the second peak of reform for Indigenous legal education, as I see it.'

As they reflected on these developments, Nokomis took her tea and held it firmly in front of her with her hands. The sun was high enough now that the dark liquid reflected the light. Faded red lipstick lined the cup's rim. After taking a sip, she looked up and smiled. 'I remember when you first went to law school. Were you ever distracted! You were like a bee in a glove, running back and forth from home to school all the time. You must have been taking lessons from that rabbit we see around here. Couldn't stay still in one place for a second. It was like you couldn't decide where you wanted to be. What was going on?'

'It was your oatmeal, grandma. I couldn't get enough.'

Nokomis laughed.

The young man went on: 'Actually, I couldn't decide if I wanted to stay at school. All through first year, I kept questioning whether I wanted to work with the law I was learning. It's hard to have much confidence in something that has been part of your dispossession. I also missed home, and everyone here. I didn't know if I really wanted to leave home and make my life elsewhere. To tell you the truth, it was also pretty hard for me intellectually. I wasn't used to looking at the world in the way my teachers did. It took some time to get the hang of it. I didn't do well, at first. But I stuck at it. It really wasn't until it was almost over that I saw there might be some value in what I had learned. And then I had a good professor, who encouraged me to go to graduate school for further study. Professor Macklem stood at the crossroads for me. I think it was only then that law started to sink in.

'Anyway,' he continued, 'that's when I realized that maybe I could teach in one of those places. I started thinking about how important it was that Indigenous issues and individuals were now a larger part of legal education. But I also knew that if things were going to change, these developments were not enough. A third crest of reform was needed. Legal institutions themselves had to become different. Ways had to be found for law schools to form partnerships with Indigenous peoples. These institutions had to change if Indigenous legal education was going to grow. And they have, to some extent, though there is still a ways to go. When I look at the Native Law Centre in Saskatchewan, the First Nations Legal Studies Program at UBC, Akitsiraq in the North, the Intensive Program in Aboriginal Governance at Osgoode, or the June Callwood Program in Indigenous Law at my school, I see there has been significant progress.[21] You can see the same thing in the United States, New Zealand, Australia, and Norway.[22] There also have been a few failures along the way, as Indigenous peoples and institutions have parted company over certain things. By and large, however, Indigenous issues and individuals are slowly being received into an institutional context that is relevant to them, which they can work to further transform. One day, we may even see an Indigenous law school or other institution where we teach our own laws, while at the same time also getting a good general legal education. That's what they're talking about at UVic.

'Which brings me to why I think writing about Indigenous ideas could be significant. Our legal traditions have something important to add to how we make decisions in this country. It's the latest challenge for legal education to surmount. It is simply not enough to have Indigenous issues, individuals, and institutions become an integral part of the academy. People need to write articles and books about our laws and the perspective we have on Canadian laws. Until our ideas – our ideologies   are part of any intellectual exchange, we are just rearranging deck chairs on the *Titanic*. Nothing much changes in the law if we just add a few more issues, individuals, and institutional variations to the mix.

'Profound legal change requires that questions be examined from perspectives that partially emerge from sources outside Western legal discourses, motivated by considerations from Indigenous normative orders. Standards for judgment must not only flow from the common law but also should spring from Indigenous legal values. Anishinabek law should guide our decision-making. Precedent should not be confined to dusty old law books but should be alive to the authority of our teachings and life-ways. The criteria for measuring what's just, fair, and equitable should not solely be drawn from non-Indigenous sources. Our codes of conduct need to be part of law's formal and informal expressions. Our traditions and stories should guide how we answer the problems we face. They are a necessary part of our internal regulation and organization. Our customs are necessary to meet challenges that lie ahead. They should be simultaneously compared, contrasted, combined with, and disaggregated from critical and constructive norms arising from many philosophical and cultural legal traditions. We should be able to dream about what our own law should look like in our contemporary lives.'

The young man looked across the table at his grandparents. He could see the approval in their eyes. He continued, 'I think that is what I should write about. I think I should report about what our own law feels like as I experience the world. I know it would only be a very small first step. Eventually, others will have to add their own voices. Furthermore, such reports will eventually have to include our codes, cases, and other deliberations from our formal judicial and governmental institutions. But we have to start somewhere. Progress in the field of Anishinabek law will be limited until Anishinabek perspectives are better understood. That is why it is important to more fully articulate our legal principles. They have the potential to deeply examine our assumptions about how to live well in the world. The contrast between Anishinabek law and the common law attempts to measure law's maturity. Intermingling and separating the insights found in these systems could create a unique venue for the exchange and exploration of ideas.[23]

'It's just like the *Indigenous Law Journal* that was recently founded at the U of T. I hope the journal does not just end up only publishing cases and comments about Canada or the national laws of other countries. That would be a sad waste of potential – like getting pushed down the last hill. Of course, any journal or book cannot stand alone. It needs to be added to a hundred other initiatives that bring Indigenous ideas forward. Yet, as part of this path, the journal has the potential to complete an important circle in Indigenous legal education, if it publishes Indigenous laws and legal commentaries. It could create feedback into how Indigenous peoples think and act in relation to issues, individuals, and institutions that make up the wider world of law. That's where I think I want to make my contribution. I want to add my voice to the journal and other Indigenous legal texts.'

Nokomis, who had been sitting quietly through this explanation, cleared her throat. 'Tell me grandson, how does all this talk about issues, individuals, institutions, and ideas relate to your dream?'

'I don't know Nokomis. I need to think about it some more. Can you help me?'

AUNAGWAUM-IZIWIN[1]

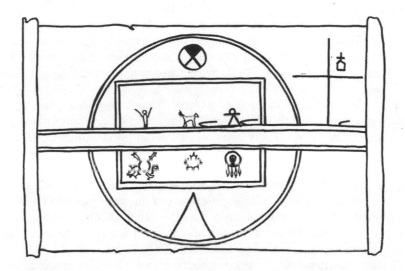

Four corners lie at the heart of the reserve. The old United Church
stands on one corner. Its limestone form sits heavily on the land, while
its tin spire rises high above the trees. Four is very prominent in the
building's design, four crowns on the main tower, four chimneys (one
at each corner), four windows on each side, as well as four windows
at the front and four at back. It is the oldest building on the reserve,
and was built by his great-grandfather over one hundred years ago. A
memorial cairn out front commemorates his contributions to the community, and those of his father. His great-great-grandfather moved the
community to the reserve from their traditional farming lands in Owen
Sound when he signed a treaty in the 1850s. His great-grandfather was
the last hereditary and first elected chief of the reserve and served on
council for fifty years.

Across the corner is the new community hall and sports arena. People still call it new, though it is over thirty years old. When he was younger, an impressive two-storey building occupied the site. It was destroyed by fire. Like the church, it had been built on modified Victorian architectural lines. It was the council hall where band meetings and official business was conducted. The church and Indian Agent's house were made of the same material, and the council hall was board and batten. When he was young, Nokomis had set up a library in the main portion of the hall so the young people of the reserve could learn to enjoy reading. This was back in the day when the only TV channel was some electrical static broadcasted from Kitchener. Nokomis bought books from all around the countryside to fill the shelves. The place was full of colour and smelled of rich, dusty pages. Now, it was transformed. The only remnant of the former building is the cenotaph standing out front, dedicated to the reserve's veterans.

The other two corners are now vacant, though they are still occupied by vivid memories. His uncle's family had lived on one corner, and ran a small grocery store. There must have been a good number of things to buy back then, but all he could remember were the Cheesies and Fanta sodas. He used to race around the building with his cousins riding bicycles, playing cowboys and Indians, tag, hide-and-go-seek, and a hundred other games. A large porch across the front provided a shady resting place when you got tired. On the other corner was Lennox's store. An old foundation at its side was where his mother high-centred a car when she was a teenager learning to drive.

Today, the intersection is once again filled with life. An all-candidates meeting for the upcoming federal election is being held in the arena. Cars fill the small parking lot and line the roads in four directions. The ground is frozen but the early snows have already receded, making it easier to crowd the area. It's *shkadni-geezis* – freezing moon. The event at the hall has attracted more people than usual. For the first time in history, a couple of people from the reserve are vying to represent them in Parliament. One is Liberal, and the other is running as an Independent. There has been a lot of talk about the election. People on the reserve wonder what it would be like to have someone from their community represent them in Ottawa. People off the reserve wonder the same thing. The press has shown a lot of interest in the contest, and a local reporter has shown up to cover the event.

The young man and his sister get out of their car and make their way towards the hall. A crowd stands about fifteen feet outside the entrance, visiting with one another. Smokers' clouds mingle with frosted breath as they chat on the sidewalk. Non-smokers themselves, the young man and his sister nevertheless stop to say hello and visit for a few moments before continuing. She has since been successful in gaining employment around the reserve. She works in the schools, the health centre, and the women's shelter. She has finally been embraced by the community and is constantly busy. Her life is balanced, and full of hope and contribution. They discuss their parents' health and confirm who will clean the snow around their house this year. When they are nearly finished visiting, they hear electric speakers crackle from inside as the meeting is called to order. Through the tangle of coats at the door they notice a few dogs in the foyer greeting the incoming guests. They squeeze their way through the entrance and step into the large hall.

Banners and flags from past community sports victories hang from the ceiling. On the walls someone has painted a few Ojibway dodems. There are about a hundred people in the room. Voices ebb as everyone takes their seats. The stage at the far end of the hall is set up with microphones and a table. The debate is being moderated by one of the band councillors, who sits between the candidates at the table. She welcomes the crowd and explains the format, before inviting the speakers to give their opening statements. They are limited to two minutes each for their introductions.

Chi Boogidiwin is the first to speak. Running on the Liberal ticket, he first offers some words of welcome and outlines his party's main platform. Next, he speaks of the need to give the community a real voice in Canada's affairs. He finishes by talking about the need to create specific opportunities for First Nations in the country. He says the people of the reserve should receive health care and educational services throughout the riding, at a level comparable to the national standard. Nimoosh Nag'anal'mot goes next. Formerly of the Conservative Party, he is now running as an Independent. He offers his welcome and stakes out his position as being above the fray of party politics. He says he decided to run as an Independent to present real alternatives at the national level. He criticizes Canada's mainstream political parties for ignoring important philosophical questions and he questions their knowledge and commitment to advancing individual development and initiative. He finishes by noting his long-time connection with the band and listing his past contributions.

After the opening statements, the moderator explains that he will direct four questions to each candidate on an alternating basis. He explains that the questions were collected from the press and community prior to the gathering. Each candidate is given ten minutes to respond to each question, with no interruption or opportunity for subsequent reply. The event will wrap up by each speaker giving a concluding statement.

The band councillor reads the first question: 'For the past few years, there have been claims that it is racist to support First Nations rights and programs directed exclusively to First Nations peoples. Can you please tell us your position on this issue? Chi, you will go first.'

Animishish boogidih. 'Thank you. I agree, racism is a terrible problem in our society and in the world. But before we begin to address the issue, let's ask: "What is racism?" Race is a socially constructed phenomenon based on the erroneous assumption that physical differences such as skin colour, hair colour and texture, and facial features are related to intellectual, moral, or cultural superiority. The concept of race has scant basis in biological reality, and thus has no meaning independent of its social definitions.[2] People define us as First Nations for social purposes, but there is really no such thing as a First Nation person, biologically speaking.[3]

'Look around you in this hall. I see brown eyes and blue, black, brown, blond, and red hair, light and dark skin – yet we are all of the Chippewa of Nawash First Nation. Some of you are even from the same families and have vastly different physical characteristics. What does that say about the concept of race? Are some here not First Nations people because we don't fit the stereotype of what a Native should look like? Are some of us "authentic" and others not, because of our physical features? Are some "purer" and have greater claims to First Nations status because of our so-called bloodlines? I think it is very dangerous to classify people in these ways. Doing so would be racist, claiming some kind of superiority because of biology. We have to be careful about that in our communities.

'There is nothing in the blood that makes us different from our neighbours in the wider world. Our blood does not distinguish us from one another. We are different because of sociological circumstances – because of our culture. First Nations is, first and foremost, a social concept. It is a political category, a construction. There are some who seek positions of political power both on and off the reserve who want to claim power on the basis of race. Some on the reserve want to prevent others from participating with us because of their ancestry. They challenge us from the opposite direction. Some off the reserve want to eliminate First Nations social and political organization by labelling us a "race." I will resist that categorization at every turn.

'Look at how we came to be the Chippewa of Nawash First Nation. We were Ojibway and were joined by Odawa and Potawatomi people in the 1600s. In fact, we were the same people. It was not long, though, before a few Wendat/Huron people joined us as they fled genocide and dispersal in 1650. In the 1700s and 1800s a few Mohawks, Seneca, and Oneida people settled here. Their descendants eventually married people in the community; then came some Delawares, Algonquin, and Shawnee individuals. Before you knew it, our people were marrying English and French people too, as they came in waves after 1800. Métis people also lived amongst us. There was a large community that made their home over by mouth of the Sauble River in what became Southampton. A Riel even settled into our reserve and some of us trace our ancestry to her – those of us who have McCloeds in our background. There are Cree, Lakota, Mi'kmaq, and Blackfoot influences, along with Polish, Hungarian, Chinese, and Latin American representation in the genealogy of our community. Look at us today: over 50 per cent marry outside our First Nation. I include my mother and myself in that number. You cannot say we are a "race" of people. We are a First Nation.

'In fact, I remember one day when the chief and council came to my office to discuss an important matter. After the business was finished, we all sat around the table and tried to identify how we were related. It turned out our most common ancestor was a woman whose family came from England in the 1830s. We were more strongly related through her lineage than we were through any other person. Facts like this should give us pause. We shouldn't keep acting as if we're all "pure" blood Indians. We're Anishinabek because of our political organization, language, culture, laws, and teachings.

'If elected, I will do all in my power to address the so-called issue of race in Aboriginal affairs. The rights, programs, and recognition we seek are not based on race. They are based on the fact that we want to continue as political entities with roots in the past, yet grafting new influences and growing into the future. We want to organize our affairs to continue the development of our political traditions. We want to sustain our languages, cultivate our culture, and live on the land in a way that respects our norms, values, and philosophies. We want Canada to organize its political affairs to sustain our political organization in contemporary terms.'

The people in the hall are quiet and attentive, if not a little bored. The speaker pauses for a moment to collect his thoughts. The man who came into the hall with his sister turns to her and asks, 'Wenesh gaaboogiyit?'

She quietly laughs and whispers, '*Kaween*, why?'
'*W'ombauzimaugozih.*'

The speaker continues. 'Some people seeking power do not want First Nations to be a political force. Their political values do not accord with ours. Their ideology of governance is different from ours. As a result, they want to eliminate our forms of organization. Let's be clear about that. The notion that we are asking for race-based entitlements puts us on the defensive. I do not want to defend First Nations rights on the basis of race, nor will I. Racism is immoral and wicked. I will, however, defend First Nations as political units. First Nations need reform but they should not be terminated. I am interested in ensuring that we exist as a political force in communities in Canada and in the world. Our world views, while they share much in common with others, also have many unique ideas relating to organization that I want to see preserved and strengthened.

'I think the rest of Canada could benefit from adopting some of our political philosophies. They would benefit from having us more clearly articulate the relevance of our laws. For example, the structure of our languages teaches us that the earth is alive, and that it has agency. I would like to see our political organization reflect that fact. We have ancient traditions relating to nation building, family organization, childcare, health, well-being, consumption, production, and transactions. They could be further developed to apply to contemporary issues. These could be of great assistance for the complex challenges we face in Canada; they may even benefit the world. I would like to see these values unburdened by government repression and given life in contemporary form, with all the vibrancy of positive inter-cultural and inter-societal contrast and comparison that we can muster. That is how I would respond to the question of race.'

The moderator thanks Mr Boogidiwin for his words and turns the question over to Nag'anal'mot.

W'mingih. 'I see my friend agrees with me. Aboriginal rights are a social construction, a legal fiction. In many places in Canada, Europeans are only the more recent arrivals than so-called First Nations. There is no reason to support the continued existence of our community just because we have interwoven some common Indigenous ancestry. As my friend confirms, many of us are more strongly related through our non-Indigenous ancestors. It is not always the case that First Nations can say "we were here first." Even if they could, prior occupancy is not a sound moral basis on which to establish political organization.'[4]

Some in the crowd look puzzled, heads titled to one side, not sure if they had heard correctly what was said. A few whispers circulate to clarify meaning.

'We should not support the recognition of so-called First Nations rights, or the development of specific First Nations programs. Look at the problems we have faced in the past because we have been singled out for so-called special treatment: residential schools, the *Indian Act*, veterans lands administration, health care, liquor offences, criminal justice, sale of agricultural and other products, the pass system, land rights, and voting rights. We of all people should know better than to demand differential treatment; it has been a disaster. It will be a disaster in the future.'

Some members of the audience are clearly angry. A few howls of derision are heard at the back. Jeers begin to scatter throughout the crowd.

'For all my friend's pretty words, the fact remains that people regard us as a race. Some have still not accepted the science that there are no biological differences that amount to race. Many still regard us as inferior on that count. Others are more charitable and do not ascribe notions of inferiority or superiority to the concept of race. Yet they still regard differences as biologically determined. They claim reverse discrimination if we receive entitlements that impact their access to goods or political power. You can see in their assumptions that they regard race as biologically real. As a result, they fear being disadvantaged if other "races" gang up on them and turn benefits upside down. They regard race as real and permanent, and want to avoid pitting "races" against each other.

'Then there are those who accept the idea that race is socially constructed. This does not make racism any less dangerous. Fascism is socially constructed, and it is still very dangerous. If people are allowed to organize around the idea of race, even on a remedial basis, we reinforce its social power. We should be trying to de-emphasize, diminish, and destroy any distinctions made on the basis of this social category. We should focus on eradicating race, racialization, and racism as a social force. Only a race-blind approach to rights and privileges will sap the concept of "race" of its life and strength. These are the reasons I oppose First Nations rights and programs.' He finishes, *w'neekimoh*: 'Racism anywhere and everywhere, and under all circumstances, is wrong. It is anathema to all democratic principles that we as a nation hold dear.'[5]

Many shocked faces dot the room. A few audibly snarl their displeasure about what's just been said. The moderator asks for calm, and the audience slowly quiets down. She turns to her next question, and asks, 'How would you improve the situation of Indigenous people? Mr Nag'anal'mot will go first this round.'

Animishish zheesheegih, and he resumes. 'Thank you. Well, that's an excellent question. My answer follows nicely from what I was just saying. So-called Indigenous people should be treated the same as other Canadians, and all distinctions in law and policy should be eliminated. This was the path Prime Minister Trudeau was on when he proposed the White Paper in 1969, before his people were overcome by guilt and lost courage. This was also the path the United States pursued under Truman in the termination era of the 1950s, before misguided notions of civil rights took over in the 1960s. It is also the course that Prime Minister Howard followed in Australia under the banner of practical reconciliation. For all their faults and political differences, Trudeau, Truman, and Howard were three very successful politicians, and their approach to this issue should not be lightly dismissed.

'In specific terms, I propose to:[6]

1　Abolish the Indian reserve system in Canada, and in particular, the abolition of our reserve.
2　Transfer ownership of reserves to us as individuals, and give us exclusive ownership of land, with freedom to lease or sell it to anyone we choose.
3　Repeal the *Indian Act*, and dismantle the Department of Indian Affairs or any bureaucratic structure meant to deal with Indians.
4　Abolish chief and council and amalgamate governance functions with the surrounding township.
5　Wind up treaty obligations by surrendering our interests to the Crown through an absolute, unqualified extinguishment of any past, present, or future rights.
6　Make a one-time per-capita distribution of the band's assets to each registered band member.
7　Immediately eliminate any policies or programs that are directed exclusively to us as Indigenous people.
8　Amend the Constitution to repeal sections 25 and 35 of the *Constitution Act, 1982*.

Taking these steps is important for us as Aboriginal people for economic and social reasons.'

Some at the back of the hall growl their disdain, while others look at the floor in embarrassment. The moderator once again asks for order before Nag'anal'mot continues.

'Economically, my proposals are necessary because the reserve system discourages investment and development. We can't get mortgages on our lands under section 89 of the *Indian Act* because they are inalienable except to the Crown. Financial institutions are unwilling to lend us money to build houses or create businesses because we can't give them collateral. A great economist, Hernando de Soto, has argued that lack of private property is the reason for poverty in the developing world and former communist countries.[7] If we as individuals owned land, we would have the incentive to improve it, because we would realize a larger gain on our investments. The liquidation of reserves and distribution of funds from our existing assets would allow individuals to have a significant initial capital pool from which to invest. The elimination of programs, policies, and constitutional rights for us as Aboriginal peoples would ensure that we permanently break the cycle of dependency. It would help us become self-sufficient. Dismantling the Department of Indian Affairs and chief and council would make economic sense because we would no longer see our financial lives politicized and over-burcaucratized. We need to clean out these levels of waste that stand in the way of our financial independence. We need to dismantle the "Indian industry." Too many elitists, like my friend here, travel the world, vacuously spouting off about Indigenous rights, while real funds are needed at home. What a waste of time and money! The only people benefiting are sycophants like him. The poorest among us suffer, while others parasitically grow rich on our misery. I know this is a strange thing for a small "c" conservative to say, but wealth needs to be redistributed. Of course, I believe the market will best perform that function.

'On the social front, my proposals are necessary because we are killing ourselves with all the petty disputes and family feuds bred on the reserve. Look at the nepotism around us. We pull one another down. Look at our levels of education, health, employment, income, and life expectancy. They are so far below the general Canadian norm that I don't think we can blame the government alone. Sure, they are responsible for some of our problems, but that's because they forced us into this rotten reserve system. Social health will only result when we break up the reserve. We will also be more socially whole when we know this safety net is no longer underneath us. We do not rely on ourselves as individuals to make changes; we always run to the government to fix our problems. I think that is unhealthy, and that it creates dysfunctional individuals, families, and communities. We need a looser social structure – one that permits more individual initiative.

'You may be familiar with the story about two men who are fishing, busy pulling up crabs from the ocean and placing them in two barrels. One man is having a difficult time getting the crabs to stay in the container while the other keeps bagging more without any escaping. After a period of time trying to keep his catch secure, the one man turns to the other in frustration and says, "I just don't get it. Here I am struggling to keep these things in the barrel while you keep fishing without a second thought of their escape. What's your secret?" The other man looks between the two barrels for a moment and notes the activity level of the crabs within each. Then, throwing another crab in his barrel he says, "There's really no secret. I don't need to worry about my crabs escaping. They're Indian crabs. Whenever I throw one in, the others claw it down and make sure it doesn't get any higher than the rest of them."

'This is the social reality created by the *Indian Act*, and this is why I think our lives would be improved if we eliminated all distinctions based on our Aboriginality.'

There is more vocal dissatisfaction from the crowd. A few people get up and leave the meeting in protest. The microphone is passed to Chi Boogidiwin, who begins his answer to the moderator's question.

Guwaetuni aepeetaunmuk. 'My proposal to improve Indigenous lives relates to the preservation and development of the reserve and its structures. We would not be better off if we followed my friend's proposals. Assimilation has been one of the main policies underlying our separate treatment since the first *Indian Act* was enacted. It is a tired, old, discreditable doctrine. I am amazed that my friend is dressing it up as new policy and proposing it once again. It has not worked. Attempts to assimilate us have caused great harm, even though we strongly resist it at every turn. The persistence of First Nations should demonstrate the folly of his proposals.

'It is morally wrong to coerce any individual or group of people into prescribed political communities when they are not unjustifiably harming themselves or others. The termination of political choice is a violent assault on agency. Freedom is diminished when people are forced to give up their peaceful political and social bonds. Democracy is threatened if people are prevented from organizing according to the dictates of their own conscience. Peace, order, and good governance are severely eroded if the rule of law within our communities is severed by abolishing our ancient legal traditions and their contemporary manifestations. Minority rights are crushed if a majority eliminates a group against their will. There have always been Indians like Mr Nag'anal'mot who have argued for assimilation. They try and transform themselves through slick political tricks. I don't believe his dogma. Fortunately, such charlatans are a very slight percentage of our people, but they will always be used by our opponents to misrepresent our clear, widespread feelings on the matter. Don't trust those tricksters.

'If elected, I will work to ensure that the inherent right to self-government is implemented. I will see that First Nations communities are freed from the oppressive structures under which we exist. If accused of being part of an "industry" or of being an "elitist" for trying to preserve our civil and political rights, then I am willing to suffer the insult. That does not mean I do not welcome targeted, constructive criticism directed at cleaning up corruption in our communities. I think it is crucial and necessary to a healthy political community. I want more of it. I do not welcome offensive stereotypes, though. There are significant problems that need to be honestly addressed and not covered up. I am deeply troubled by those who have abused their positions of trust in our communities, but that does not mean that everyone who works to ensure the vitality and health of First Nations should be tarred with the same brush, should be called elitist and part of an industry.

'While we are certainly not without our problems, there is great value in supporting the political growth and development of First Nations. In the world today, people are becoming alienated from one another and the earth. In highly urbanized societies, people often live in extreme social isolation. Well-being is diminished by the intense individualism evident in many political structures. Many people move every few years, and live next to people they barely know. They work in environments where the social rules are set by profit rather than friendship. It is almost as if neighbours and workers are regarded as interchangeable units. People sacrifice potentially deeper social satisfaction for mortgages, cars, and bright shiny toys. It seems like an empty existence when compared with the richness we enjoy, even in our material poverty and in the midst of our conflicts. And think of how they are surrounded by concrete and cars. They rarely connect with the land or feel its rhythms. Now I don't want to romanticize nature – it can sometimes be very harsh in its extremes. But we should not underestimate the land's value in our lives. We would *not* be better off if we assimilated, and sought the social and physical world in which much of Canada lives. Trudeau admitted his attempt was wrong, the tribes Truman tried to terminate have re-emerged, and Howard's actions have caused great damage to Australia's Aboriginal peoples. Assimilation must be rejected.

'Our form and unit of political organization is a real alternative. Our basic social structure remains stable but dynamic, as people join our community from different places every generation. Our laws contain deep wisdom. We need to better integrate each of these things more strongly into our lives in a contemporary fashion. Through our laws, we have enjoyed relationships with this land for generations, and will for generations more. As I said before, it is not as if everyone is originally from here; we have interwoven continuity with change. Yet we know one another and our surroundings in a deep and profound way. Most of us can count on the fact that we will know one another and this land throughout our whole lives, even if we move off the reserve for decades. Most of us will get to know those who move into our community, or at least we should attempt to do so. Our liberal ties of political kinship can connect our past to the future.

'If elected I would defend our form of political organization. I would extend our laws. There is an implication that First Nations politics are inferior and undemocratic, synonymous with nepotism, corruption, coercion, and all that is wasteful. All politics are susceptible to these abuses of power, including First Nations politics. I will work at the national level to reinforce the positive aspects of political organization as First Nations. That does not mean we should reject reform. We need tribal courts to facilitate accountability. An independent, well-resourced dispute resolution body that makes decisions in accordance with Anishinabek legal traditions would improve our internal and external relations. We also need a stronger, more independent media, a professional civil service, and a more stable social service delivery network. These reforms would enhance our social structures.

'We also need economic reform. Land, labour, and capital are the traditional sources of development. With land, I believe we should have more flexibility in our land use structures. It is ironic that some commentators castigate us for attempting to combine individual land rights within a collective structure, when condominiums are one of the fastest growing forms of land use in Canada. They effectively combine individual and collective ownership. Collective control of individual land rights is also evident through zoning, development agreements, easements, trusts, and restrictive covenants. We should search for solutions to our land use problems by studying these and other analogies, and then applying aspects of them in a culturally appropriate manner. While I would certainly not counsel the wholesale adoption of Western models that combine these interests, I do think these examples bear further study. We should determine if they have some potential to be partially adapted to our circumstances. I don't think our future development should be written off just because we insist that land be collectively held; we should study the innovative ways being used to create material wealth using collective regulation.

'On the issue of labour and its role in development, we should consider that knowledge is the greatest asset people possess in today's world. People earn money from work because they have emotional and intellectual skills that enable them to direct and coordinate sophisticated activities requiring specialized information. We need to ensure that our people can effectively participate in wealth creation by having access to various forms of knowledge. This occurs through access to land, Elders, and formal schooling, as each teaches important ideas about how to take care of others and our own selves in society. We should ensure that people within our communities do not stand in the way of education and create barriers to acquiring these skills.

'On the issue of capital, we could learn from successful communities that share some similarities with us, like Membertou, Rama, Westbank, Millbrook, Cowichan, Nisga'a, Moose Deer Point, Chippewas of the Sarnia, and others. We can also do more as a First Nation to rework fiscal relations with the federal government. It would be interesting to explore a tax treaty with the federal government to supplement our other treaties. There is much we could propose. For example, we could extend tax immunities in exchange for our continued agreement that others share our territories. We could create innovative taxation structures for our membership. For example, 50 per cent of our people live and work off the reserve, some of them earning decent incomes. If the federal government collected their income tax, then remitted it to the First Nation, this could provide an important supplement to the First Nation's operation. Many community members would be happy to see their income applied in this fashion.

'If elected, I would defend the development of our political structures. These are the initiatives I would work on to improve the situation of Indigenous people if I were elected to federal Parliament.'

When Boogidiwim is finished the people in the hall signal only slight agreement. Most like what he has to say better than Nag'anal'mot's proposals, but they remain unconvinced. At that point, an Elder stands up from her seat and asks for the floor. She loudly proclaims, 'There's something not right about either of these speeches. This isn't how we talk about ourselves. They're both forgetting something important. Can I address the group for a moment?' The moderator acknowledges the request, and invites the woman to take the floor. The assembled group respectfully watches as she slowly makes her way to the tables, helped by her young granddaughter.

Facing the group, she is handed the microphone and begins, 'I never heard our parents or grandparents talk like these fellows are talking to-day. Their words are all directed to our heads, there's nothing about the heart. You wouldn't choose a relationship with someone based on your thoughts alone; you'd need to feel something to make that decision. You also wouldn't choose relationships based on your feelings alone, or at least you shouldn't; there'd need to be some thought there. These men are asking us to make important decisions about our political rela-tionships without talking to our hearts. I even heard that when I went back to school a few years ago.

'Learning's not complete if you don't address the whole person. In the old days, we used to weave lessons from the natural world into our teachings. Our leaders would expand our understanding by telling sto-ries. They understood that stories could appropriately combine reason and emotion when they correlated with one another. We need more true stories to help us make sound decisions. That's where our real law re-sides. Our leaders need to knit them into their teachings. The only story I have heard so far is about crabs, and I didn't like it. It didn't feel right. It was disrespectful and demeaning. Aside from that, all we've heard are dry phrases with no colour or life. They don't make me dream. I don't trust ideas detached from their context, with no emotional gauge to weigh and evaluate them; just as I also don't trust stories that don't accord with reason. Emotion and reason must work in balance.[8]

'Our hearts and minds have to line up when we make a decision; these men are not helping us. They are too one-sided, too focused on reason alone. Stories may be hard for some to understand, and may be too open-ended for others, but that's part of their beauty. They gener-ate innovation and creativity. They leave some of the work in making judgments to those who're listening to them. Stories don't force your mind to the speaker's conclusions in the same way that words alone do. Stories respect a person's agency. I wish more of our people would function in this way once again.

'It's like when I was a young woman and my father was concerned about a job I was thinking about taking. The Indian Agent had asked me to clean his house each morning and he was offering good money. As I was thinking about the job, I talked to my father. He said it was my decision, but he also explained the reasons behind his concern. The Agent was known to pry and gossip to try and extract information. He was always trying to find out what we were doing, because we tried to keep our lives as free as possible from his interference. As the chief's daughter, he was concerned that the Agent might pressure me to reveal some inappropriate secret. He was worried that if I let something slip, I might find myself ostracized by the community. What he said sounded logical, but I still wasn't convinced. Then he told me a story. It was about dogs and their relationship with humans.

'It seems that one time there was this big council. All the animals were there, the bear, deer, beaver, moose, wolf, otter, and so on. They were all worried about the people who were living among them. Too many of their brothers and sisters were being taken by them and the animals were becoming fewer and fewer. They decided that they would not as freely give themselves to humans. They would warn one another when the people approached.[9] Just as the meeting was ending, the dog snuck away from the council to tell the people what the animals decided. As a result of the dog's disclosure, the people changed their hunting habits and took as many animals as before. As the months passed the animals still felt no relief, so they once again called a council. Everyone attended. They spoke of how their numbers were still too low, and they devised yet another plan to remedy their problem. This time, as the council was breaking up, the wolf became suspicious when he saw the dog leave early. Meiigun followed him through the woods at a safe distance so that he would not be detected. As they drew closer to the people's village, the wolf saw the dog greet the humans and speak to them. Drawing closer, he heard the dog divulge the animal's new secret plan. He was furious, but crept away undetected.

'The next day the wolf called a council, and once again all the animals attended. The wolf told the group about the dog's actions. The dog was given a chance to reply. He did not deny the charge, stating only that he felt obligated to help his friends. The council deliberated about the dog's breach of trust, and the action they should take. They decided they could not live this closely to a trickster-transformer who tried to live his life through shifting loyalties – to the animals and the humans. It was too dangerous. To save their lives, the council's decision was to banish him from their councils and association. From that day forward, the dog was no longer as the other animals. He would spend the rest of his days living like a human, but it would come with a twist. Animoosh would live like those humans who were most oppressed and subject to the whim of others.

'If we participate in Canadian politics in the way that these candidates are asking us, without our values and methods being prominent, we might find ourselves living at the whim of others for another seven generations. We might find that we are policing our own oppression. If our affairs become even more tightly entwined with Canada without our stories setting the course, the pressures may be too great to withhold our consent when we would not otherwise agree. If we're going to form closer relationships with Canada, I want to *feel* right about that decision. I want my heart to be in agreement as well as my head. It doesn't mean I won't listen to reason, but I need more. When people also start talking with their hearts, then I'll be encouraged to consider more fully what they have to say. Think about this and the other stories you may have read or heard as you make your decisions – what do they tell you about how we should think and act in the future? That's how we practise Anishinabek law.

'That's all I wanted to say. I hope we will think about these things as we sort through our feelings on what we're hearing.'

As the Elder finished speaking, the candidates shifted nervously in their chairs. They looked to one another and to the back of the room. Nag'anal'mot conspicuously scratched behind his ear and tilted his head as he heard a dog bark at the back of the hall.

Just as the moderator was about to take back the microphone, the fire alarm shrieked out its warning. Sound reverberated off cinder-block walls and chased through steel rafters. For a few seconds, the people of the reserve looked at each other and glanced about the room, wondering what to do. From that moment, it didn't take long until the group saw one of the band councillors stand and race into the street through the doors at the back. Following his example, one or two band members hurried out of the hall at full speed. After that pandemonium set in and a full stampede developed. The entire crowd panicked.

In the rush to leave the room, most of the audience got stuck in the bottleneck at the gymnasium doors. Their exit was complicated by a few stray dogs that blocked the outgoing surge. They rushed in the doors from the opposite direction at the same moment. They ran around in confusion, yelping at the high-pitched siren. Finally the blockade was broken when a second door at the foyer was opened. For some minutes, a steady stream of people poured out of the building into the cold November evening, randomly grabbing at coats in the foyer to keep themselves warm when they emerged. When the building was finally empty, they milled in the street outside at the four corners, searching for signs of smoke and trouble from inside the band hall. Nothing appeared to be happening. The only smell of smoke anyone could detect came from the cigarette cloud that began to emerge from the mingling crowd. For a few minutes there was relative quiet, until the band fire truck was heard in the distance. When the volunteer brigade finally arrived, the truck parted the crowd to let the men through. For the next half an hour they checked out the hall, at length declaring that it had been a false alarm. When the word was finally passed around the assembled crowd, they continued to mingle in noisy pandemonium.

Anarchy reigned as people checked with one another, going round and round in circles to see who had grabbed their coats.

WINDIGOS[1]

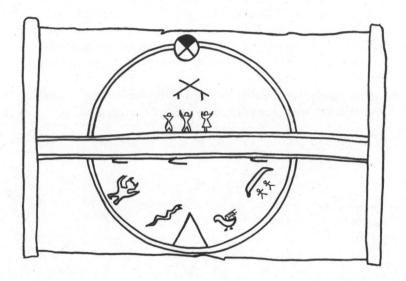

The old refrigeration fan whines in the background as she checks the window seals. Frost coats the panes from the inside, and a skin of ice covers the glasses in the sink. The fire went out in the old stove last night, allowing the winter to seep through the walls.

Her house is slowly deteriorating. The upkeep is getting more difficult each year. The cabin's south-western corner is gradually being undermined through accumulated years of natural settling, invasive cedar roots, and percolating water and ice. Time had a way of wearing most everything down. The result was a noticeable tilt in her living room. Nokomis had asked her son to backfill the crumbling foundation. Now, below her window, a steel shovel pushes against crushed stones, signalling her son's work. It is a comforting sound; she could always count on her boy's help. She lights the propane stove to prepare him some tea, while enjoying the sound of her son's memory.

He was her oldest, a father of six and a general contractor on the peninsula. He was known as a careful person. Living at the edge of the reserve in a big new house, he was taking his place in the community. He had built the house himself – it wasn't one of those Indian department specials. Its basement had above-ground windows. A chalet-style roof covered its bulk and guarded spacious rooms. The project was almost complete. He just needed some spare time and a few more dollars to clad it in new siding. He had even placed the order at the building store.

As the rocks sing their reburial, Nokomis is relieved to hear his work. He had been missing for two days. He had gone fishing with his brother and hadn't returned.[2] Yesterday, all the men in the community launched their boats in search of them. The volunteers stayed out dangerously late, past dusk, eventually returning without any news. Later that evening, they patrolled the shores around the reserve with their flashlights. Others scanned the horizon, looking for signal fires on Hay, White Cloud, Griffith and Rabbit Islands. It was well past midnight by the time the search parties returned to her house. They visited for an hour or so, offering what comfort they could before eventually retiring for the night. Nokomis had finally fallen asleep around three in the morning, too tired to fight exhaustion any longer.

Now, hearing the sound outside her window, she is overcome with relief. Her son has returned. She knew Lake Huron's waters were dangerous this time of year. *Mishi-bizheu* was at his most unforgiving. Many a boat had been lost in November's sudden, fierce gales. The Bruce Mines, Jane Miller, and the Steamer Jones, being some of its more famous victims, she also remembered other, more intimate tragedies.

The digging stops, and Nokomis walks to the porch to call her son.

There is no answer.

She calls again, and still receives no reply. She puts on her boots and walks outside, calling his name once more. There is no sound but the wind. For the first time she notes that there is no car in the driveway. She looks over the ground; there are no footprints in the snow. Her heart beats faster. She hurries around the house to the corner that needed repair. The stones in the hole lie unturned. A skiff of snow covers the rocks.

Everyone in the community attended the funeral. A day earlier they had gathered at the old store on the four corners for the wake. Bear meat sandwiches were served. There were many songs and stories, a few jokes and laughter. People spoke about the brothers' lives and reflected on their deaths. One of the bodies had been found along the shore. The other was picked up by the coast guard, caught in the rocks just off the beach. It was 11 November, Remembrance Day.

A few weeks later, the young man and his grandmother were sitting in her old cabin kitchen, discussing recent events. A picture of the two brothers sat on the table between them. Looking at their image, each recalled their personalities, goals, and fears. They reminisced about good times together. Nokomis spoke about her sons' childhood, and the people they left behind. As the conversation drifted, the subject turned to deeper things.

'Nokomis, how do you get through the pain and challenges of life?' the young man asks his grandmother. 'Tell me about the fourth hill again. We haven't spoken about it for ages.'

'What do you want to know, grandson?'

'I'm thinking about the scrolls in the cave. I remember thunderbird was the guide and guardian of the fourth realm. From my dream, I also remember the peace of the fourth hill. It was white, with lots of snow. There were fewer people on that hill than the others, and many of them became frail the higher they rose. Some fell by the wayside. Those at the top were joyful, standing in the sun. Sweetgrass smoke rose from the pinnacle. I sensed purity in the scene. I'm wondering what it takes to make it up the fourth hill.'

Nokomis smiles at her grandson. 'That's a big question you're asking, too big for words. I could get lost in them, trying to explain the answer to you.'

The young man takes his uncles' picture in his hands as he ponders her response. He sets it back on the table and asks, 'If it's hard to explain, how am I to learn how to rise above this life?'

'The answer to that question partly depends on you, grandson. Each person has different gifts they use to reach their destination. There's uniqueness in every journey. Some of what it takes to reach that goal will only come from you. You need to discover and develop what is distinctively yours.'

Nokomis laughs as she thinks about what she's just said. 'We sound like a couple of Hollywood Indians, full of stoicism and wisdom. Your grandfather would get a kick out of that. He spent years becoming one when he was in California,' she laughs again.

'Anyway, they can't take away our teachings. Even if your journey is your own, there are some general guides that have been passed down to us. Our dreams and experiences teach us specifics; the scrolls, stories, and songs express ideas from which everyone can learn. There is also wisdom in many cultures from which we can draw strength and guidance. These ideas can be used to judge how we should live. They contain criteria to evaluate our course in life. In fact, I think that's what you told us when you first recounted your dream. Do you remember?'

The porch door opens and a blast of December wind fills the room. Wisps of snow flash across the floor and die at the stove. Mishomis rushes in, slamming the door behind him, locking out the storm. Unwrapping his scarf and shrugging off his coat, he drapes them over hooks on the wall. He sits on the stool by the coats and pries off his boots. 'The snow's really getting heavy out there,' he says. 'It's a real blizzard; you can hardly see the house. It's really whipping in from off the lake. I'm sure we'll be nearly buried by morning.'

Mishomis stands and makes his way to the kitchen table. He sits down and pours himself a cup of tea, wrapping his fingers around its warmth. They talk of his trip back from town, and of the mounting storm. They discuss the latest forecast. Eventually the conversation fades into silence, while they listen to the blowing snow.

After a few minutes, Mishomis turns to his grandson. 'So, what are you writing about these days?' he asks. 'Still trying to finish that book?'

'Yeah, it's been pretty slow. I'm not sure if anyone will understand what I'm saying. When you try to write about law in Anishinabek terms, it doesn't come out the same as you're taught in law school. I'm struggling to give some insight into our legal world without being completely confusing. I can't imagine what Professors Macklem, McNeil, or Slattery would think about my work, though they encouraged innovation and creativity. I'd hope they understand it as legal literature, even if it has a different feel. They were my graduate supervisors.'

'You've had a lot of teachers,' Mishomis answers. 'I'm sure it's complicated to incorporate all you've learned. Anyway, even if some of them don't understand, I think you should press on. Our traditions are alive and relevant when they interact with the world around them. Our legal perspectives would be lost if we didn't use them. I've always had a problem with the notion of trying to preserve traditions in their pristine form. You preserve jam – you live traditions.'

'That's true, but we have to be careful about how our traditions are expressed,' Nokomis interjects. 'You know it can be a challenge to do it properly. We have to keep true to their spirit, even as they are translated through the generations. Our traditions are abused when they aren't cross-referenced and woven together. Their meaning should be drawn from how they interact with one another. They should be wound tightly around their subject, not just scattered here and there. Since our ideas embody a world view, they must interact with all parts of the world. Of course, some details change as they are applied to new situations. Our grandson's life is different from our grandparents'. But there are aspects that remain constant.' Turning to her grandson she says, 'I'll be interested to see if you succeed.'

Mishomis looks at the young man. 'I'm sure he'll do fine, as long as he doesn't quote us. What are you writing about now?'

'I've already written about issues, individuals, and institutions,' the young man answers. 'Now, I'm writing about ideas, about how our laws need to re-emerge and infuse our issues, lives, and institutions. We need their guidance to chart our journeys. Nokomis and I were just discussing my dream about the hills. I was asking her how she deals with the pain of death. I can't imagine how sad you must feel right now. The climb looks difficult from where I sit. There are so many obstacles, and the path is steep. Do you have any ideas, Mishomis?'

'There are no easy answers,' Mishomis replies, 'but one thing you might consider writing about is healing. It's spoken about so often in our communities, and there's a reason for that. Deep laws are attached to that teaching. We have grand medicine societies that teach knowledge about healing, but this idea runs through much of our society. You know our family is from the otter dodem. We have special responsibilities for healing because of our affiliation. The otter dodem is a medicine dodem. You have a responsibility to look at the laws and see where you can find healing. I know it is a struggle for you, but I am glad to see you are trying to live up to your duty. Tell me what you have learned about law and healing.'

The young man ponders the question for a moment before responding. 'There's a lot to say, Mishomis, but when you ask the question, my mind goes to my childhood. When I was a boy, I remember exploring our barn out back. Whenever you entered, the birds would fly all over the place, from rafter to rafter, throwing dust into shafts of light. I would spend days finding all sorts of secret chambers in the hay. I found baby mice, newborn kittens, freshly hatched chicks, and a hundred varieties of spiders and bugs. The place was full of magic.

'Anyway, one day, when I was about ten, I was exploring the chicken coop on the second floor. It had two windows, each one about three feet off the floor. I wanted to see outside. I jumped up to rest my stomach on one of the windowsills while I took in the view. You could see out to the ravine, along the creek, and to the forest beyond the fields at the back. My feet were dangling about a foot off the floor. When I was finished, I pushed myself back down off the windowsill and felt a sharp pain in my foot. A rusty nail had pierced my old North Star shoes. It was driven an inch into the centre of my foot. It hurt so bad I could hardly stand, but there was no one around to help. I had to extract the nail from my foot and make my way back to the house on my own. And to add insult to injury, I remember going to the doctor and getting the biggest tetanus shot anyone had ever seen. I had difficulty walking for a few weeks. That curbed my enthusiasm for the barn for a while.

'It wasn't until a few years later that I started going into the barn again. One day, when Mom was walking in the ravine, she came to one of those old white pine trees that grew on its slope. They towered over the land. At the bottom was a fledging red-tailed hawk that seemed to have fallen and damaged its wing. She approached it and it didn't resist, so she picked it up. She held it by the legs, with the talons away from her body, and cradled it in her arms. She then walked back to the barn, and placed the injured bird in the empty chicken coop. She called a man from the Ministry of Natural Resources to see if he could do anything to help, but he was fairly pessimistic. He said the bird's wing was broken, and that it would probably never fly. He said there was no place to care for such a bird, so we might as well dispose of it. Mom had no such intent, and did what she could to help. She read about its dietary needs, and spoke to people she thought might know something about these birds. Every day she gave it cat food and fresh water.

'When you entered the coop, the hawk would just stare at you. When you left, you could spy through the cracks and watch it hop over to its meal. As the months passed it seemed to get stronger, until one day it tried to fly to its food. It was awkward at first, but eventually it got the hang of it. Through time, we could see the bird was getting better. With its health seemingly restored, Mom made a plan to release it. We threw open the main barn doors and opened the chicken coop door, placing some food in front of it to tempt it out. We left a trail of food to freedom, Hansel and Gretel style. Following the food the hawk hopped out of the coop, and seemed content to sit amongst the bales of hay for a while. Its movements were tentative, so we made a lot of noise, waving our arms and yelling for it to leave. Our actions shook its complacency, and it jumped to the door's threshold, looking over the barnyard and ravine. Again, it seemed hesitant to leave. Then, something must have sparked its intuition. All at once, it jumped and glided across the barnyard. It landed on the old hand pump near the well house, and looked back towards the open barn. Then, with a mighty force it sprung into the air, beating its wings and catching the wind currents. It rose higher and higher. It circled the barn, looking down on us below. It did this for five or ten minutes before heading out over the fields in complete freedom. I remember thinking how majestic it looked as it soared away. The image is etched in my mind. From that time forward, I had no fear of the barn, and it became a favourite place once again.

'I think this experience helped me learn about healing, though I'm sure I didn't realize it at the time. A place of pain does not always have to remain that way. It can be transformed through knowledge, care, and time. This experience has since become a significant reference point in my thoughts about healing. It's a little like that dream you once had about throwing the baby eagle from the nest, Mishomis.

'Anyway, I don't think much of what we teach in law school does a very good job of addressing Anishinabek notions of healing. That's one reason I am writing the book. I think our practices and teachings can help remedy this deficiency. The Canadian legal system seems to be so oriented around material concerns. It's a large bureaucracy, filled with professionals, paper, management, and delay. In criminal matters, it primarily apportions blame or guilt. In civil matters, its remedies are mainly monetary. The system has many strengths, but it has a hard time staying focused on people and their relationships. It needs an infusion of other ideas. There is a search going on right now for alternative processes. Our system seems to be more oriented around relationships. To recover this focus, I believe the development of our laws and systems should once again be the mainstream of legal thought in our territories. We should resolve our disputes by judging them by these broader principles.'

Mishomis nods his agreement and adds, 'Healing will expand when our people judge the lessons behind their experiences by these principles.' Mishomis looks at the picture in front of him, his sons in front of the church his father built. 'Your story about the barn is a good one. We can be healed from our carelessness and wrongdoing. Knowledge, the right care, and time are important prescriptions. But that's not enough. Sometimes we don't recognize when we're hurting ourselves or others. Heaven knows I haven't. You need good ideas as a reference point to help you realize the harm you're causing, or you need someone like your mother around, who knows our principles and has the knowledge about how to apply them.'

'I wish Canada would recognize all the harm they've caused our people,' the young man interjects. 'Maybe they would see the harm if they viewed things from our perspective and were attentive to our laws and traditions. Their laws don't seem to acknowledge the systemic harm. Canada's legal system doesn't appear to be capable of framing the issue in broad enough terms to provide relief.'

'Your point's a good one, grandson, but we can't get caught up in constantly blaming others when they bring us pain. Healing has to move in two directions. On the one hand, when we cause harm, we need to restore what we've taken to the extent that we can. On the other hand, when someone has harmed us, balance is restored by getting on with our lives, and not letting another's exercise of agency poison us.

'I'll always remember an example about this from a man in Arizona.[3] A group of young people decided to spend a day in the desert. They drove out of the city, through the flatlands, and into some canyons. They put on their hiking boots and set out on foot across the harsh terrain. They had a great day, enjoying the beauty of the land. Late in the evening they returned to their cars and prepared for their journey home. Just as they were about to leave, one of the girls stepped on a snake that had been sunning itself on a rock. It lashed out in defence, biting her on the ankle and sinking its venom deep into her leg. It took a moment for the others to realize what had occurred, but when they did, they set about trying to find and destroy the snake. Their intent was good, as they didn't want others to come after them and be harmed by the snake's strike. They spent about twenty minutes looking for the snake, but it had disappeared.

'Then they remembered their friend who had been hurt, so they returned to help her. When they got to the car, her leg had started to swell and she was becoming delirious. On the two-hour journey back to the city, her condition rapidly deteriorated. Finally, they arrived at the hospital. She was taken into emergency, where she received all the assistance they could give her. She survived the snake bite, but not all was well. Unfortunately, she had to have her leg amputated because there was no other way to stop the flow of venom from reaching her heart. The doctor said that if she had only arrived twenty minutes earlier, they probably would have been able to save her leg.'

'I've heard you tell that story before, Mishomis,' the young man said. 'It always feels sad when I hear it. The time they spent searching for the snake was the amount of time needed to save her leg. I can see what you mean about healing. Not only do we have to take action when we hurt others, but we also have to take action so others don't unduly harm us, and we have to take that action as quickly as we can. We can poison our lives if we try to fight every injustice we encounter. We have to be wise, and choose when to strike back. No one can face every challenge alone, and you have to leave some wrongs behind so you get on with your life. I am not excusing injustice and harm, these have to be addressed, but you may not be the one best prepared to remedy every wrong. That's why we work together, and have communities of relationships. Chances are there's someone out there who's willing and able to address the harm we've suffered. It's one reason others must start to recognize our laws, because they can work with us to eliminate injustice. It's also why our communities need to become healthier, so that we can pool our talents and gifts. We all need to work together, to take action and restore relationships.'

'That reminds me of something I read in the band newsletter the other day,' says Nokomis. 'It's an old story from the 1830s that actually happened in the French River area on the other side of the bay. It relates to what you said about working together to take action and restore relationships. Let me see if I can find it.'

Nokomis stands and heads for her new desk. A laminated map of the world covers its entire top surface, so she can see where things happen in the world. She opens a drawer, and rifles through her files. She pulls a few pages of photocopied paper from a file. 'This is it! I knew it was in here somewhere.' She sits back down at the kitchen table, and passes the clipping to her grandson. 'Read this, it's a story about a Windigo and how our people used their laws to deal with people who threatened individuals and the community. Windigos were people who went mad and took the lives of others, becoming cannibals. They're also a symbol of greed and consumption because they're constantly hungry and devour all around them, but are never satisfied. I think your cousin Darlene found the story, and passed it on to the newsletter.'

The young man takes the document in his hands, and turns to the article. He begins reading it aloud:

Account given by Mayamaking of the murder of an Idiot last winter by a band of Indians near French River, during the winter of 1838, recorded by Jarvis, Superintendent of Indian affairs.

  He came among us at the very beginning of last winter, having in most severe weather walked six days, without either kindling a fire, or eating any food.

During the most part of this winter he was quiet enough, but as the sugar season approached got noisy and restless. He went off to a lodge, and there remained ten days, frequently eating a whole deer at two meals. After that he went to another [lodge] WHEN a great change was visible in his person. His form seemed to have dilated and his face was the color of death. At this lodge he first exhibited the most decided professions of madness; and we all considered that he had become a Windigo (giant). He did not sleep but kept on walking round the lodge saying 'I shall have a fine feast.' Soon this (caused) plenty of fears in this lodge, among both the old and growing. He then tore open the veins at his wrist with his teeth, and drank his blood. The next night was the same, he went out from the lodge and without an axe broke off many saplings about 9 inches in circumference. [He] never slept but worked all that night, and in the morning brought in the poles he had broken off, and at two TRIPS filled a large sugar camp. He continued to drink his blood. The Indians then all became alarmed and we all started off to join our friends. The snow was deep and soft and we sank deeply into it with our snow shoes, but he without shoes or stockings barely left the indent of his toes on the surface. He was stark naked, tearing all his clothes given to him off as fast as they were put on. He still continued drinking blood and refused all food eating nothing but ice and snow.

We then formed a council to determine how to act as we feared he would eat our children.

It was unanimously agreed that he must die. His most intimate friend undertook to shoot him not wishing any other hand to do it.

After his death we burned the body, and all was consumed but the chest which we examined and found to contain an immense lump of ice which completely filled the cavity.

The LAD, who carried into effect the determination of the council, has given himself to the father of him who is no more: to hunt for him, plant and fill all the duties of a son. We also have all made the old man presents and he is now perfectly satisfied.

This deed was not done under the influence of whiskey. There was none there, it was the deliberate act of this tribe in council.[4]

When the young man finishes reading, he places the paper on the table in front of him. 'Does that tell you something about our principles and how we used to exercise our laws?' his grandmother asks.

The young man thinks for a moment before responding, and scans the paper once again. 'This is quite exciting, Nokomis,' he begins. 'Look at the problem they faced. The community had no other resources for their protection but themselves, their extended family, and friends. The onset of their problems with the man was slow and gradual, and developed over most of the winter. His health and mental state seems to have worsened as time went by, until he began uttering threats. They did not take action right away, but seemed to wait for two or three weeks. They exercised watchfulness and patience despite the threat they were under and the harm the man was causing himself. When it finally became clear he was not getting any better, rather than taking action on their own, they went to council together. Their method of making judgment was collective, not individualized. They relied upon one another's viewpoints. They obviously thought it was very important to decide in this manner, because they travelled through heavy snow to meet together.

'When the group finally deliberated, notice what motivated their decision to kill the man. It was not retribution or anger, but defence and compassion. The man's closest friend was charged with the duty. Then there's the restorative part of the action. The father received gifts from the community, and the man who killed his son stepped into his role. Imagine if judges or lawyers had to take the place of those they prosecuted or sent to jail! This shows how Anishinabek law can be so very different. And to top it all off, the man who lost his son seemed to be satisfied with the council's decision.

'After reading this example, I think it's important to focus on the process and principles that guided their actions, rather than concentrate on the specific outcome. I am sure we would approach psychological illness very differently than our ancestors; like others, we have developed a more refined understanding of mental disorders. However, we can take guidance from the underlying principles in this account. Windigos come in different forms today. There are other harmful forms of cannibalistic consumption that destroy lands and people. The principles here could be applied to those problems. What do you think about Windigos, Nokomis?'

At that moment, a strong gust of wind buffets the windows, shaking them in their frames. Nokomis casts an anxious look around the room, pulling her sweater more tightly around herself. Another blast rattles the windows, and she gets up to test the door latches. She takes a few towels from the drawer and places them under the windows as she walks around the room. Before she sits back down at the table she checks the fire, adding another log.

As she resettles at the table, Nokomis says, 'I still think Windigos stalk the land. I have felt their presence over the last month. Sometimes I feel as if I am being frozen from the inside out, the pain is so hard to bear. I am grateful for our stories and ideas, they do help me move forward, but I understand blood running from wrists and a hunger that can never be filled. It's easy to sit here and philosophize about healing, and talk about how our stories should guide our actions. But it's more difficult than words. Don't get me wrong, it's a very important thing you are trying to write about and understand. You should keep working at your book; it may do some good, as long as you remember that words are never sufficient to convey the complexity of our laws. You also have to practise law. It has to be experienced. It has to be lived. How many people do you think will believe Windigos still shadow the land, even with your explanations, grandson? We can't dismiss Windigos lightly, but many will doubt their existence.'

As Nokomis finishes speaking, the blizzard redoubles it rage outside the small log cabin at the edge of the lake. Driving snow sticks to the windows and pushes against the door, while the howling wind tears at the roof. Ice and snow slowly work their way further under the south-west corner of the house, undermining its foundation. The world outside is chaotic and dangerous. Inside, the young man and his grandparents are safe, for the moment, protected by the stove's warmth and their stories.

CHEEBY-AKEENG[1]

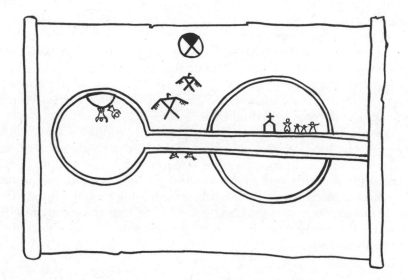

The snow sleeps peacefully on the branches as Nokomis and Mishomis
climb through the forest. They had arisen early to begin their journey.
Tiny creatures greet the sun as the new morning light lengthens shadows across the land. White rabbits, brown mice, and small chickadees
leave a complex network of tracks as they scurry through the snow. An
otter slide is visible along the banks of the river. The world feels new.
Everything is bright, crisp, and clean as they start their journey.

   Nokomis and Mishomis walk lightly through the bush as they start
along the path that climbs up the escarpment. Though it is still winter,
a flock of large birds has been seen circling the bluff in the past few
days. Nokomis and Mishomis have watched them from a distance, seeing black flecks catching currents at the high cliff's edge. Most birds fly
south for the winter and, curious, Mishomis and Nokomis have awok-
en early to get a closer look.

'I always love this time of day,' Nokomis says. 'The Creator feels close in the new light of morning. It's almost as if he remakes the world each day. You can feel his lingering presence. When I was a little girl, I believed that if I woke early enough I would catch him working. Now I realize I see his work whenever and wherever I look, but daybreak still brings that special closeness.'

'I know what you mean,' Mishomis responds. 'I feel it, too; it is truly miraculous. But this day also feels different, somehow. Have you ever felt so alive? There's something extraordinary in the air. Listen to the blue jays in the trees. Their calls sound distant, as if they're echoes from another world. And look at this snow. Have you ever seen anything so white and pure?'

Nokomis looks around her as they walk through the drifts, sun glinting off the soft powdered banks lining their path. 'It really is beautiful, isn't it? It's been a long time since we've been out walking this early, especially this time of year. I think we've just forgotten how inspiring it is out here. We're not as young as we used to be. Memory fades, even as it intensifies.'

Mishomis nods in agreement as they walk on. The path narrows as it rises. 'I'm afraid the years have taken their toll on me; it's not easy growing old. I've lost so much vitality. I've trudged up similar hills so many times, as a child, in my youth, as a younger man; you'd think all that climbing would have made me stronger. But here I am, an old man: *akiwenzie*. I find it hard to get around most days. I haven't had the energy to make my way up here until today. It is good to be back on the land like this again. I feel so peaceful. I think we're in for a special experience. I can't wait to see what kind of birds are up here.'

As the sun rises higher, spreading its warmth through the bush, clumps of snow gently fall to the forest floor, cascading from the branches around them. The woods are bathed in the aroma of pine and cedar, which strengthens as the morning advances. Nokomis inhales deeply, drawing new life from the trees. She looks back at Mishomis. 'Our grandson would love this place. It's too bad we didn't see him this morning. I was hoping he could join us. Everything was so quiet around his place, though. Since that storm, we haven't seen much of him. *Ishpau-goonugauh*, the snow has been so deep. We haven't really seen many people at all, since we were buried that day.'

As she speaks, Mishomis notes the radiance in his wife's eyes. He has never felt stronger about their relationship. He loves her deeply. He renews his pace as she leads him up the path. 'I'm glad it's just you and

I today,' Mishomis says. 'I think our grandson will be just fine. It's nice to spend the day together, just you and I.'

They pass by an abandoned farm house that once belonged to his brother Jack. A mantle of snow covers the ruin. A couple of dogs run out from the crumbled structure, keeping them company and ushering them along their way. Nag'anal'mot takes the lead.

As they watch the dogs run ahead of them, Nokomis turns the conversation. 'Remember that story about Odaemin? This path reminds me of him, *agidau-akeewae-ummoh*. There was a large dog that sat beside the path, remember? He made sure no one returned to the land of the living once they had gone too far. It must have been quite an experience for Odaemin to travel the path of souls, reach the land of the dead, and then return.'

'I haven't thought about that story for a while,' Mishomis says. 'He was lucky to return. Death is a long journey.'

Nokomis reflects on her husband's answer as the dogs depart from the path, chasing through the undergrowth and branches, barking at some snowbound soul.

A snowy white owl, *kookookoo*, swoops from the trees above the dogs. It crosses their path and glides deeper into the woods. Mishomis suddenly recalls the baby eaglets he tried to rescue in his youth. It was good to come to life's end and witness the strength that still surrounded him. While too many had been prematurely cast from the nest, the owl reminded him that others had reached the height of their potential. They had grown to become grandmothers and grandfathers. Nokomis and Mishomis stopped to listen to the owl's receding call. When the voice was gone, a gentle stillness settled around them. They pressed forward, crossing *kookoogaupigun*, and continued their journey up the escarpment.

E-nuh-mah-buh-kee-zis: See How the Morning Sun. Strains of the hymn fill the church as the congregation focuses their attention on the conductor. The young man sits beside his mother, father, and sister, as their voices mingle with the congregation. Shafts of light stream through the stained-glass windows, refracting their many colours.

At the front of the church, the bodies of Nokomis and Mishomis lie in separate caskets. A young child escapes her mother's arms and runs up the aisle. She reaches out to her great-great-grandmother and grandfather, and runs her hand over their coffins. She calls their names, but the bodies remain still. Looking back at her mother, the young child gives a questioning look. Then, raising her blanket, she turns and places it over her father's grandmother's body.

When the service is finished, the caskets are carried into the cold winter day, and loaded into the waiting cars. The congregation follows, spreading out over the four directions from the church at the heart of the reserve.

The people look around them. The four hills surrounding the reserve stand out in the crisp winter light. The northern-most escarpment seems particularly bright, bathed in dappled sunlight and wrapped in quiet serenity.

Cheeby. Nokomis and Mishomis climb higher as they near their destination. They feel like they have been climbing for ages. The path has been long and they have laboured hard to make it this far. They now walk silently, struggling against the deep gravity of the incline. The dogs stop in their tracks, near the edge of the bluff, watching the two old people approach the escarpment's pinnacle. Its upper reaches are bathed in sunlight. Nokomis and Mishomis stop, and look out over the vista below them. They turn to each other and join hands, as a smile passes between them. They inch forward. At the edge of the bluff, on the top of the hill, they survey the reserve spread out below. Their eyes trace the line of the shore, following its contour around the peninsula. Their attention is drawn to a large bird passing below them. Its wing span is immense: Animikee – Thunderbird, the guardian of the fourth realm. Another bird comes into sight, and then another. Seven birds glide on the winds rising off the escarpment. They swirl and soar upon the ever-changing currents. Nokomis and Mishomis stand at the pinnacle, looking down on the thunderbirds and the people of the land below. As they gaze out over the reserve, they notice that the gentle sound of laughter begins to fill the air. They soon hear the quiet whispers of familiar and loving voices from their childhood. A fine mist gently blows over them. Sweetgrass smoke curls and blends with the breeze. Past generations slowly become visible around them. The people standing at the crown of this last hill wear the lines and furrows of the terrain they crossed. The white of the stone-ashen sky adorns their heads, purified through their experiences.

Notes

Preface

1 He dreams and welcomes spirits into his presence. See Basil Johnston, *Anishinaubae Thesaurus* (Lansing: Michigan State University, 2007), 181.
2 David Treuer, *Native American Fictions: A User's Manual* (St Paul, MN: Graywolf Press, 2006). What Treuer sees as a debate between authentic and inauthentic voices in Native American writing, I view as different styles and methods of writing within Anishinabek genres and traditions. Recognizing diversity within Anishinabek expression allows for variations between authors, including the use of mixed metaphors, misplaced dialects, fragmentary memories, and fluid identities. For further comment, see Matthew L.M. Fletcher, '"Native American Fiction" Tough on Indian Culture,' *Indian Country Today* (August 2007), retrieved 20 January 2009 from http://works.bepress.com/matthew_fletcher/22.
3 An earlier draft of chapter 2 was published as 'Taking What's Not Yours' (2003–4) 22 *Windsor Yearbook of Access to Justice* 253, and 'Indian Agency: Forming First Nations Law in Canada' (2001) 24 *Political and Legal Anthropology Review (PoLAR)* 9. A previous draft of chapter 13 was published as 'Practical Recolonization: Indigenous Rights in Australia' (2005) 28 *University of New South Wales Law Review* 614. An earlier version of chapter 14 was published as 'Fourword/Foreword: Issues, Individuals, Institutions, Ideologies' (2002) 1 *Indigenous Law Journal* 1.
4 Francis Densmore, *Chippewa Customs* (St Paul: Minnesota Historical Society, 1979), 78–86.

1. Daebaujimoot

1 The storyteller: a friend of Nokomis (Nanabush's grandmother) and tutor

to Nanabush. Daebaudjimoot began the practice of Anishinabek storytelling and is a guardian of the nation's traditions, though he is seldom taken seriously. See Basil Johnston, *Anishinaubae Thesaurus* (Lansing: Michigan State University, 2007), 16.

2 Meaning 'beautiful point of land partly surrounded by water.' Located on the southern shores of what is now called Lake Huron, and part of the larger Anishinabek/Ojibway nation surrounding the Great Lakes.

3 Basil Johnston, *Ojibway Heritage* (Toronto: McClelland and Stewart, 1976), 109–18.

4 Dan. 2:1, King James Version.

5 Anne McGillivary and Brenda Comaskey, *Black Eyes All the Time: Intimate Violence, Aboriginal Women and the Justice System* (Toronto: University of Toronto Press, 1999); see also *Voices of Aboriginal Women: Aboriginal Women Speak Out About Violence* (Ottawa: Canadian Council on Social Development and the Native Women's Association of Canada, 1991); Joyce Green, ed., *Making Space for Indigenous Feminism* (Halifax: Fernwood Publishing, 2007).

6 Kathleen MacMillan et al., 'Prevalence of Child Physical and Sexual Abuse in the Community: Results from the Ontario Health Supplement' (1997) 278 *Journal of the American Medical Association* 131.

7 John Borrows, *Recovering Canada: The Resurgence of Indigenous Law* (Toronto: University of Toronto Press, 2002), 56–7.

8 An excellent version of this story is told in Basil Johnston's *Tales the Elders Told: Ojibway Legends* (Toronto: Royal Ontario Museum, 1981), 12–16.

2. W'aud-issookae

1 To call on the manitous for their assistance in the creation and narrative of a story; see Basil Johnston, *Anishinaubae Thesaurus* (Lansing: Michigan State University, 2007), 141.

2 For some purposes, Indian Agents were often referred to as superintendents under the *Indian Act*, R.S.C. 1985, c. 32. For a list of their regulatory authority over Indians, see ss. 2(1), 32, 63, 50(2), 40, 86, 103(1), 108, 117(b), 122(c).

3 Francis Paul Prucha, *The Great Father: The United States Government and American Indians* (Lincoln: University of Nebraska Press, 1984), 91, 97, 113, 140, 143, 159–63, 298–9; Royal Commission on Aboriginal Peoples, *Final Report of the Royal Commission on Aboriginal Peoples*, vol. 1, *Looking Forward, Looking Back* (Ottawa: Supply and Services, 1996), 297–9.

4 Prucha, *The Great Father*, 512–19, 522–9.

5 George Manuel and Michael Posluns, *The Fourth World: An Indian Reality* (Don Mills: Collier-MacMillan, 1974), 54.
6 John Borrows, 'A Genealogy of Law: Inherent Sovereignty and First Nations Self-Government' (1992) 30 *Osgoode Hall Law Journal* 291, 345–6; Peter Schmalz, *The Ojibwa of Southern Ontario* (Toronto: University of Toronto Press, 1991), 208–26.
7 The Anishinabek language divides itself into the animate and inanimate. Many things that English speakers would consider inanimate are animate in Anishinabek, such as rocks, household utensils, or tools.
8 See *R. v. Sparrow*, [1990] 1 S.C.R. 1075, 1103: 'For many years the rights of Indians to their aboriginal lands were virtually ignored.'
9 *Reference Re Quebec Secession*, [1998] 2 S.C.R., para. 74.
10 *Logan v. Styres* (1959), 20 D.L.R. (2d) 416 (Ont. H.C.) (upholding forcible eviction of traditional Haudenosaunee government).
11 For example, Joseph Trutch, in denying Aboriginal title in B.C., observed: 'The title of the Indians in the fee of the public lands, or any portion thereof, has never been acknowledged by Government, but, on the contrary, is distinctly denied.' *British Columbia, Papers Connected with the Indian Land Question, 1850–1875* (Victoria: Government Printer, 1875), appendix, 11.
12 John S. Milloy, *A National Crime: The Canadian Government and the Residential School System, 1879–1986* (Winnipeg: University of Manitoba Press, 1999).
13 Aboriginal people are constantly charged with criminal offences for hunting and fishing in traditional economic pursuits. Some high-profile cases are *R. v. Syliboy*, [1929] 1 D.L.R. 307 (N.S. Co. Ct.); *Simon v. The Queen* (1985) 24 D.L.R. (4th) 390 (S.C.C.); *R. v. Horseman*, [1990] 1 S.C.R. 901 (S.C.C.); *R. v. Cote* (1996) 138 D.L.R. (4th) 185 (S.C.C.); *R. v. Badger* (1996) 133 D.L.R. (4th) 324 (S.C.C.); *R. v. Marshall*, [1999] 3 S.C.R. (S.C.C.).
14 *Thomas v. Norris*, [1992] 2 C.N.L.R. 139 (B.C.S.C.) (Aboriginal spirit dancing not protected by *Charter*); *Jack and Charlie v. The Queen* (1985) 21 D.L.R. (4th) 641 (S.C.C.) (taking fresh deer meat for Aboriginal death ceremony not protected).
15 Many bands were kept apart or relocated to prevent their association because of a government fear that they would organize to resist impingements of their rights.
16 A Crown fiduciary duty has been articulated in an attempt to cure violations of Aboriginal rights stemming from differences in the way Aboriginal people hold and access their rights. Significant cases in this regard are *Guerin v. The Queen*, (1984) 13 D.L.R. (4th) 321 (S.C.C.); *Kruger v. The Queen*, (1985) 17 D.L.R. (4th) 591 (F.C.A.); *Blueberry River Indian Band v. Canada*

(1995) 130 D.L.R. (4th) 193 (S.C.C.). For a fuller discussion, see Len Rotman, *Parallel Paths* (Toronto: University of Toronto Press, 1996).

17 *Canada (A.G.) v. Lavell*, [1974] S.C.R. 1349 (invidious distinctions in *Indian Act* on basis of sex upheld).

18 *Reference Re Quebec Secession*, [1998] 2 S.C.R., para. 74.

19 Indians could not vote for the first seventy-five years after Confederation. See, for example, British Columbia's *Qualification and Registration of Voters Amendment Act*, 1872, s. 13. Indians did not generally enjoy federal voting rights until 1960, when the federal franchise was finally extended to them without qualification. The provinces extended the franchise to Indians at different dates: British Columbia 1949, Manitoba 1952, Ontario 1954, Saskatchewan 1960, Prince Edward Island and New Brunswick 1963, Alberta 1965, Quebec 1969. The Inuit were excluded from the federal franchise in 1934, but had the vote restored to them in 1950. Métis were always considered citizens able to vote in federal and provincial elections. Indians also had restricted access to legal remedies. For example, see section 141 of the *Indian Act* 1927, which read:

> Every person who, without the consent of the Superintendent General expressed in writing, receives, obtains, solicits or requests from any Indian any payment or contribution or promise of any payment or contribution for the purpose of raising a fund or providing money for the prosecution of any claim which the tribe or band of Indians to which such Indian belongs, or of which he is a member, has or is represented to have for the recovery of any claim or money for the benefit of said tribe or band, shall be guilty of an offence and liable upon summary conviction for each such offence to a penalty ...

For commentary, see Brian Titley, *A Narrow Vision: Duncan Campbell Scott and the Administration of Indian Affairs in Canada* (Vancouver: UBC Press, 1986), 59.

20 See Royal Commission on Aboriginal Peoples, *The Final Report of the Royal Commission on Aboriginal Peoples*, vol. 3, *Gathering Strength* (Ottawa: Supply and Services, 1996).

21 The most prominent example of Indigenous concerns being concealed by Canadian federalism is found in the earliest and at one time leading case *St Catharines Milling and Lumber Company v. The Queen* (1888) 14 App. Cas. 46 (J.C.P.C.).

22 John Borrows, *Recovering Canada: The Resurgence of Indigenous Law* (Toronto: University of Toronto Press, 2002).

23 John Borrows, 'A Genealogy of Law: Inherent Sovereignty and First Na-, tions Self-Government' (1992) 30 *Osgoode Hall Law Journal* 291.

24 *Indian Act, Statutes of Canada*, 39 Victoria, c. 18, now as amended, R.S.C. 1985, c. I-5.

25 In 1920, the deputy superintendent of Indian Affairs (the highest non-elected official dealing with Indians) stated, 'Our objective is to continue until there is not a single Indian in Canada that has not been absorbed into the body politic and there is no Indian question, and no Indian Depart-ment, that is the whole object of this Bill.' Duncan Campbell Scott, deputy superintendent general of Indian Affairs, testimony before the Special Committee of the House of Commons examining the *Indian Act* amend-ments of 1920, National Archives of Canada, Record Group 10, volume 6810, file 470-2-3, volume 7, pp. 55 (L-3) and 63 (N-3).

26 Sections 20 to 41 of the *Indian Act* are largely concerned with real property on Indian reserves. While the *Indian Act* does not allow for the alienation of reservation land to non-Indians, as under the provisions of the *General Allotment Act* in the United States 24 St. 388 (1887), it did attempt to con-vert collectively held Indian land to individual ownership. Fortunately, the act has not always been successful in converting Indian lands to individual ownership, as many people still hold their land under customary prac-tices. For cases interpreting the act's sections dealing with individual land ownership, see Shin Imai, *The 2000 Annotated Indian Act and Aboriginal Con-stitutional Provisions* (Toronto: Carswell, 2000), 50–79.

27 Sections 74 to 86 of the *Indian Act* deal with matters of governance; see Imai, ibid., 103–21.

28 Douglas Cole and Ira Chaikin, *An Iron Hand Upon the People: The Law against the Potlatch on the Northwest Coast* (Vancouver: Douglas and McIn-tyre, 1990), 5–13; Katherine Pettipas, *Severing the Ties That Bind: Govern-ment Repression of Indigenous Religious Ceremonies on the Prairies* (Winnipeg: University of Manitoba Press, 1994).

29 Sarah Carter, *Lost Harvests: Prairie Indian Farmers and Government Policy* (Montreal: McGill-Queen's University Press, 1993); Peter Douglas Elias, *Development of Aboriginal People's Communities* (North York: Captus Press, 1991).

30 Royal Commission on Aboriginal Peoples, *The Final Report of the Royal Commission on Aboriginal Peoples*, vol. 4, *Gathering Strength* (Ottawa: Supply and Services, 1996), 24–34; Larry Gilbert, *Entitlement to Indian Status and Membership Codes in Canada* (Toronto: Carswell, 1996); F. Laurie Barron, 'The Indian Pass System in the Canadian West, 1882–1935' (1988) 13 *Prairie Forum* 27–8.

31 Fortunately, many of the Indian Agents at Cape Croker were very ineffec-
tive, as they were absentee administrators who suffered from substance
abuse and thus were incapable of performing their duties, or were not able
to secure the cooperation of the community in their efforts. Indian Agents
were removed from Indian band council structures in the 1960s.

32 For an account of efforts to retain governance, see John Borrows, 'A Genealogy of Law: Inherent Sovereignty and First Nations Self-Government in
Canada' (1992) 30 *Osgoode Hall Law Review* 291–354.

33 *Calder v. The Attorney General of British Columbia* (1973) 34 D.L.R. (3d) 145,
[1973] S.C.R. 313.

34 Jurisprudence in the United States is mixed on this point; see *United States
v. Santa Fe Railroad* 314 US 339 (1941); *Tee-Hit-Ton v. United States* 348 US
272 (1955).

35 See *R. v. Sparrow*, [1990] 1 S.C.R. 1075 at 1104: 'It took a number of judicial
decisions and notably the *Calder* case ... to prompt a reassessment of the
position.'

36 *Calder v. The Attorney General of British Columbia* (1973) 34 D.L.R. (3d) 145,
[1973] S.C.R. 313, 156.

37 Ibid., 200.

38 The fact that an Aboriginal presence might be a permanent feature of
Canadian society is contrasted with the Court's adoption of the Royal
Commission on Aboriginal Peoples statement (see *The Final Report of the
Royal Commission on Aboriginal Peoples*, vol. 1, *Looking Forward, Looking Back*
at 137–91) that describes the relationship between the federal government
and Aboriginal peoples during the period from the early 1800s to 1969 as
one of 'displacement and assimilation.'

39 The Supreme Court itself identified this process and wrote, in *R. v. Sparrow*
at 1105:

It is clear, then, that s. 35(1) of the Constitution Act, 1982 represents the
culmination of a long and difficult struggle in both the political forum
and the courts for the constitutional recognition of aboriginal rights. The
strong representations of native associations and other groups concerned
with the welfare of Canada's aboriginal peoples made the adoption of s.
35(1) possible ...

For a discussion on the rise of Aboriginal advocacy since the early 1970s,
see Michael Asch, *Our Home and Native Land* (Toronto: Methuen, 1984).

40 The text of section 35(1) reads: 'The existing aboriginal and treaty rights of
the aboriginal peoples of Canada are hereby recognized and affirmed.'

41 Section 37 of the *Constitution Act, 1982* mandated these conferences, and
    four were held between 1983 and 1987. For a discussion, see Kathy Brock,
    'The Politics of Aboriginal Self-Government: A Canadian Paradox' (1991)
    34 *Canadian Public Administration* 272.
42 *R. v. Sparrow,* [1990] 1 S.C.R. 1075, 1103.
43 *Oregon Jack Creek Indian Band v. Canadian National Railway,* [1990] 1 S.C.R.
    117; *R. v. Horseman,* [1990] 1 S.C.R. 901; *R. v. Sioui,* [1990] 1 S.C.R. 1025; *R. v.
    Sparrow,* [1990] 1 S.C.R. 1075; *Mitchell v. Peguis Indian Band,* [1990] 2 S.C.R.
    85; *Ontario (A.G.) v. Bear Island Foundation,* [1991] 2 S.C.R. 570; *Williams v.
    Canada,* [1992] 1 S.C.R. 877; *Quebec (A.G.) v. Canada (N.E.B.),* [1994] 1 S.C.R.
    159; *R. v. Howard,* [1994] 2 S.C.R. 299; *Native Women's Association v. Canada,*
    [1994] 3 S.C.R. 627; *C.P. v. Matsqui Indian Band,* [1995] 1 S.C.R. 3; *Blueberry
    River Indian Band v. Canada,* [1995] 4 S.C.R. 344; *R. v. Badger,* [1996] 1 S.C.R.
    771; *R. v. Lewis,* [1996] 1 S.C.R. 921; *R. v. Nikal,* [1996] 1 S.C.R. 1013; *R. v.
    Vanderpeet,* [1996] 2 S.C.R. 507; *R. v. N.T.C. Smokehouse,* [1996] 2 S.C.R. 672;
    R. v. Gladstone, [1996] 2 S.C.R. 723; *R. v. Pamajewon,* [1996] 2 S.C.R. 821;
    R. v. Adams, [1996] 3 S.C.R. 101; *R. v. Cote,* [1996] 3 S.C.R. 139; *Opetchesaht
    v. Canada,* [1997] 2 S.C.R. 119; *St. Marys v. Cranbook,* [1997] 2 S.C.R. 657;
    Delgamuukw v. British Columbia, [1997] 3 S.C.R. 1010, *R. v. Williams,* [1998]
    1 S.C.R. 1128; *Union of New Brunswick Indians v. New Brunswick (Minister
    of Finance),* [1998] 1 S.C.R. 1161; *R. v. Sundown,* [1999] 1 S.C.R. 393; *R. v.
    Gladue,* [1999] 1 S.C.R. 688; *Corbiere v. Canada,* [1999] 2 S.C.R. 203; *Westbank
    First Nation v. British Columbia Hydro,* [1999] 3 S.C.R. 134; *R. v. Marshall (I),*
    [1999] 3 S.C.R. 465; *R. v. Marshall (II),* [1999] 3 S.C.R. 533; *R. v. Wells,* [2000]
    1 S.C.R 207; *Musqeaum Indian Band v. Glass,* [2000] 2 S.C.R. 633; *Lovelace v.
    Ontario,* [2000] 2 S.C.R.; *Mitchell v. M.N.R.,* [2001] 1 S.C.R. 911; *Osoyoos In-
    dian Band v. Oliver,* [2001] 3 S.C.R., 746; *Kitkala Indian Band v. B.C.,* [2002] 2
    S.C.R. 146; *Ross River Dena Council Band v. Canada* 2002 SCC 54; *Wewaykim
    Indian Band v. Canada* 2002 SCC 79.
44 John Borrows, 'Sovereignty's Alchemy: Delgamuukw v. British Columbia'
    (1999) 37 *Osgoode Hall Law Review* 537.
45 *Delgamuukw v. British Columbia,* 1111; emphasis in original. For commen-
    tary, see Catherine Bell, 'New Directions in the Law of Aboriginal Rights'
    (1998) 77 *Canadian Bar Review* 36, 62. For a critique of the infringement of
    constitutional Aboriginal rights, see Kent McNeil, 'How Can the Infringe-
    ments of the Constitutional Rights of Aboriginal Peoples Be Justified?'
    (1997) 8 *Constitutional Forum* 33.
46 I would like to thank the Honourable Justice Tony Mandamin of the
    Federal Court, formerly of the Calgary Criminal Division of the Provincial
    Court and of the Peacement (Tsuu T'ina First Nation) Court, for sharing

with me the story of 'Nanabush and the Dogs,' on which the event at the
end of this chapter is based. Judge Mandamin is from the Wikwemikong
First Nation, a neighbouring band to Cape Croker, also located on Lake
Huron in Georgian Bay.

3. Pauwauwaein

1 Revelation: An awakening; a vision that gives understanding to matters
   that were previously obscure. See Basil Johnston, *Anishinaubae Thesaurus*
   (Lansing: Michigan State University, 2007), 19.
2 Thanks to Basil Johnston for bringing this word to my attention.
3 US, 120 S.Ct. 2597 (USSC).
4 *R. v. Morgentaler*, [1988] 1 S.C.R. 30, per Wilson J.
5 The right to life was interpreted by Wilson J in *R. v. Morgentaler*, [1988] 1
   S.C.R. 30 in the following terms:

   … the right to liberty contained in s. 7 guarantees to every individual a
   degree of personal autonomy over important decisions affecting their
   private lives. The question then becomes whether the decision of a
   woman to terminate her pregnancy falls within this class of protected
   persons. I have no doubt it does. This decision is one that will have profound psychological, economic and social consequences for the pregnant
   woman. The circumstances giving rise to it can be complex and varied
   and there may, and usually are, powerful considerations militating in opposite directions. It is a decision that deeply reflects the way the woman
   thinks about herself and her relationship to others and society at large.
   It is not just a medical decision; it is a profound social and ethical one as
   well.

6 Section 7 of the *Charter* states: 'Everyone has the right to life, liberty and
   security of the person, and the right not to be deprived thereof except in
   accordance with the principles of fundamental justice.' For an interpretation of security of the person, see Dickson J in *R. v. Morgentaler*, [1988] 1
   S.C.R. 30, who writes: 'Forcing a woman, by threat of criminal sanction,
   to carry a foetus to term unless she meets certain criteria unrelated to her
   own priorities and aspirations, is a profound interference with a woman's
   body and thus a violation of security of the person.'
7 See Margaret MacMillan, *Paris 1919: Six Months that Changed the World*
   (New York: Random House, 2001).
8 Ibid.

4. Daeb-awaewin

1 To tell what one knows according to his perception and fluency; see Basil Johnston, *Anishinaubae Thesaurus* (Lansing: Michigan State University, 2007), 73.

2 For an alternative discussion of this issue, see John Borrows, 'With or Without You: First Nations Law (in Canada)' (1996) *McGill Law Journal* 630.

3 Of course, this is technically an endnote, not a footnote. For more information about the justification for footnotes, see Anthony Grafton, *The Footnote: A Curious History* (Cambridge, MA: Harvard University Press, 1997).

4 For an exploration of Holocaust denial, see Erna Paris, *Long Shadows: Truth, Lies and History* (Toronto: Knopf, 2001).

5 Ursula Hegi, *Stones from the River* (New York: Scribner, 1994), 286–7.

6 Jan Wong, *Red China Blues* (Toronto: Doubleday, 1996), 307; Hagonda Harry Wu, *The Chinese Gulag* (Boulder, CO: Westview Press, 1992).

7 Premier Li Peng, cited by Wong, *Red China Blues*, 236.

8 The text supporting note 5 from Hegi could be rephrased in an Indigenous context as follows: Aboriginal peoples are marked, even if they have 'blond hair and straight noses,' and look like many non-Aboriginal people around them. No doubt, this marking is often invisible to non-Aboriginal people, but is carried deep within individuals whose parents and communities have transmitted the horror of colonialism and cultural abuse. The marking is even more dramatic if you happen to have copper skin and deep brown eyes. You might have this differentiation thrown back at you on a daily basis by others from outside your family and community. But when we look at the situation even more deeply, we see that the results of legal differentiation are more than just a matter of skin colour.

9 J. Rabin, 'Job Security and Due Process: Monitoring Discretion through a Reasons Requirement' (1976) 44 *University of Chicago Law Review* 60, 77.

10 As Chief Justice John Marshall of the United States Supreme Court observed: 'It is difficult to comprehend the proposition that the inhabitants of the globe could have rightful claims of dominion over the inhabitants of the other, or over the lands they occupied; or that discovery should give the discoverer rights in the country discovered which annulled the pre-existing rights of its ancient inhabitants.' *Worcester v. Georgia* 31 US (6 Pet.) 518.

11 For an insight into Aboriginal possession of land prior to British assertions of sovereignty in northern North America, see Cole Harris and Geoffrey Matthews, eds., *Historical Atlas of Canada: From the Beginning to 1800* (Toronto: University of Toronto Press, 1987).

12 John Borrows, 'Wampum at Niagara: The Royal Proclamation, Canadian

Legal History and Self-Government,' in Michael Asch, ed., *Aboriginal and Treaty Rights in Canada: Essays on Law, Equality and Respect for Difference* (Vancouver: UBC Press, 1997), 155–72.

13 To understand how vagueness and unintelligibility relate to the rule of law, see *R. v. Nova Scotia Pharmaceutical Society*, [1992] 2 S.C.R. 606, 643: 'A law will be found unconstitutionally vague if it so lacks in precision as not to give sufficient guidance for legal debate.'

14 Jared Diamond, *Guns, Germs, and Steel: The Fates of Human Societies* (New York: W.W. Norton, 1997).

15 For further information, see Kirk Cameron, *Northern Governments in Transition: Political and Constitutional Development in the Yukon, Nunavut and North-west Territories* (Montreal: Institute for Research on Public Policy, 1995), chap. 4.

16 Kelly Gallagher-MacKay, 'Affirmative Action and Aboriginal Government: The Case for Legal Education in Nunavut' (1999) 14 *Canadian Journal of Law and Society* 21.

17 For a critical assessment of the Nisga'a Treaty, see Paul Rynard, 'Welcome In, But Check Your Rights at the Door: The James Bay and Nisga'a Agreements in Canada' (2000) 33 *Canadian Journal of Political Science*; Niel J. Sterritt, *Tribal Boundaries in the Nass Watershed* (Vancouver: UBC Press, 1998).

18 *Indian Act*, R.S.C. 1985, c. I-5. For a general discussion of the agreement, see Tom Molloy, *The World Is Our Witness: The Historic Journey of the Nisga'a into Canada* (Calgary: Fifth House, 2000).

19 See section 31.1 (2.1) of the *Fish Licencing, Ontario Regulations 664/98*, passed pursuant to the *Fish and Wildlife Conservation Act*, S.O. 1997, c. 41.

20 In many ways, the opposition to the Chippewa fishery in Ontario is reminiscent of the opposition faced by Chippewa fishers in Wisconsin in the 1970s and 1980s, and Minnesota in the 1990s. See Larry Nesper, *Walleye War: The Struggle for Ojibwe and Spearfishing Rights* (Lincoln: University of Nebraska Press, 2002).

21 *R. v. Jones*, [1993] 3 *Canadian Native Law Reporter* 182 (Ont. H.C.).

22 For a discussion of residential schools in Canada, see J.R. Miller, *Shingwauk's Vision* (Toronto: University of Toronto Press, 1996); John S. Milloy, *A National Crime: The Canadian Government and the Residential School System, 1879–1986* (Winnipeg: University of Manitoba Press, 1999).

23 Nicholas Flood Davin, *Report on Industrial Schools for Indians and Half-Breeds*, 14 March 1879, 35428–45. National Archives of Canada, Manuscript Group 26A, Sir John A. Macdonald Papers, vol. 91.

24 Royal Commission on Aboriginal Peoples, *Final Report of the Royal Commission on Aboriginal Peoples*, vol. 1, *Looking Forward, Looking Back* (Ottawa: Supply and Services, 1996), 334.

25 Ibid., 335. The graduate referred to is the late George Manuel, past president of the National Indian Brotherhood (precursor to the Assembly of First Nations) and founder of the World Council of Indigenous Peoples.
26 Ibid., 339.
27 This happened at the Port Alberni Residential School on Vancouver Island. See A.C. Hamilton and C.M. Sinclair, 'Child Welfare,' in Aboriginal Justice Implementation Commission, *Report of the Aboriginal Justice Inquiry of Manitoba*, vol. 1, *The Justice System and Aboriginal People* (Winnipeg: Queen's Printer, 1999), 514.
28 Royal Commission on Aboriginal Peoples, *Final Report of the Royal Commission on Aboriginal Peoples*, vol. 1, *Looking Forward, Looking Back* (Ottawa: Supply and Services, 1996), chap. 10, 'Residential Schools,' 365–76.
29 Leading cases which opened up the path for finding liability and remedies for Aboriginal peoples abused in residential schools are *Bazley v. Curry*, [1999] 2 S.C.R. 534 (S.C.C.); *Jacobs. v. Griffiths*, [1999] 2 S.C.R. 570 (S.C.C.); *Re Christian Brothers of Ireland* 47 O.R. 3d 674 (Ont. C.A.); *F.S.M. v. Clarke*, [1999] B.C.J. No. 1973 (B.C.S.C.); *B (WR) v. Plint* (1998) 161 D.L.R. (4th) 538 (B.C.S.C.); *P (V) v. Canada*, [2000] 1 W.W.R. 541 (Sask. Q.B.); *DW v. Canada* (1999) 107 Sask. R. 21 (Sask. Q.B.); *Re Indian Residential Schools* (2000) 287 Alta. L.R. (3rd) 62 (Alta. Q.B.).
30 For example, my friend Dr Alfred Scow, the first Aboriginal judge in British Columbia, has expressed his gratitude for certain aspects of the educational experience he had at residential school.
31 Basil Johnston, *Indian School Days* (Toronto: Key Porter Books, 1988).
32 R. Foot, 'Ottawa Plans Two Billion Dollar Abuse Bailout,' *National Post*, 31 January 2001, 1.
33 Joel Bakan, 'You Can't Always Get What You Want (or even what you need)' (1989) *Canadian Bar Review* 307.
34 John Borrows, 'With or Without You: First Nations Law (in Canada)' (1996) 41 *McGill Law Journal* 630.
35 *R. v. Van der Peet*, [1996] 2 S.C.R. 507 at 546.
36 Ibid., citing Mark Walters, 'British Imperial Constitutional Law and Aboriginal Rights: A Comment on *Delgamuukw* v. B.C.' (1992) 17 *Queen's Law Journal* 350, 412–13.

5. Pauguk

1 The flying skeleton, emaciated, sparse. See Basil Johnston, *Anishinaubae Thesaurus* (Lansing: Michigan State University, 2007), 17.
2 The version of Pauguk found in this chapter draws from Basil Johnston, *The Manitous: The Spiritual World of the Ojibway* (Toronto: Key Porter Books,

1995), 195. I also heard this story growing up, and have read it in numerous books, including Mentor L. Williams, ed., *Schoolcraft's Indian Legends* (East Lansing: Michigan State University Press, 1991), 236.

6. Aud-waudjimoowin

1 To speak allegorically; see Basil Johnston, *Anishinaubae Thesaurus* (Lansing: Michigan State University, 2007), 93.
2 *R. v. Moses*, (1992) 71 CCC (3d) 347 (Yukon Territorial Court).
3 *R. v. Gladue*, [1999] 1 S.C.R. 688 (S.C.C.) at para. 51.

7. Animikeek & Mishi-Bizheu

1 Thunderbirds and the Great Water Lynx: 'Thunderbirds are the guardians of Mother Earth's well-being … also known as the grandfathers.' The Great Lynx is a manitou of the underworld who dwells in the waters, and is the nemesis of Nanabush and humans. See Basil Johnston, *Anishinaubae Thesaurus* (Lansing: Michigan State University, 2007), 16–17.
2 This example is taken from 'Freedom to Choose,' *Gospel Principles* (Salt Lake City, UT: Church of Jesus Christ of Latter-Day Saints, 1997), 23.

8. W'pishebaubee-aushih

1 He flies in circles; see Basil Johnston, *Anishinaubae Thesaurus* (Lansing: Michigan State University, 2007), 182.
2 *U.S. v. Lara*, 324 F.3d 635 (U.S.S.C.); for commentary, see Robert Williams Jr, *Like a Loaded Weapon: The Rehnquist Court, Indian Rights and the Legal History of Racism in America* (Minneapolis: University of Minnesota Press, 2005), 149–60.
3 *Washington v. Confederated Bands and Tribes of Yakima Nation*, 439 U.S. 463, 470–1 (U.S.S.C.).
4 For analysis, see David Wilkins, *American Indian Sovereignty and the U.S. Supreme Court: The Unmasking of Justice* (Austin: University of Texas Press, 1997).
5 *Ex Parte Crow Dog* (1883) 109 U.S. 556 (U.S.S.C). See Sidney Harring, *Crow Dog's Case: American Indian Sovereignty, Tribal Law, and United States Law in the Nineteenth Century* (Cambridge: Cambridge University Press, 1994).
6 Johann Georg Kohl, *Kitchi-Gami: Life among the Lake Superior Ojibway* (St Paul: Minnesota Historical Society, 1985), 39.

9. Augoonaet-waendumoowin

1 To be suspicious, sceptical, or dubious; to disbelieve, mistrust, renounce, or repudiate. See Basil Johnston, *Anishinaubae Thesaurus* (Lansing: Michigan State University, 2007), 85.
2 Brian Bucknall, Thomas Baldwin, and David Lakin, 'Pedants, Practitioners and Prophets: Legal Education at Osgoode Hall to 1957' (1968) 6 *Osgoode Hall Law Journal* 138; Harry Arthurs, 'The Affiliation of Osgoode Hall Law School with York University' (1967) 17 *University of Toronto Law Journal* 194.
3 Though one must be careful not to romanticize this view of time and conclude that Indigenous peoples have no history. This was a problem in the work of Claude Levi-Strauss, *The Elementary Structures of Kinship* (London: Eyre and Spottiswoode, 1969).
4 John Borrows, 'Fourword/Foreword: Issues, Individuals, Institutions, Ideologies' (2002) 1 *Indigenous Law Journal* 1.
5 In this regard, I am intrigued by the Mayan calendar, which is described in Ronald Wright, *Time among the Maya: Travels in Belize, Guatemala and Mexico* (Toronto: Penguin Books, 1989).
6 Thomas Peacock, *The Four Hills of Life: Ojibwe Wisdom* (Afton, MN: Afton Historical Society Press, 2006).

10. Ashawa-munissoowin

1 To be forewarned; see Basil Johnston, *Anishinaubae Thesaurus* (Lansing: Michigan State University, 2007), 126.
2 Ibid., 12.
3 Richard White, *The Middle Ground: Indians, Empires, and Republics in the Great Lakes Region, 1650–1815* (Cambridge, UK: Cambridge University Press, 1991).
4 Darlene Johnston, *Litigating Identity: The Challenge of Aboriginality* (Vancouver: UBC Press, 2009).
5 *R. v. Kapp*, [2008] S.C.C. 41.
6 *Law v. Canada (Minister of Employment and Immigration)*, [1999] 1 S.C.R. 497.
7 Ibid., 25.
8 *Andrews v. Law Society of British Columbia*, [1989] 1 S.C.R. 143, 165, per MacIntyre J.

11. Maemaegawahsessiwuk

1 The little people, who dwell in nature and are the guardians of those who

believe; see Basil Johnston, *Anishinaubae Thesaurus* (Lansing: Michigan State University, 2007), 93.

2 This speech is a composite of three speeches Dr Frank Calder gave at the University of Victoria, from 13 to 16 October 2003, for a conference called, Let Right Be Done: The Calder Decision at 30. For the published essays from the conference, see Hamar Foster, Heather Raven, and Jeremy Webber, eds., *Let Right Be Done: Aboriginal Title, the Calder Case and the Future of Aboriginal Rights* (Vancouver: UBC Press, 2007).

12. Iskugaewin

1 To set afire; see Basil Johnston, *Anishinaubae Thesaurus* (Lansing: Michigan State University, 2007), 103.

2 Deborah Bird Rose and Shannon D'Amico, *Country of the Heart: An Indigenous Australian Heartland* (Canberra, AU: Aboriginal Studies Press, 2002), 41.

3 Shepard Kresh III, *The Ecological Indian: Myth and History* (New York: W.W. Norton, 1999).

4 Deborah Bird Rose and Shannon D'Amico, *Country of the Heart: An Indigenous Australian Heartland* (Canberra, AU: Aboriginal Studies Press, 2002), 21.

5 Ibid., 45.

6 Ibid., 23.

13. Mauz-aubindumoowin

1 A dream in which the vision is incomplete; further visions are required to clarify or complete the message. See Basil Johnston, *Anishinaubae Thesaurus* (Lansing: Michigan State University, 2007), 19.

2 The story about the four hills is found in Basil Johnston, *Ojibway Heritage* (Toronto: McClelland and Stewart, 1976), 109–19. The version in the first five paragraphs draws very strongly from this account.

3 Other academically based journals that deal with certain aspects of Indigenous legal issues are the *American Indian Law Review* based at the College of Law, University of Oklahoma (founded in 1973), the *Tribal Law Journal*, an electronic journal published by the University of New Mexico School of Law at http://tlj.unm.edu/ (founded in 2000), and the *Indigenous Law Bulletin* from the University of New South Wales (founded in 1981). The *Canadian Native Law Reporter* published academic submissions up until the late 1990s, when the large number of reported cases started crowding them

out. Their discontinuation made room for the creation of the *Indigenous Law Journal* in Canada.

4 *Calder v. A.G.B.C.*, [1973] S.C.R. 313 (S.C.C.).

5 *Mabo v. Queensland No. 2* (1992), 107 A.L.R. 1 (H.C. Aust.).

6 *Williams v. Lee* (1959) 358 U.S. 217 (U.S.S.C.). For an explanation of the pivotal role this case played in the revitalization of Indian jurisprudence in the United States, see Charles Wilkinson, *American Indians, Time and the Law* (New Haven, CT: Yale University Press, 1987), 1.

7 In those countries where the justiciability of Indigenous rights is a recent development, this is transforming the treatment of Indigenous peoples in those states. See Paul Havemann, ed., *Indigenous Peoples' Rights in Australia, Canada and New Zealand* (Oxford: Oxford University Press, 1999); Kent McNeil, *Emerging Justice: Essays on Indigenous Rights in Canada and Australia* (Saskatoon: Native Law Centre, 2001); Patrick Macklem, *Indigenous Difference and the Constitution of Canada* (Toronto: University of Toronto Press, 2001); 'Case Note, Native Title in Malaysia: Adong's Case' (2001) 3 *Asian Law Journal* 198.

8 An early source for teaching Indigenous legal issues in Canada was Peter Cumming and Neil Mickenburg, *Native Rights In Canada* (Toronto: Indian-Eskimo Association of Canada, 1971). Doug Sanders was the primary writer of the first edition, and taught a course in Native Peoples and the Law in the early 1970s. In the United States, Ralph Johnson was a pioneer in the field. For a brief description of the importance of his work, see David Getches, 'Dedication to Ralph W. Johnson' (1997) 72 *Washington Law Review* 995. For a description of Indigenous people teaching Indigenous law, see G. William Rice, 'There and Back Again: An Indian Hobbit's Holiday, Indians Teaching Indian Law' (1996) 26 *University of New Mexico Law Review* 169.

9 Robert Williams Jr, 'Vampires Anonymous and Critical Race Practice' (1997) 95 *Michigan Law Review* 741.

10 The attention the U.S. Supreme Court has paid to Native Americans has not been without its problems; see David Wilkins, *American Indian Sovereignty and the U.S. Supreme Court* (Austin: University of Texas Press, 1997); Frank Pommersheim, *Braid of Feathers: American Indian Law and Contemporary Tribal Life* (Berkeley: University of California Press, 1996); Robert Williams Jr, *Discourses of Conquest: The American Indian in Western Legal Thought* (New York: Oxford University Press, 1990); David Getches, 'Beyond Indian Law: The Rehnquist Court's Pursuit of States' Rights, Color-Blind Justice and Mainstream Values' (2001) 86 *Minnesota Law Review* 267; Philip Frickey, 'A Common Law for Our Age of Colonialism: The

Judicial Divestiture of Tribal Authority over Non-Members' (1999) 109 *Yale Law Journal* 1.

11 *Oregon Jack Creek Indian Band v. Canadian National Railway*, [1990] 1 S.C.R. 117; *R. v. Horseman*, [1990] 1 S.C.R. 901; *R. v. Sioui*, [1990] 1 S.C.R. 1025; *R. v. Sparrow*, [1990] 1 S.C.R. 1075; *Mitchell v. Peguis Indian Band*, [1990] 2 S.C.R. 85; *Ontario (A.G.) v. Bear Island Foundation*, [1991] 2 S.C.R. 570; *Williams v. Canada*, [1992] 1 S.C.R. 877; *Quebec (A.G.) v. Canada, (N.E.B.)*, [1994] 1 S.C.R. 159; *R. v. Howard*, [1994] 2 S.C.R. 299; *Native Women's Association v. Canada*, [1994] 3 S.C.R. 627; *C.P. v. Matsqui Indian Band* [1995] 1 S.C.R. 3; *Blueberry River Indian Band v. Canada*, [1995] 4 S.C.R. 344; *R. v. Badger*, [1996] 1 S.C.R. 771; *R. v. Lewis*, [1996] 1 S.C.R. 921; *R. v. Nikal*, [1996] 1 S.C.R. 1013; *R. v. Vanderpeet*, [1996] 2 S.C.R. 507; *R. v. N.T.C. Smokehouse*, [1996] 2 S.C.R. 672; *R. v. Gladstone*, [1996] 2 S.C.R. 723; *R. v. Pamajewon*, [1996] 2 S.C.R. 821; *R. v. Adams*, [1996] 3 S.C.R. 101; *R. v. Cote*, [1996] 3 S.C.R. 139; *Opetchesaht v. Canada*, [1997] 2 S.C.R. 119; *St Marys v. Cranbook*, [1997] 2 S.C.R. 657; *Delgamuukw v. British Columbia*, [1997] 3 S.C.R. 1010; *R. v. Williams*, [1998] 1 S.C.R. 1128; *Union of New Brunswick Indians v. New Brunswick (Minister of Finance)*, [1998] 1 S.C.R. 1161; *R. v. Sundown*, [1999] 1 S.C.R. 393; *R. v. Gladue*, [1999] 1 S.C.R. 688; *Corbiere v. Canada*, [1999] 2 S.C.R. 203; *Westbank First Nation v. British Columbia Hydro*, [1999] 3 S.C.R. 134; *R. v. Marshall (I)*, [1999] 3 S.C.R. 465; *R. v. Marshall (II)*, [1999] 3 S.C.R. 533; *R. v. Wells*, [2000] 1 S.C.R. 207; *Lovelace v. Ontario*, [2000] 2 S.C.R.; *Mitchell v. M.N.R.*, [2001] 1 S.C.R. 911; *Osoyoos Indian Band v. Oliver (Town)*, [2001] 1 S.C.R.

12 Paul McHugh, *The Maori Magna Carta: New Zealand Law and the Treaty of Waitangi* (Oxford: Oxford University Press, 1992); Matthew Palmer, 'The Treaty of Waitangi in Legislation' (2001) *New Zealand Law Review* 207.

13 Erica-Irene Daes, 'Equality of Indigenous Peoples under the Auspices of the United Nations – Draft Declaration on the Rights of Indigenous Peoples' (1995) 10 *St Thomas Law Review* 175; Indigenous Declarations have also been drafted for specific issues; see Marie Battiste and Seigfried Wiessner, 'The 2000 Revision of the United Nations Draft Declaration on the Protection of Heritage for Indigenous Peoples' (2000) 13 *St Thomas Law Review* 383. For a more general treatment of Indigenous peoples in international law, see S. James Anaya, *Indigenous Peoples in International Law* (New York: Oxford University Press, 1996).

14 The *Awas Tingni* case from the Inter-American Court of Human Rights ordered Nicaragua to demarcate traditional communal lands of the Awas Tingni and to pay compensation for the granting of logging rights to foreign companies. See No. 67 *Casa La Communidad Mayagna (Sumo) Awas Tingni*, retrieved 7 March 2002, from www.corteidh.or.cr/serie_c/C_67_

ESP.html. For commentary about the development of this and other cases
before the Inter-American courts, see S. James Anaya and Robert Williams
Jr, 'The Protection of Indigenous Peoples' Rights over Lands and Natural
Resources under the Inter-American Human Rights System' (2001) *Harvard
Human Rights Journal* 33.

15 T. Svennsson, 'The Attainment of Limited Self-Determination among the
Sami in Recent Years' (1995) *Law and Anthropology* 267.

16 For a discussion of Indigenous peoples' actions during so-called occupations, see John Borrows, 'Crown and Aboriginal Occupations of Land: A
History and Comparison,' retrieved 11 July 2008 from www.attorney
general.jus.gov.on.ca/inquiries/ipperwash/policy_part/research/pdf/
History_of_Occupations_Borrows.pdf.

17 The Royal Commission on Aboriginal Peoples, *Bridging the Cultural Divide:
A Report on Aboriginal People and Criminal Justice in Canada* (Ottawa: Supply
and Services, 1996), 26–53; A.C. Hamilton and C.M. Sinclair, *Report of the
Aboriginal Justice Inquiry of Manitoba,* vol. 1 (Winnipeg: Queen's Printer,
1991), 509–48; Amy Standefer, 'The Federal Juvenile Delinquency Act: A
Disproportionate Impact on Native American Juveniles' (1999) 84 *Minnesota Law Review* 473; Manuel Guerriro, 'Indian Child Welfare Act of
1978' (1979) 7 *American Indian Law Review* 51, 57, 66–73; M.M. Slaughter,
'Contested Identities: The Adoption of American Indian Children and the
Liberal State' (2000) 9 *Social and Legal Studies* 227; Marlee Kline, 'Child Welfare Law: "Best Interests of the Child Ideology" and First Nations' (1992)
30 *Osgoode Hall Law Journal* 375; Philip Lynch, 'Keeping Them Home: The
Best Interests of Indigenous Children and Communities in Canada and
Australia' (2001) 23 *Sydney Law Review* 501.

18 P.S. Deloria and Robert Laurence, 'What's an Indian? A Conversation
about Law School Admissions, Indian Tribal Sovereignty and Affirmative
Action' (1994) 28 *Georgia Law Review* 1107.

19 For reflections of Indigenous law students' experiences in law school,
see Patricia Monture, 'Now That the Door Is Open: First Nations and the
Law School Experience' (1990) 15 *Queen's Law Journal* 179; Tracy Lindberg,
'What Do You Call an Indian Woman with a Law Degree? Nine Aborigi-
nal Women at the University of Saskatchewan College of Law Speak Out'
(1996) 9 *Canadian Journal of Women and the Law* 301; Leah Whiu, 'A Maori
Women's Experience of Feminist Legal Education in Aotearoa' (1994) 2
Waikato Law Review 161.

20 Lawrence Boca, 'American Indians Over-represented in Law Schools?
How Can That Be?' (2000) 29 *Student Lawyer* 17; Daniel Lavery, 'The
Participation of Indigenous Australians in Legal Education' (1993) 4 *Legal*

Education Review 1; Heather Douglas, 'Indigenous Australians and Legal Education: Looking to the Future' (1996) 7 *Legal Education Review* 225; Carolyn Penfold, 'Indigenous Students' Perceptions of Factors Contributing to Successful Law Studies' (1996) 7 *Legal Education Review* 155.

21 For comments on different Indigenous law programs in Canada, see Roger Carter, 'University of Saskatchewan Native Law Centre' (1980) 44 *Saskatchewan Law Review* 135; Donald Purich, 'Affirmative Action in Canadian Law Schools: The Native Student in Law School' (1986) 51 *Saskatchewan Law Review* 79; Hugh MacAulay, 'Improving Access to Legal Education for Native People in Canada' (1991) 14 *Dalhousie Law Journal* 133. The Native Law Centre has both a research and a teaching mission. It offers a pre-law summer program for Indigenous students interested in admission to law schools. It also publishes the *Canadian Native Law Reporter*, theoretical and technical legal texts, and has an excellent resource library. The University of British Columbia's First Nations Legal Studies Program has operated since 1975. Originally an admissions program, it has assisted over 150 Indigenous law students to graduate from its school. UBC is now developing a Centre for International Indigenous Legal Studies to further its mission. Akitsiraq is a law program offered by the University of Victoria to Inuit people in Canada's newest territory, Nunavut. Fourteen Inuit students are studying there, entirely at home in their own territory, and will graduate with a UVic law degree in four years. UVic also offers a joint law degree and a master's degree in Indigenous governance at its main campus. Osgoode Hall Law School at York University has offered the Intensive Program in Aboriginal Governance since 1994. This clinically based program immerses students in an Indigenous legal experience for all their credits over an entire semester. The June Callwood Program at the University of Toronto provides graduate scholarships for advanced Indigenous legal studies. It also facilitates internships and applied experiences with Indigenous communities.

22 Robert Laurence, 'Preparing American Indians for Law School: The American Indian Center's Pre-Law Summer Institute' (1992) 12 *Northern Illinois University Law Review* 278. There are now two graduate LLM programs in Indigenous Legal Studies in the United States (U of Arizona and Tulsa), with numerous JD programs specializing in Indian law (New Mexico, ASU, Washington, Wisconsin, Kansas, Iowa, South Dakota, Vermont) or Indian law clinics (Colorado, Idaho, Montana). The University of Waikato in New Zealand was created for the purpose of advancing Maori legal studies in a bicultural environment, though it has been slow in establishing itself. The University of New South Wales has an Indigenous Law

Centre. The University of Tromsø, in Norway, has led the way in teaching Sami legal issues.

23 The stated objectives of the *Indigenous Law Journal* are as follows:

Our central concerns are Indigenous legal systems and legal systems as they affect Indigenous peoples.
We are governed by core values that include recognition:
- that Indigenous legal systems are best learned from Indigenous peoples;
- that to ensure balance and cultural authenticity, both First Nations and non First Nations participation is required in all of the journal's editorial and business decisions; and
- that the pursuit of excellence in scholarship requires not only continuity with the past, but also a commitment to innovation.

To compare and contrast this with the purposes of the *American Indian Law Review*, see Robert A. Fairbanks, 'American Indian Law Review: Purposes and Goals Revisited' (1995) 20 *American Indian Law Review* 1.

14. Aunagwaum-iziwin

1 To be cautious, wary, mindful, prudent. See Basil Johnston, *Anishinaubae Thesaurus* (Lansing: Michigan State University, 2007), 63.
2 *Declaration on Race and Racial Prejudice*, adopted and proclaimed by the General Conference of the United Nations Educational, Scientific and Cultural Organization at its Twentieth Session, on 27 November 1978; Peter Li and B. Singh Bolaria, *Racial Oppression in Canada* (Toronto: Garamond Press, 1988), 13–25; Frances Henry, Carol Tator, Winston Mattis, and Tim Rees, eds., 'Terminology and the Forms of Racism,' in Frances Henry and Carol Tator, eds., *The Colour of Democracy: Racism in Canadian Society* (Toronto: Harcourt, Brace and Company, 1995), 3–4.
3 For a somewhat contrary view, see Vincent Sarich and Frank Miele, *Race: The Reality of Human Difference* (Boulder, CO: Westview Press, 2004).
4 Patrick Macklem, *Indigenous Difference and the Constitution of Canada* (Toronto: University of Toronto Press, 2001), 76–106; Tom Flanagan, *First Nations, Second Thoughts?* (Montreal: McGill-Queen's University Press, 2000), 11–26.
5 Mel Smith, *Our Home and Native Land: What Government's Aboriginal Policy Is Doing to Canada* (Toronto: Stoddart Publishing, 1996), 250.
6 For similar proposals, see Mel Smith, *Our Home and Native Land: What Government's Aboriginal Policy Is Doing to Canada* (Toronto: Stoddart Publishing,

1996); Tom Flanagan, *First Nations, Second Thoughts?* (Montreal: McGill-Queen's University Press, 2000); Tanis Fiss, 'Apartheid: Canada's Ugly Secret' (Calgary: Centre for Aboriginal Policy Change, April 2004); Francis Paul Prucha, *The Great Father: The United States Government and American Indians* (Lincoln: University of Nebraska Press, 1984), 1013–59; Charles Wilkinson and Eric Biggs, 'The Evolution of the Termination Policy' (1977) 5 *American Indian Law Review* 139; Prime Minister Pierre Elliott Trudeau, 'Remarks on Aboriginal and Treaty Rights,' excerpt from a speech given 8 August 1969 in Vancouver, British Columbia, in Peter Cumming and Neil Mickenburg, *Native Rights in Canada*, 2nd ed. (Toronto: Indian-Eskimo Association, 1972), appendix IV; Sally Weaver, *Making Canadian Indian Policy: The Hidden Agenda, 1968–1970* (Toronto: University of Toronto Press, 1981).

7 Hernando de Soto, *The Mystery of Capital: Why Capitalism Triumphs in the West and Fails Everywhere Else* (New York: Basic Books, 2000).

8 Antonio Damasio, *Emotion, Reason and the Human Brain* (New York: Penguin, 1994); Anotonio Damasio, *The Feeling of What Happens: Body and Emotion in the Making of Consciousness* (New York: Harcourt, 1999); Martha Nussbaum, *Upheavals of Thought: The Intelligence of Emotions* (Cambridge: Cambridge University Press, 2003).

9 See Basil Johnston, *Ojibway Heritage* (Toronto: McClelland and Stewart, 1976), 7.

15. Windigos

1 The Giant Cannibal. For more information, see Basil Johnston, *Anishinaubae Thesaurus* (Lansing: Michigan State University, 2007), 18.

2 It was a little earlier in the season than usual, but they heard the catch was good around Lion's Bay. They had been going there for years. In fact, many times it had been their lifeline, especially when their dad was lost to drinking. Fishing was the only thing that had kept their family alive.

Now, the fall's harvest had long been consumed. Welfare wasn't an option for them. Bear and deer had been too scarce to be of much sustenance. Their supply of fish was nearing depletion. The only hope they had was to brave the winds, and set nets in the cold November waters.

Despite the hardships, they had some good memories of those times. As children they had been fairly close, and tried to do what they could to help. The older brother taught his younger sisters how to snare rabbits and catch squirrels. They often cut wood in the bush together, too. It was hard work, hauling the load back through the spring snow, but it created its own warmth that was deeply fulfilling. The oldest had taken on this special role in his father's absence. He was proud he had helped keep some things together. That had been twenty years ago. They now had young families of their own. As they set out that day, his thoughts turned to those earlier times. He was happy to have his younger brother at his side.

3 This story is found in H. Burke Peterson, 'Removing the Poison of an Unforgiving Spirit,' *Ensign Magazine* (November 1983), 59.

4 Jarvis Papers, Metro Toronto Reference Library, Collection # S-125, Volume B57. Jarvis was superintendent of Indian Affairs in the 1840s. My thanks to Professor Darlene Johnston of the University of Toronto, Faculty of Law, for bringing this document to my attention.

16. Cheeby-akeeng

1 A place of peace and tranquillity. For further information, see Basil Johnston, *Anishinaubae Thesaurus* (Lansing: Michigan State University, 2007), 19, 153.

Index